"Longenecker's work has always provided a model for the thoughtful, careful, and persuasive use of material culture as key evidence to explore issues of religious observance in the Roman world. His current book is no exception. Its masterful treatment of the material culture from Pompeii and Herculaneum and the role of that material in informing us about early Jesus-worship is once again superb. Although this lavishly illustrated book is written for an interested nonprofessional audience, I found new insights and perspectives that will shape my own research and teaching."

—**Steven L. Tuck**, Miami University;
author of *Pompeii: Daily Life in an Ancient Roman City*

"Longenecker has made an outstanding contribution to understanding the development of early Christianity in the Roman world, taking seriously both stone and story. True to its goal, select texts are examined alongside detailed archaeological evidence from Pompeii and Herculaneum. The book is beautifully enriched with images of frescoes, monuments, inscriptions, and 'newsy' graffiti. Appreciation for student perspectives and questions guides the style and organization of the volume. Interpretive challenges are addressed with great lucidity on topics ranging from ancient deities to spiritual identities to literacy and concepts of housing and space. Longenecker's study is deeply informed by his knowledge of early Christianity and his breadth of understanding of contemporary scholarship. The thematic approach offers innovative opportunities for teaching and learning, with the emergence of new associations and interfaces that can shed light on the rise of early Jesus-devotion. I know of no other book like it, and I am eager to discuss its rich contents with students."

—**Margaret Y. MacDonald**, Saint Mary's University

"The circumstances of Pompeii's destruction in 79 CE meant that Pompeii and the adjacent towns of Herculaneum and Oplontis were frozen in time, and houses, shops, temples, and industrial complexes were preserved along with their contents and decorations. Pompeii thus provides better and more detailed evidence of ancient urban life than any other site from the ancient world. Longenecker expertly employs the findings from Pompeii not only to produce an engaging picture of the social, religious, economic, and political life of this town but also to show how a detailed understanding of ancient urban life casts light on the activities and beliefs of early Jesus-followers, who in some respects fit comfortably into ancient society and in other respects offered different perspectives on social relationships, piety, politics, and commerce. *In Stone and Story* normalizes the picture of early Christians by giving due scope to the many ways they were aligned with ancient society, which allows their distinctives to stand out with particular clarity. An excellent teaching resource."

—**John S. Kloppenborg**, University of Toronto

In Stone and Story

In Stone and Story

EARLY CHRISTIANITY IN THE ROMAN WORLD

Bruce W. Longenecker

B
Baker Academic
a division of Baker Publishing Group
Grand Rapids, Michigan

© 2020 by Bruce W. Longenecker

Published by Baker Academic
a division of Baker Publishing Group
PO Box 6287, Grand Rapids, MI 49516-6287
www.bakeracademic.com

Printed in the United States of America

Library of Congress Cataloging-in-Publication Data
Names: Longenecker, Bruce W., author.
Title: In stone and story : early Christianity in the Roman world / Bruce W. Longenecker.
Description: Grand Rapids : Baker Academic, a division of Baker Publishing Group, 2020. | Includes bibliographical references and index.
Identifiers: LCCN 2019014370 | ISBN 9781540960672 (cloth)
Subjects: LCSH: Church history—Primitive and early church, ca. 30–600. | Pompeii (Extinct city)—Church history. | Pompeii (Extinct city)—Civilization.
Classification: LCC BR182 .L66 2020 | DDC 274.5/7301—dc23
LC record available at https://lccn.loc.gov/2019014370

Cover photo: A fresco of Medea and the daughters of King Pelias (from the *triclinium* of the House of the Group of Glass Vases in Pompeii, MANN 111477)

20   21   22   23   24   25   26   27   7   6   5   4   3   2   1

For Richard Bauckham
and Philip Esler

Contents

Looking Ahead

An Introduction

A little painting on the wall of a small house in Pompeii is one of the most delightful artifacts among the many treasures buried by the volcanic eruption of Mount Vesuvius in the late first century. The painting (shown below) depicts two little cupids pulling rings and a mirror out of a jewelry box and examining them with curiosity.

That charming vignette can serve as an analogy of what transpires in this book. Like those two cupids, the chapters of this book pull out selected archaeological resources from the treasure chest of Vesuvian artifacts, examining them for what they reveal about the ancient Roman world. Moreover, when configured in relation to selected texts of early Christianity, those artifacts (graffiti, inscriptions, statues, temples, paintings, tombs, and more) help to foster fresh angles of vision regarding the slow but steady rise of early Jesus-devotion within its earliest historical contexts. Relating texts of the early Jesus-movement to selected Vesuvian resources offers the opportunity to explore ways in which Jesus-devotion was getting a foothold within that world and, at times, infusing fresh resources into it.

In the process, readers of this book may learn as much about Pompeii as they do about the early followers of Jesus and the theological library they bequeathed to the world (that is,

Figure Intro.1. Two cupids inspecting jewelry and a mirror (from the House of the Prince of Naples in Pompeii, located at 6.15.8; for an explanation of this numbering system [Fiorelli's], see chapter 3 under the heading "Designations Frequently Used")

1

Figure Intro.2. Mount Vesuvius today rising above the Bay of Naples (see credits)

the New Testament). That will be no bad thing, since understanding how an ancient urban center "worked" will inevitably help to highlight the issues of Christianity's emergence within similar urban centers throughout the Mediterranean world of the first century.

If readers of this book are anything like the author of this book, they will find what lies ahead to be a stimulating journey of discovery. I am sometimes asked whether I consider myself to be a researcher of early Christianity or of the Vesuvian towns of Pompeii and Herculaneum. Because the two are not mutually exclusive, I usually respond by saying that I consider myself to be a better scholar of early Jesus-devotion precisely because I am also a scholar of the Vesuvian towns. It is my hope that readers of this book will also come to a better understanding of the early Jesus-movement as the Vesuvian towns become increasingly familiar.

PART ONE

Protocols of Engagement

Human Meaning in Stone and Story

Throughout history, people have told stories to help them interpret their lives within the cultures in which they were embedded. These were stories about who they were, where they came from, what's wrong with the world, how they were connected with other people, how they were different from other people, and where things were going. The more those stories could explain their world, the more powerful they proved to be; the more powerful those stories were, the more useful they were for interpreting people's life stories.

Earliest Christianity, even in its various forms, began to get a foothold in a world very different from our own. It told its stories in a context far removed from the twenty-first century. Appreciation for the contributions of early Christian voices to the articulation of human meaning grows when those voices are heard in relation to their own world—the Greco-Roman world of the first century. That world was animated by a tournament of narratives about the world and its supposed deities. It was in relation to that tournament that a small number of Jesus-followers began to tell stories alongside the many others that were already on offer. Arguably, if Christian stories can contribute to the quest for meaning in contexts other than the first-century world, their potential is augmented when those stories are informed by an understanding of their significance within their original context.

There are a number of ways to become immersed in that first-century world. Two standard methods for approaching the Roman world include (1) the study of ancient classical texts and (2) the study of archaeological discoveries from that ancient world. This book primarily adopts the second of these—exploring the material culture of the Roman age through the illumination provided by the archaeological site of Pompeii, with assistance from Pompeii's sister town, Herculaneum (and at times artifacts from nearby first-century Vesuvian villas). Literature from the Roman age will be referenced occasionally, in instances when it significantly aids interpretation of the material evidence of the two Vesuvian towns.

Through these two spellbinding Vesuvian sites, the first-century configuration of Roman culture comes to life in concentrated form. No other ancient site comes close to offering the vast historical resources that the Vesuvian towns offer. Roughly 150 miles south of the

Figure 1.1. Two photos depicting Mount Vesuvius behind the material remains of Pompeii today

bustling city of Rome, these two towns died when their local mountain, Mount Vesuvius, erupted in the year 79 CE. Volcanic debris from that eruption suffocated the Vesuvian towns, burying them under heavy blankets of volcanic pumice (in the case of Pompeii) and flows of dense pyroclastic ash (in the case of both Pompeii and Herculaneum). Now largely uncovered by archaeologists, these first-century towns sit on the doorstep of our twenty-first-century world, boldly displaying much of what life was like in two small urban contexts of the Greco-Roman world.

This book will offer windows into the Greco-Roman context in which Jesus-devotion was getting its initial foothold. It will do this by highlighting selected Vesuvian artifacts that best illustrate aspects of the Roman world and that, in turn, impact our understanding of early Christian texts and phenomena. Pompeii and Herculaneum were, after all, urban centers vibrantly alive at the very time that the early Jesus-movement was

first getting some traction in urban centers of the Roman world. The Vesuvian remains are a treasure trove of life from two urban centers and various rural villas of the first century CE. They access that ancient world in a way that matches anything we might wish for, and they supplement the great literary texts of Greek and Latin writers with the everyday life of ordinary people who would otherwise be largely invisible to us. Moreover, Vesuvian artifacts reveal Greco-Roman contexts in an organic, interrelated fashion; the inner sinews connecting first-century urban culture are on display at Vesuvius's base in a fashion unequalled at any other ancient site. In short, when it comes to understanding the world of the first century, no other urban site offers anything close to the Vesuvian resources of Pompeii and Herculaneum.

In addition, today there are exciting opportunities for exploring those Vesuvian towns by means of internet resources. Those opportunities allow people with curious minds to delve deeply into the Vesuvian archaeology from the window of their own digital screens, making the study of the Roman world easier than ever before. More will be said about this in chapter 3.

Before we get too far, however, I want to highlight my motivation for writing this book by recalling the words of one of my former undergraduate students. Toward the end of a university course I had taught, I asked my students to write reflections on what they had learned about the early Christian texts in their historical context. One perceptive undergraduate included the following in her larger reflections: "I'm starting to realize that taking these [New Testament] writings and directly applying them to our modern context without thinking about the 'interpretative bridge' of time and culture is about as helpful as taking a scale to the moon. Weight is going to be different there, because gravity is different there!"

Much might be said in relation to this observation, but this is not the place for that. Instead, borrowing this student's analogy, I simply note my hope that this book will help readers construct that "interpretative bridge" to the Roman world, in the enterprise of reading early Christian texts in their first historical

Figure 1.3. Skeletons of some of the people killed in the eruption of Vesuvius, who had sought shelter in the storage bays on the seafront at Herculaneum

contexts. Placing early Christian discourse in its historical setting will allow the force of that discourse to be more readily apparent. And in this task we will be assisted by those people of Pompeii and Herculaneum who will act as our guides, our "key informants" of the Roman world, even though many of them lost their lives in a horrific tragedy of unimaginable proportions.

A Glance at Our Guides

In this book, we will have the honor of entering into the Roman world through the lives and lifestyles of the people who populated the residences of Pompeii and Herculaneum. These people, who were often neighbors to each other, will act as our guides into a world that had at least as many differences from our own world as similarities. We will recognize many parts of their world, but at times we might also scratch our heads and wonder about other aspects. Within this very foreign world, some people had big dreams, clear

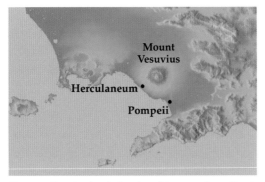

Figure 1.2. Map showing the location of the towns Pompeii and Herculaneum on the seacoast and in their proximity to Mount Vesuvius

Figure 1.4. A plaster cast of a young child whose body decomposed in the volcanic debris (from the House of the Golden Bracelet, 6.17.42)

schemes, and high hopes for the future, while many others must have been discouraged by the drudgery of their situations. Some of them were eager to think through the complexities of life. Some of them looked forward to the next party they would attend. Some of them expressed their hatred for their competitors. Some of them were desperately in love. Some of them were stuck in loveless marriages, and some of them were desperately bitter at the way love had treated them. These aspects of their lives, and more, are on display as we enter the spaces of the Vesuvian residents.

At times we get glimpses into their ordinary lives by means of graffiti that they left on walls throughout their towns. The Roman biographer Plutarch encouraged his readers to avoid glancing at the graffiti all around them, since those graffiti only encouraged "the practice of inquiring after things which are none of our business" (*On Curiosity* 520E). But "the practice of inquiring after things" like first-century graffiti is precisely the "business" of historical inquiry. Those graffiti give us access to first-century lives, revealing the everyday occurrences of ordinary people. So, for instance, out of the thousands of graffiti from the Vesuvian towns, one graffito reads: "A copper pot went

missing from my shop. Anyone who returns it to me will be given 65 bronze coins [literally, *sestertii*]; twenty more will be given for information leading to the capture of the thief" (*CIL* 4.64; for an explanation of the "CIL" enumeration, see chapter 3). Some of the residents of these towns were honest and helpful, as in this graffito: "If anyone lost a mare laden with baskets on November 25, apply to Quintus Decius Hilarus, freedman of Quintus . . . at the Mamii estate on the other side of the Sarno Bridge" (*CIL* 4.3864).

Many graffiti were not so courteous, as in this one directed to someone named Chios: "I hope your hemorrhoids rub together so much that they hurt worse than they ever have before!"

Figure 1.5. Portraits (with damage to the right portrait) of two children (boy on the left and girl on the right) depicted on the walls of their bedroom (from Pompeii's House of Marcus Lucretius Fronto, 5.4.a)

(*CIL* 4.1820). Still other graffiti get to the point even more quickly: "May you be crucified" (*CIL* 4.2082); "Curse you" (*CIL* 4.1813); and "Samius to Cornelius: go hang yourself" (*CIL* 4.1864). In some ways, the world has not changed very much from the days when early Christianity was struggling to get a foothold within first-century society.

Nowhere is that more clear than in graffiti about love. "No young buck is complete until he has fallen in love," one Pompeian resident advised (*CIL* 4.1797). Around the town, graffiti reveal that the town's residents were often enmeshed in relationships of love. One man described his darling as the "sweetest and most lovable" girl (*CIL* 4.8177), while another referred to his sweetheart Noete as "my light" (*CIL* 4.1970). A man named Caesius declared that he "faithfully loves" his partner, whose name has not survived beyond the first letter, M (*CIL* 4.1812). Yet another gave a wonderful compliment to his partner, referencing a famous painting in the Temple of Aesculapius on the island of Cos that was greatly discussed in the ancient world: "Anyone who has not seen the painting of Venus by Apelles should take a look at my girl: she is equally radiant" (*CIL* 4.6842).

Clearly, then, there were romantics among the population of the Vesuvian towns. One of them saluted another with this little gem, written on a column in the back of a Pompeii residence: "May you, girl, thrive, and may you have the goodwill of Pompeian Venus" (*CIL* 4.4007). One graffito illustrates how someone would have willingly compromised his/her own prospects in order to be with the love of his/her life: "Love dictates what I write, and Cupid guides my hand: I would rather die than be a god without you" (*CIL* 4.1928). On another occasion, a woman named Livia posted greetings to a man named Alexander, adding that if his life should start to falter, she would "come running" (*CIL* 4.1593).

Love was a fragile thing in many circumstances, especially for slaves embedded within households. Two graffiti that speak of "the vetoing of love" seem to capture this point.

Figure 1.6. Part of a Latin graffito scratched onto a Pompeii wall (*CIL* 4.2175)

Figure 1.7. A fresco depicting the myth of the cupid Eros being led into the presence of Venus, who will reprimand him for shooting his arrow of love at the wrong target; his brother, the cupid Anteros, looks on from behind Venus with seeming amusement at the punishment of his brother (from 7.2.23, MANN 9257; for an explanation of the MANN numbering system, see chapter 3 under "Designations Frequently Used").

On the wall of the residence of one of Pompeii's private auctioneer-bankers, someone scratched this catchy memo: "May prosperity come to those who love; may death come to those who cannot love; and may those who veto love die twice" (*CIL* 4.4091). Another graffito tells us that the attempt to veto love was not an uncommon thing: "He who vetoes love, he who keeps a watch on lovers . . . is by no means unique" (*CIL* 4.4509). The phrase "to veto love" may refer to the efforts of any householder who prevented romance to develop either (1) between slaves within his own household or (2) between a slave in his household and a slave belonging to a different household. But love often transpired among slaves nonetheless, as in the case of the female slave Methe (who was literate) and Chrestus (whose status is uncertain but who was most likely servile as well): "Methe of Atella, slave of Cominia, loves Chrestus. May Venus of Pompeii smile favorably on their hearts and let them always live in harmony" (*CIL* 4.2457). Love can sometimes take hold in even the most difficult of situations. One Pompeian resident claimed that the power of love could never be held back, making the point with poetic sarcasm: "He who dissuades lovers can also fetter the winds and stop the perennial flow of spring" (*CIL* 4.1649).

Sometimes graffiti testify to affection between partners who lived near each other. On the exterior wall of one residence, a man named Secundus declared his love for his mistress Prima ("Secundus greets his Prima everywhere; I beg you, my mistress, to love me"; *CIL* 4.8364, outside 1.10.7), and four doorways down the street Prima seems to have responded favorably ("Prima sends very many greetings to Secundus"; *CIL* 4.8270, outside 1.10.3).

Sometimes graffiti testify to affection between partners who were spread out over the miles. One woman inscribed a wish about her lover who was soon to make a sea voyage (he may have been a merchant or a sailor on a merchant vessel). The woman, named Ario, fears that while he is away he will find many alluring sexual temptations: "Venus is a weaver of webs; from the moment that she sets out to attack my dearest, she will lay temptations along his way: he must hope for a good

voyage, which is also the wish of his Ario"
(*CIL* 4.1410, depicted in figure 1.9). Ario's
clever intellect is evident in this short graffito.
In her prose, the motif of distance acts both
literally (her lover is physically going away on
a journey) and metaphorically (he might lose
sight of his affection for her, in view of the web
of sexual temptations that Venus will weave
for him along the way). At the metaphorical
level, the phrase "he must hope for a good voyage" moves from being about physical safety
to being about his emotional fidelity, as does
the closing sentiment, "which is also the wish
of his Ario."

Another graffito articulates passion over
the miles of separation and expresses the desire for relational reunion. Although it was
inscribed on a wall in Pompeii, the graffito
voices the emotion of being distant from a
specific Pompeian resident:

> Wagon driver, if you could only feel the fires
> of love, you would increase your speed to
> enjoy the pleasures of Venus. I love my young
> Charmer, so please get the horses going; let's
> get on! You've had your drink, let's go. Take
> the reins and crack the whip. . . . Take me
> to Pompeii, where my sweet love lives. (*CIL*
> 4.5092)

Of course, in many instances love was not
all it was advertised to be. Whereas one romantic person held the view that "lovers, like
bees, lead a honeyed life," below that graffito
someone else added the words, "If only that
were true" (*CIL* 4.8408a and b). And heart-
break is all over this brave inscription against
Venus, the deity of sexual passion and love:
"Let all who love go to blazes! As for Venus, I
want to break her ribs with cudgel blows and
maim her loins. If she can pierce my tender

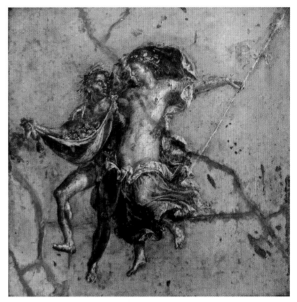

Figure 1.8. A stylized fresco of a couple in amorous flight (from 6.9.6, MANN 9135)

heart, why shouldn't I split her head with my
stick?!" (*CIL* 4.1824).

The people who will be our guides into
this first-century world are people who loved,
often passionately, often caringly. They had
hopes and dreams of one kind or another.
They philosophized about life. One of them
offered this observation: "To be discerning in
life, one must know something of death" (*CIL*
4.8832). Another, this: "Whoever disdains life
will easily despise the divine" (*CIL* 4.5370).
One captured the ironies of progress: "Nothing is as hard as stone, and nothing is as soft
as liquid; and yet, hard stones are hollowed
out by soft water" (*CIL* 4.1894).

We will see more of our guides' graffiti in
the following chapters. Along the way, as we
enter their world cognizant of some of its
particular strengths and peculiar weaknesses,
we should also enter the world of their lives
respectfully. Sometimes even their wisdom

11

Figure 1.9. Ario's inscription appears on the left of this fresco (*CIL* 4.1410); the fresco itself (MANN 4694) is from the House of Hercules (6.7.3).

overreaches the boundaries of their world. Consider, for instance, this poetic reflection on the changing tides of life (*CIL* 4.9123, a graffito found at 9.13.4):

> Nothing can last for all time:
> The dazzling sun returns to the
>   ocean;
> The once-full moon wanes to a
>   crescent;
> The most passionate of storms often
>   becomes the lightest of breezes.

Before we begin exploring the historical context of early Jesus-devotion by way of the Vesuvian towns of Pompeii and Herculaneum, a few things need to be set out in advance to ensure the maximal effectiveness of our journey. The next chapter (chapter 2) highlights a central feature of Roman society—what has been called "the fire in the bones" of those

Figure 1.10. An artist's depiction of the excavations of Pompeii with Mount Vesuvius in the distance (by Giuseppe Laezza [1835–1905], now in the public domain; see credits)

who lived in the world that we will be exploring. That chapter stands at the outset of our journey because, in many ways, it is the glue that holds together many aspects of the case studies that follow. Having registered that central feature of the first-century world, the subsequent chapter (chapter 3) lays out a few of the "tools" necessary to access the first-century world. With those preliminaries in hand, the chapters that follow will explore life in a Vesuvian town in order to capture a sense of the world in which Christianity began to emerge, telling its controversial stories about new opportunities to live meaningfully.

2

Fire in the Bones

It will be helpful to foreground at the outset what is arguably the most important social phenomenon of the ancient world: status capture. The acquisition and accumulation of status was central to the main workings of the Roman world. Cicero (the popular philosopher, orator, and politician, 106–43 BCE) said it like this: "By nature we yearn and hunger for honor. Once we have glimpsed . . . some part of honor's radiance, we are prepared to bear and suffer anything in order to secure it" (*Tusculanae disputationes* 2.24.58).

Simply put, the world of the first urban Jesus-followers was a world enmeshed in the quest for status. It is only the slightest exaggeration to say that no matter what ancient stone you uncover, no matter what ancient inscription you decipher, no matter what ancient painting you interpret, status capture lies at the heart of it. The people of the Roman age saw status as the essential commodity of life. The more status someone could accumulate, the more power and security he or she would stockpile. Conversely, people with lesser status were usually more vulnerable to forces beyond their control.

Differences in status are on display everywhere in the Vesuvian towns, as we will see

throughout this book. One intriguing example will suffice for now. One of Pompeii's most powerful politicians prior to the eruption of Mount Vesuvius was a man named Gaius Julius Polybius, who lived in one of Pompeii's finest houses (at 9.13.1–3). As he walked from his residence to the town's main forum, Polybius and his entourage would have passed some political endorsements that encouraged other residents of the town to vote for him in a forthcoming election. One of Polybius's supporters was a woman named Zmyrina. Her endorsement of him was painted on the external wall of a small pub where she and other women worked. (The endorsement has the inventory number *CIL* 4.7864, and the inventory number of the pub is 9.11.2; these enumerations will be explained in chapter 3.) Although Zmyrina was probably a barmaid, her endorsement testifies to Polybius's prominence among the townspeople, since the endorsement references him not by name but only by the three initials of his Roman name. Curiously, however, after Zmyrina commissioned her endorsement, someone covered her name with plaster (faint traces of the plaster were still visible when archaeologists first excavated the site). This meant that the endorsement of Polybius no longer mentioned this particular endorser. Evidently the status differential between Polybius and Zmyrina was too great in Polybius's eyes, causing him to have her name struck out of the endorsement, since she was a lowly barmaid and unworthy to be included in his sphere of influence. (For a Pompeian fresco of a barmaid, see figure 15.8.)

In this instance, we first see a low-status woman articulating her political preference. In that action, however, she was simultaneously attempting to elevate her own status as someone whose opinion might be worthy of some public notice. But her efforts were derailed when the very man whom she had supported took steps to remove her name from public discourse, while simultaneously accepting her public praise as a means of elevating his own status. Status capture is all over this single graffito.

That is not the last we hear of Zmyrina, however. In a later election, another barmaid named Asellina, who worked in the same tavern, decided to express her support for a different political candidate (this time, Gaius Lollium Fuscum). This election endorsement included a clause that suggested, "Zmyrina is back; you can't keep a good woman down" (literally, "Asellina asks you to elect Gaius Lollium Fuscum, not without Zmyrina"). This endorsement (see figure 2.1), which was placed near Zmyrina's earlier endorsement, has the effect of reasserting this barmaid's significance, despite Polybius's earlier attempt to remove her voice from the canvassing of political opinion.

People everywhere did whatever they could to leverage increasing amounts of status for themselves. Some had little or no chance of doing this. Others had a variety of strategies

Figure 2.1. The second political endorsement mentioning Zmyrina, this time with Asellina (spelled "Asellinas"); the top line still reveals a part of the name of her preferred candidate (the "Loll . . ." of "Lollium," for instance), while the third and fourth lines read "Asellinas rogant [plural] nec sine Zmyrina" (translated in the main text; *CIL* 4.7863, at 9.11.2, in situ).

for capitalizing further on whatever status they already had in order to heighten their standing among their peers.

It was the civic elite who benefited from having a variety of strategies for capitalizing on their status. Because they had significant control of social structures, numerous options were at their disposal to ensure that their public status was reinforced and augmented at every turn. For instance, when people attended gladiatorial contests in Pompeii's amphitheater or dramatic presentations in Pompeii's theater, a prescribed seating plan ensured that the civic leaders were in prominent positions. In Pompeii's amphitheater, the elite sat in a separate section closest to the action in the arena (in what today might be called "box seats"), while others sat in the rows behind, leading all the way to the upper seats, where those with the lowest configuration of status would have sat (see figure 2.2).

Moreover, the non-elite walked up the huge external staircases to get to the sections of

Figure 2.2. The stratified seating in Pompeii's amphitheater; the elite sat in the section reserved for them closest to the action, while people with lesser status sat higher up behind them.

the amphitheater where they were to sit; the elite, however, accessed their privileged seating through special internal tunnels attached to separate entrances, ensuring that the elite did not have to mix with the ordinary people of inferior social status (see figure 2.3).

Status came in a variety of kinds. In one sense, certain kinds of status were configured as binary opposites—for instance, slave or free. People were either one or the other, never both simultaneously in different mixtures of each. The binary contrast between

Figure 2.3. Left: the public access by means of the exterior staircases; right: elite access by means of the interior passageways leading to the amphitheater's front seats

these two particular kinds of identity is evident in a public inscription placed near a water tower in Herculaneum. The inscription, erected by two local magistrates, was an official decree against leaving garbage at the base of the water tower, and it itemized the penalties for failing to comply with the order. Those penalties were articulated with reference to whether a person was free or in servitude: "We declare a fine of twenty denarii for free citizens . . . [and] we will punish slaves with lashes" (CIL 4.10489; a similar decree appears in CIL 4.10488, shown in figure 2.4). These contrasting penalties (monetary fines versus physical floggings) differentiated the binary opposites of free or freed persons on the one hand and slaves on the other. Perhaps this differentiation was thought to be necessary in view of the fact that many slaves would not have had economic resources of their own, thereby requiring that their punishment be physical in nature rather than economic.

Other kinds of status were not as contrastive, being configured along a spectrum. For instance, one's family heritage, occupation, or

Figure 2.4. A public notice (now highly damaged and faded, with an Italian translation on its protective glass) placed on a street column, detailing the punishments to be meted out to individuals who dumped garbage at this public place in Herculaneum (CIL 4.10488)

age in relation to others—these were generally spread out across a spectrum of honor.

But, in fact, even within most forms of status, there was often a kind of spectrum of identity. For instance, there was a variety of slave identities, since the spectrum of servile tasks and positions varied widely. And there was a spectrum of status within the category of those who were "free," since (all else being equal) those born free were superior to those who were born in slavery and later freed.

There was also variety within the category of "citizen." Two episodes from the narrative of the Acts of the Apostles make the point with clarity, highlighting both the binary dimension of citizenship and non-citizenship on the one hand and the spread of status within citizenship on the other hand. The binary contrast between citizen and non-citizen is evident in this exchange between the apostle Paul and city magistrates:

> Paul said to the officers: "They beat us publicly without a trial, even though we are Roman citizens, and threw us into prison. . . ." The officers reported this to the magistrates, and when they heard that Paul and Silas were Roman citizens, they were alarmed. They came to appease them and escorted them from the prison. (Acts 16:37–39 NIV)

This story illustrates that citizenship was a status-enhancing commodity in binary or contrastive fashion over against non-citizen identity. If magistrates in the story deemed it acceptable to beat someone whom they took to be a non-citizen, they would never knowingly have permitted such a punishment to be meted out on a citizen.

In another episode from Acts, however, two different forms of citizenship are displayed along a spectrum of status:

The commander went to Paul and asked, "Tell me, are you a Roman citizen?" "Yes, I am," he answered. Then the commander said, "I had to pay a lot of money for my citizenship." Paul replied, "I was born a citizen." (Acts 22:27–28 NIV alt.)

This story illustrates that there were variables even within citizenship status. Though citizenship was a status-enhancing commodity, there were nonetheless degrees of status even within that form of identity.

This is where the first-century audience hearing this story would be intrigued, since social nuances of challenge and contest animate this encounter. The two men are not just trading information casually. Instead, a Roman commander is seeking to outdo Paul with regard to citizenship status. First-century audiences would have heard his statement "I had to pay a lot of money for my citizenship" as an attempt at one-upmanship. The commander must have assumed that Paul's citizenship had been acquired cheaply—perhaps as an inexpensive payoff to a poor master who needed quick access to resources and therefore agreed to release a slave in return for a small payment. The commander is, in effect, insulting Paul and trumpeting his own claim to status over what he assumed to be Paul's inferior claim. Paul's simple reply, however, put an end to the contest: "I was born a citizen." Paul did not acquire citizenship through strategic means. He inherited it by birth within a Roman family. Paul's citizenship, then, ran deeper than the commander's. An audience sympathetic to Paul is given the opportunity to chuckle as they watch a Roman commander initiate a contest of status, only to lose that contest to their hero,

Figure 2.5. A list of names of the local male citizens who were eligible to vote was inscribed in marble and hung in the basilica of Herculaneum; this broken fragment is only a small part of that lengthy list, which was a very public record of a certain form of civic status.

Paul, in his understated yet poignant riposte to the commander.

One of the best ancient examples of status differentiation, even within a single category of identity, comes from the case of one man who once resided in Herculaneum. A few particulars about the man will help us to understand his fuller story. He had once been a slave. When he earned his freedom, his slave name (Ennychus) was joined to the first two names of his master (Lucius Venidius), giving him the new name Lucius Venidius Ennychus. Whereas slaves almost always had only one name (a common slave name being Felix, ironically meaning "happy," or Faustus, meaning "lucky"), freemen and freedmen had at least three names (for example, Gaius Julius Caesar). So upon earning his freedom, Ennychus gained a fully Roman name to match his Roman citizenship (since slaves freed by masters who were Roman citizens usually gained Roman citizenship in the process of being released from slavery, unless they had been notably insubordinate at any point during their time of slavery).

But as we have already seen, there were various kinds of Roman citizenship, and this is where Ennychus's story becomes interesting. Ennychus's problem was that he had been freed from servitude before his thirtieth birthday. This meant that his citizenship was deemed by his peers to be second-rate, more like a pseudo-citizenship. Upon gaining his freedom, Ennychus would have had the status of a "Junian Latin"—that is, he had gained a form of citizenship, but it was inferior to full citizenship (because he was younger than thirty when he gained his freedom). The origins of this category of citizenship lay in the fact that some influential people felt that ex-slaves were becoming Roman citizens far too

easily, leading to a growing number of people who could boast of possessing citizenship. Because of that concern, the category of Junian Latin was created to introduce further stratifications of status and, ultimately, to try to protect the currency of full Roman citizenship. The path of Ennychus's upward advancement was blocked at the level of a Junian Latin unless or until he could remove that stigma and move forward to become a full Roman citizen.

This is where a stash of documents from Herculaneum's House of the Black Salon helps shed light on Ennychus's story. Of the thirty-nine wooden tablets found in that house, three of them record various business transactions and important moments in Ennychus's life.

- One document was dated July 24 in the year 60. It recorded the birth of Venidia, a baby girl, to Ennychus and his wife, Livia Acte.
- A second document was dated July 25 in the year 61, a year and a day after the first document. In it, the magistrates of Herculaneum certified that the baby Venidia had survived beyond her first birthday.
- The third document was dated March 22 in the year 62. It recorded the decision of an official in Rome, who had been approached by magistrates of Herculaneum regarding the status of Lucius Venidius Ennychus and Livia Acte. The official in Rome confirmed three things: (1) Venidius Ennychus and Livia Acte had a legitimate marriage; (2) their daughter had survived beyond the age of one year (as testified to by the first and second documents); and (3) as a consequence, Venidius

Figure 2.6. Part of the courtyard in the House of the Black Salon, where Venidius Ennychus, Livia Acte, and Venidia resided

Ennychus was now a full-fledged Roman citizen, no longer a Junian Latin.

From this point forward, a considerable obstacle in Ennychus's rise in social status was removed, and he was free to rise to further challenges as he ascended to the next level of Roman society. The story of Ennychus gives us unique insight into one of the many complexities of status and status manipulation in the Roman world.

————

We have seen that status capture ran through the veins of many in the Roman age. It was the "fire in the bones" that drove the machinery of the world that the early Jesus-movement was infiltrating. In some very practical and challenging aspects, the message proclaimed by early Jesus-followers ran against the cultural grain of the Roman world. The texts of early Christianity often depict moments in which the relationship between the "good news" (or "gospel") and Roman culture is being negotiated. As we will see, early Jesus-followers did not apply an overarching template to every situation. When considering particular issues that faced the nascent Jesus-movement, apostolic voices sometimes spoke with a fair degree of unanimity; certain theological perceptions were foundational for shared forms of discourse (for instance, early Christian discourse about the Greco-Roman deities; see the chapters in part 2). But on other pressing issues, their reflections sometimes differed, with the mixture of theological ingredients being combined in different ways (as we will see in certain chapters of part 4 especially). This is one of the things that makes early Christian texts so engaging—a "one size fits all" master stencil was rarely overlaid onto every situation. Instead, a spectrum of voices sought to negotiate the impact of Jesus-devotion within the Roman culture that early Jesus-followers were beginning to infiltrate, challenge, and, at times, perhaps even enhance.

3 Accessing the First-Century World

As the first followers of Jesus Christ began to emerge from Judea and Galilee in the 30s, their numbers grew rather impressively. Roughly one thousand people may have self-identified as Jesus-followers by the year 40 (ten years or so after the death of Jesus), with that number growing to ten thousand by the year 100, to two hundred thousand by the year 200, and to perhaps as many as five million by the year 300. These estimates are largely guesswork, of course, but guesswork based on informed inference. At the same time that Christianity was gaining traction within the Roman world, other forms of devotion were also on the rise—including devotion to the Egyptian deities Isis and Osiris, devotion to the Roman emperor, and (especially in the second through fourth centuries, but already in the late first century) devotion to the Persian deity Mithras. Among this influx of devotional fervor was the reverence for Jesus Christ, inculcating various forms of expression across a spectrum of beliefs and practices.

Those who self-identified as Jesus-followers embedded themselves within urban centers dotted around the Mediterranean basin. Some Jesus-followers must also have inhabited rural areas. Nonetheless, the historical record shows us almost nothing of rural forms of Jesus-devotion in the earliest generations of the Jesus-movement; it is only in the second and third centuries that we catch significant glimpses of Christians in rural contexts. In the first century, our evidence of Jesus-followers coalesces around urban centers almost exclusively (which were themselves closely interlocked with rural contexts). Even though Jesus-followers must certainly have been resident in rural contexts as well, our sources deal predominately with situations in which Jesus-devotion was being negotiated within vibrant urban contexts of the Roman world.

Some small groups of Jesus-devotees were beginning to spring up in these urban centers—places like Rome (with an estimated population of 1,000,000), Alexandria (600,000), Antioch of Syria (500,000), Ephesus (400,000), Corinth (250,000), Smyrna (200,000), Thessalonica (200,000), and more. These urban centers were obviously large cities. The town of Pompeii (together with its sister town, Herculaneum) was relatively small by comparison, being neither a large city on the one hand nor a small village on the other. The population of Pompeii was probably ten thousand to twelve thousand (something of the size of Philippi, perhaps, where some Jesus-followers resided). Herculaneum had a much smaller number of residents, four thousand to five thousand.

It almost goes without saying that each urban center of the Roman world was different from others in ways that go beyond their differences in size. For instance,

- deities were given reverence in different combinations and concentrations in the various urban centers;
- the populations of those centers differed in their demographic makeup;
- the narratives of local history were distinctive;
- "inter-city" political affiliations and alliances of concord were particular to each urban center; and
- the forms of commercial activity varied according to a variety of factors in each locality.

The list of differences in urban profiling could go on. Contributing to the vibrancy of the Roman age was the conviction that an overarching imperial order could serve as the umbrella within which diverse forms of indigenous identities could thrive in a pact of peaceful coexistence. The strengths and weaknesses of this conviction might be debated, but it coincides with what we know to be true from the archaeological and literary records of the Roman world and from simple common sense: different places were different.

But despite the diversity of urban centers throughout the Mediterranean basin, certain features characterized life in Roman urban contexts in general—features that tended to transcend the particularities of distinct urban centers. The Romans seem to have prided themselves on ensuring that civic centers around the Mediterranean basin shared certain characteristics that reinforced the value system of the Roman imperial order. A person could travel from one urban center to another and, with only a few accommodations to the indigenous configuration of things, operate within that new setting with fluent familiarity. So while the Vesuvian towns were distinct from other urban centers of the time (even differing from each other in some important ways), they also shared many features of Roman life that were widespread throughout the first century. The chapters

Figure 3.1. An ancient access tunnel leading down into Pompeii's amphitheater (a metaphor for our own access into the archaeological remains of the Vesuvian towns)

that follow touch on some of the areas where what was practiced in one urban center must have looked very much like what was practiced in another. Every place was different, but for many urban centers of the Roman world, many things were comparable.

Since this book allows readers to access the first-century world through the material remains of Pompeii and (to a lesser extent) Herculaneum, a few issues pertaining to those towns need to be mentioned at this point in order to enhance the process along the way. While we are at it, a few other preparatory matters about this book will also be registered in this chapter. With these issues in hand, we will then be able to set off to the first-century world by way of the historical probes undertaken in the following chapters.

What This Book Is and Is Not

The first thing to set in place is an understanding of what this book is and what it is not. It is neither a complete introduction to the material remains of the Vesuvian towns nor a complete introduction to early Christianity in the Roman world. It does not delve into every nook and cranny of the Vesuvian towns, nor does it lay out a history of the spread of Jesus-devotion throughout the Mediterranean basin. Instead, it selectively explores some points of the interface where the world of the Vesuvian towns intersects with themes and issues evident in New Testament texts. Through a series of "snapshots," or close-up vignettes, it highlights illustrative and exemplary Vesuvian artifacts (inscriptions, graffiti, frescos, etc.), explores their relevance in a first-century context, and brings certain New Testament texts into conversation with those artifacts. The process is intended to add

depth and focus to our understanding of those early Christian texts.

The selected issues presented in this book, then, are those that have strong footholds in both spheres of study. This book does not offer reflections on areas where there is little substantial overlap. For instance, the New Testament says things about widows that might provide some insight into early Christianity, but because the material remains of Pompeii do not lend themselves to much solid data regarding widows, there is very little in this book to introduce the readers to the issues early Christians faced regarding how to care for widows.

It goes without saying, then, that there is more to the study of both Vesuvian towns and early Christianity than the issues that fall within this interdisciplinary interface. Nonetheless, the interface of issues shared by Vesuvian material culture and New Testament texts takes us to the heart of many issues pertaining to the influx of Jesus-devotion within the Roman world, even if there is always more to learn beyond the interface. Readers of this book are invited to explore this correlation of Vesuvian material and New Testament texts where the two most fruitfully intersect.

This book is informed by much current scholarship on the Vesuvian towns and by much scholarship on early Jesus-devotion, but it is not an academic book. Its goal is not to propose a stimulatingly novel argument for academic scholars but, instead, to assemble a helpfully creative resource for interested learners (including scholars). In other books, I have presented academic arguments offering new interpretations of both Vesuvian materials and early Christian literature, but that is not my goal here. Instead, this book brings together two spheres of scholarship in order to allow the resonances between them to be audible, or, to change the imagery, to permit the two to lean into each other productively. In my teaching experience, explorations at this interface have proven exceedingly profitable for eager thinkers at any stage in their learning.

Chapter by Chapter

Although the following chapters of this book probe the interface of the Vesuvian towns and New Testament texts, they do not probe that interface with a single template. Readers will not find, for instance, a self-contained section on the Vesuvian realia that is then followed by a self-contained section on early Jesus-devotion, or vice versa. Because the Vesuvian towns and the New Testament offer different mixes of resources on any given issue, the format of each chapter will have its own internal

structure. To best accommodate the relevant data on any given issue, I have avoided using a single organizational template in the chapters that follow.

It might appear from the chapter titles that individual sections of this book focus on relatively self-contained issues. While there may be some truth to that general impression, in reality any particular issue will merge with others in a number of ways. Aspects of ancient life were organically interrelated, rather than being demarcated into particular self-contained boxes. Take, for instance, gladiatorial competitions. These were athletic games, so perhaps they could be analyzed in terms of sport. But other cultural dimensions also pertained to them: death in the ancient world, slavery, power, status, drama, and (last but not least) the primacy of the Roman imperial order. There is, then, some artificiality in

Figure 3.2. An eighteenth-century painting depicting the 1764 excavation of the temple of the deity Isis in Pompeii (painting by William Hamilton [1757–1804], now in the public domain; see credits)

splitting things into separate chapters. But this is a necessary artificiality. A whole meal is not to be eaten in a single bite. Similarly, the issues pertaining to Christian engagement with the Greco-Roman world cannot be encountered in toto. Consequently, the reader will occasionally find that issues discussed in one chapter overlap with issues discussed in another chapter. This simply reflects the realities of Roman culture.

Although every book of the New Testament is mentioned at some point within the following chapters, there is a noticeable lean toward the letters of Paul, which themselves constitute about a third of the New Testament. Of course, other parts of the New Testament have a strong foothold here too—not least the Gospels, Revelation, 1 Peter, the letter of James, and the Acts of the Apostles. (Even the often overlooked texts of Jude and 2 Peter get mentioned.) But if the Pauline letters often come to the fore, that is because they were written to Jesus-followers in the Roman urban society more evidently, more extensively, and more relevantly than most other New Testament texts. For instance, the audience of 1 Peter includes first-century urban residents, but that text is only five chapters long. The four canonical Gospels were written to Jesus-followers in urban society and were deemed relevant to that audience, but they do not offer sustained views of urban society in the Roman world. For reasons of this sort, this gentle lean toward the letters of Paul is virtually inevitable by the very nature of the subject matter.

If you want to probe New Testament texts further than the discussion within the following chapters, you may want to consult the questions raised in the appendix, "Questions to Consider." Three questions per chapter are listed there for chapters 4 through 19. The questions take the contents of those chapters a step further by considering other texts and issues of some relevance.

Designations Frequently Used

We will make extensive use of inscriptions and graffiti from the Vesuvian towns. These inscriptions and graffiti have been collected by archaeologists in particular volumes of *Corpus Inscriptionum Latinarum*, or "the corpus of Latin inscriptions." In particular, the fourth volume of this massive project (together at times with the tenth volume) contains the majority of graffiti, inscriptions, and other phenomena found in Pompeii and Herculaneum (which collectively comes to over eleven thousand entries). So when an inscription is mentioned and a reference appears next to it, such as "*CIL* 4.5112," the reader knows that this inscription can be found in the fourth volume of *Corpus Inscriptionum Latinarum* (*CIL*), where it appears as inscription number 5112. (You have seen this convention used already in this book.)

Most of the Vesuvian artifacts that are housed in the National Archaeology Museum of Naples have been given inventory numbers by the museum's curators. Wherever possible, those inventory numbers have been included in the discussions that follow. They are clearly referenced by the four letters "MANN," which abbreviate the Italian name of the museum, Museo Archeologico Nazionale di Napoli. For instance, the discussion in chapter 18 considers the artifact MANN 9987, whose number indicates that it resides in the museum and is identified by the inventory number 9987. This information will enable you to search several websites, as discussed below. Some artifacts discussed in this book are not currently accessible at internet sites—as is the case for the fresco displayed in figure 3.3, for instance, which was discovered in the temple of the deity Isis (whose excavations are depicted in figure 3.2).

Other abbreviations will also appear in this book, although much less frequently; these are explained in the list of abbreviations at the back of the book. The glossary can be referenced if you find the need to clarify the meaning of a technical word (for instance, *triclinium* or *columella*—although such terms are often defined within the main text where they are first introduced).

It will frequently be helpful to discuss particular locations in the Vesuvian region, and several points arise in this regard.

1. In the mid-nineteenth century, the famous archaeologist Giuseppe Fiorelli divided Pompeii into nine regions for ease of reference, and this categorization has stuck ever since. (A plan of these nine designated regions of Pompeii appears in figure 3.4.) Within those nine regions, Fiorelli assigned specific numbers to street blocks (or *insulae*, literally "islands," the singular being *insula*); within those street blocks, the entryways into houses and businesses were enumerated as well. So, for instance, the large house that archaeologists named "The House of the Faun" is situated in Region 6 of Pompeii and in block number 12, with its main entrance being entryway number 2 within that block—meaning that the main entrance into the House of the Faun is located at 6.12.2 in Pompeii. On rare occasions, a letter may be included as part of the designator for a particular location—such

Figure 3.3. A Vesuvian fresco of a worship ceremony being conducted in the temple of the deity Isis (MANN 8919)

as 5.4.a, which is Region 5, block number 4, entryway "a."

2. Sometimes residences have more than one entryway, so the third number in a location designation might include multiple entries (as in the case of the House of the Golden Cupids at 6.16.7/38).

3. Usually Vesuvian villas (as opposed to residences of whatever size) do not have location designators but are referred to simply by their titles (for instance, the Villa of the Mysteries or the Villa of the Papyri).

4. Tombs are designated by the town gates that they lie beyond, so the tomb of Mamia (seen in figure 7.6) is the fourth tomb beyond Pompeii's Herculaneum Gate (HG) on the west side of the street (W) and is therefore designated HGW04 (HG, W, 04).

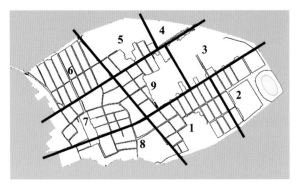

Figure 3.4. Pompeii divided into nine regions (blank areas within Regions 1, 3, 4, 5, and 9 are areas that have not yet been excavated)

5. Locations in Herculaneum have only two enumerators rather than Pompeii's three (so, for instance, the location 5.6 designates one of Herculaneum's wine shops).

6. Occasionally whole insulas (or *insulae*) in Pompeii will be referred to using the location of the insula itself (such as the country club of Julia Felix at insula 2.4).

Pompeii in Pictures

Residents of the Vesuvian towns loved beauty. Artistic scenes and ornamental decorations were usually painted directly onto the walls of residences, shops, and workshops. Although we might think of these as "paintings," they are actually frescos and will be referred to in that way throughout this book. A fresco is created by embedding the paint into the plaster just after the plaster is set on the wall and while it is still wet. In that way, the paint becomes embedded within the plaster itself, rather than sitting on the surface of the plaster. This technique has ensured the relative longevity of so many beautiful pieces of Vesuvian artwork.

The fantastic thing is that anyone can access many of these frescos and the majority of the Vesuvian material structures (residences, workshops, temples, tombs, public baths, etc.) simply through the convenience of the internet. Of course, visiting the physical sites is the best thing, but accessing it through the internet is not a shabby second best. So, whenever a location is referred to in this book, the reader can check that location and explore it further at the tremendous online resource called "Pompeii in Pictures."

Let's say, for instance, that you read something that intrigues you about "the House of the Faun" at 6.12.2 and want to know more about that residence and take a look inside it. In that case, simply go to the "Pompeii in Pictures" website, scroll down to the map of Pompeii and click on section 6, then insula 12, then entryway 2, and the website opens up pages of photos that take you into every sector of that magnificent residence. Similarly, if you want to explore the Temple of Isis further, go to the website, scroll down to the map of Pompeii and click on "Temples in Pompeii" and then "Temple of Isis," at which point photos of the temple are available in a series of web pages. Or perhaps you are intrigued by the agony displayed in the contorted corpse of the dog chained near the entrance of a Pompeian residence (see figure 3.5), in which case you can explore the magnificent residence in the web pages dedicated to the House of Vesonius Primus at 6.14.20. The first of those web pages provides photos of the bust of Vesonius Primus that was centrally displayed within the house, so we can even see what this dog's owner might have looked like.

This convenient way of accessing the Pompeian material allows readers of this book to amplify their reading experience with further

28

Figure 3.5. The contorted body of a dog who died in the eruption is captured by this nineteenth-century plaster in-fill of the cavity left by the dog's body years after the eruption, after it had decomposed (from 6.14.20).

investigations. That might involve checking to see what frescos were displayed on a residence's walls, what interior shrines a residence enjoyed, or what graffiti were scratched or painted onto the exterior walls of a residence—the kind of things that give further glimpses into the experiences of the people whose lives we are observing. In this way, the website "Pompeii in Pictures" can act as a rich and rewarding supplement to your reading and learning experience.

The same site can be used to check on artifacts that are not graphically displayed in this book. For instance, in chapter 10 you will read about an election campaign fresco that has the designation *CIL* 4.9885. Although that artifact is not depicted in this book, if you type "9885" into the "Pompeii in Pictures" search

Figure 3.6. The large forum of Pompeii, as seen from its southern side looking north (northwest) with Mount Vesuvius in the background (from a nineteenth-century photo, now in the public domain; see credits)

engine, you will be shown the web page where that election notice can be seen. You will not be able to do this for every fresco, election notice, or graffito, since there has been no attempt to make "Pompeii in Pictures" a depository for photos of all the Vesuvian realia (and many of them are no longer visible anyway). Nonetheless, a search of this kind is worth a try, and sometimes you will get lucky. Usually the inscription is also cited in its original language (usually Latin). (Also, when using the "Pompeii in Pictures" search tool, search for the *CIL* inscription number that appears after the volume number—so, "9885" rather than "4.9885"; alternatively, since that website uses the standard form of citing *CIL* volumes by Roman numerals, you could also search for "IV 9885.")

There is also a "Herculaneum in Pictures" website, which can be usefully consulted along the same lines. The "Catalogue of the Museo Archeologico di Napoli" on Wikimedia Commons gives online access to many of the artifacts held in the Naples archaeological museum.

Terminology

In this book, we will use "the Common Era" as our temporal reference point. Traditionally, the abbreviations "BC" ("before Christ") and AD ("Anno Domini," or "in the year of the Lord") have been used for this purpose. So, for instance, the emperor Augustus was born in the year 63 BC and died in AD 14. Rewritten with reference to "the Common Era," we would say that the emperor Augustus was born in the year 63 BCE ("sixty-three years before the Common Era") and died in 14 CE ("in the fourteenth year of the Common Era"). At times no temporal designation is required in the chapters that follow, and in those instances the designation "CE" is implied and left unstated.

Another terminological convention pertains to words that refer to the gods and goddesses of the Roman world. In this book, these "gods" will be referred to as "deities," and the same word will be used when referring to the "God" of Judeo-Christian theology (as in the phrase "the deity proclaimed by the early Jesus-followers"). This terminology avoids an inbuilt distinction between the Roman "gods" and the Judeo-Christian "God"—with the traditional capital *G* reflecting a theological commitment that does not suit the conceptual framework of most people in the first century of the Common Era. (So too, the authors of first-century Christian texts did not have the luxury of capitalizing the word in some instances and not in others, since all letters were written in capital formation—as was the convention of the day.) Of course, one of the leading contributions of early Christian theological discourse was the attempt to make devotion to the deity of Jesus-followers exclusive—which, in a sense, was equivalent to capitalizing the *G* in discourse about the divine reality (although even here there were some precedents within Greco-Roman philosophical discourse). Distinguishing "God" from "the gods" was precisely the terrain where the first Jesus-followers did some of the most creative and engaging spadework in their theological discourse. Their efforts may eventually have been rewarded, with the establishment of the Christian empire under the auspices of emperor Constantine in the early fourth century. But in the first century, there seemed to be no guarantee that the Christian movement would succeed (except for theological convictions about the eventual triumph of the Judeo-Christian deity). Historically speaking, the Christian voice could just as easily have died out, just as so many other voices of that day eventually did. The simple avoidance of the term "God" within this book will go some way in helping us to replicate that first-century situation, allowing us to hear voices of early Jesus-followers in their original context without predetermining the inevitable legitimacy of their contributions. The word "God" with a capital *G* does appear at times in subsequent chapters of this book but only in English translations of the Greek New Testament, where it is in keeping with the convictions (although not the conventions) of those first-century authors.

Terminology pertaining to "the Jews" needs to be explained briefly, since the default within this book will be to replace that term with "the Judeans." In the ancient world, forms of what we call "religion" were often embedded within larger ethnic contexts—that is, many deities were associated with particular ethnic identities. In this frame of reference, the Greek term *Ioudaios* (usually translated "Jew"; the plural is *Ioudaioi*) referenced forms of identity that were traceable (or claimed to be traceable) to Judea and the ethnic people whose corporate origins derived from there. The temple of the deity of the *Ioudaioi* was based in Judea (specifically, in the Jerusalem temple), and it was there that the presence of that deity was, in one sense, most densely concentrated (specifically, in the temple's innermost sanctuary, "the holy of holies"—although qualifications were sometimes applied to this conviction). Any "religious" practices that came with the claim to be a *Ioudaios* were practices derived from within a broader ethnic framework of relationality—both relationality between people of that ethnic group and

Figure 3.7. Excavation of Vesuvian sites continues to this day, as at this site near Pompeii, a villa (Oplontis Villa B) is currently being uncovered below ground level.

relationality between that ethnic group and the deity attached to that ethnic group. If a person decided to become a *Ioudaios*, for instance, he/she would not have been seen as simply adopting a new form of "religion"; instead, he/she would have been seen as embedding himself/herself within a particular ethnic group—with its own cultural heritage, its Judean homeland, and its ethnically distinctive forms of devotion to an ethnic deity, whose primary residence was in Judea. Because of this, at times it will serve us better to translate the term *Ioudaios* as "Judean" rather than "Jew," in an effort to perceive situations in accordance with the perceptions of people in

Figure 3.8. The west side of the Eumachia building (to the left of the photo, facing onto Pompeii's forum) was demolished in the earthquake of 62 and was rebuilt after the earthquake using red brick rather than the original brick (plaster would have covered the wall and kept these differences from being visible).

the Roman world. The weakness of the term "Judean," of course, is that it does not permit easy differentiations between "Judeans" who lived in Judea itself and "Judeans" who lived beyond that geographical territory throughout the Mediterranean basin. In a sense, however, for many *Ioudaioi* of the ancient world, that was precisely the point.

The word "pagan" will be used at points in the following chapters. This word, however, is not completely "fit for purpose" for two reasons. First, it suggests a kind of monochrome sameness to the Roman setting, rather than inviting us to expect and explore the rich diversity of devotional systems. Second, pejorative connotations and derogatory baggage are often imported into the term, especially when judged from a perspective of monotheistic convictions. Nonetheless, no one has yet found a better term to replace "pagan." In this book, I tend to write in ways that allow the word "pagan" to be avoided, but at times I found the need to resort to it, for lack of a better word.

With reference to the Pauline letters themselves, I will use different terminology to refer to the author of various Pauline texts. This is because the authorship of some of Paul's letters is not wholly clear. There is no dispute that Paul wrote at least seven letters that have survived and are part of the New Testament—these include (in their order within the New Testament) Romans, 1 and 2 Corinthians, Galatians, Philippians, 1 Thessalonians, and Philemon. Other Pauline texts are less clear with regard to authorship. It is possible that some of them were written by disciples of Paul who sought to extend Paul's voice and address situations that transpired after his death in a way they imagined Paul would have done. These are thorny issues whose complexities need not detain us here. In my view, 1 Timothy and Titus derive from the last two decades of the first century, when a disciple of Paul thought it necessary to extend facets of Paul's theology in order to address some pressing needs of that day; 2 Timothy might be similar in this regard, although it might also derive from one of Paul's own letters. The letter to the Ephesians probably slots into place somewhere in the 70s or 80s, and perhaps Colossians (itself something of a template for Ephesians) is best placed there as well. I err on the side of thinking that 2 Thessalonians was written by Paul. Not much hangs on these issues for the most part, except at three points:

- Chapter 15 discusses early Christian discourse about slaves, and there the later date of Colossians comes into play.
- Chapter 16 discusses early Christian discourse about family relationships, and there the later date of Ephesians comes into play.
- Chapter 17 discusses early Christian discourse about women, and there the later date of 1 Timothy and Titus comes into play.

Figure 3.9. The large marble paving slabs in Pompeii's forum include damage marks from a bomb explosion during an Allied air raid in 1943.

Other than these three points, the proposed dates of these texts do not affect the presentation very much. But I mention the issue in order to explain the terminological distinction between "Paul" (the name used when discussing the undisputed letters) and "the author of . . ." (the phrase used when discussing the disputed letters, as in "the author of 1 Timothy").

Miscellaneous Things

A few other points can be made quickly here.

- The photos of Vesuvian artifacts are usually my own, although some black-and-white drawings have been included as well, originating from books that are now in the public domain. The credits for those drawings appear in the credits at the back of this book. The photos are not to be replicated, by instruction of the Superintendency of the Vesuvian towns.

- Whenever house names or locations are mentioned in this book, they are from Pompeii unless specifically listed as being from Herculaneum.

One final word before the explorations begin. Although each of the following chapters deals with a particular slice of the pie of Roman urban life in relation to New Testament features, it might be good to keep in mind one other question that keeps trying to nuzzle in: Why might someone have been attracted to a form of Jesus-devotion in the Roman world? We cannot address that question in any depth here, since it requires the accumulation of much fuller resources in order to give it the necessary consideration. But it is ultimately the question that stands over many of the discussions in subsequent chapters, and it teases and taunts us to think further at each and every point.

Timeline of Events, People, and Texts of Pertinence to the Rise of Early Christianity

Note that the dates given here are only approximations, based on what seems to be the most plausible interpretation of a variety of data.

30	The death of Jesus
32	Paul encountered one whom he subsequently called "our Lord Jesus Christ"
50	Paul wrote 1 Thessalonians, probably his earliest extant letter
	Paul wrote 2 Thessalonians soon after 1 Thessalonians (although this letter may have been written after his death by one of his disciples)
50/51	Paul wrote Galatians
54/55	Paul wrote 1 Corinthians
55/56	Paul wrote 2 Corinthians
57	Paul wrote Romans
60–62	Paul wrote Philippians and Philemon (although both could have been written in the mid-50s, especially Philemon)
70–75	The Gospel of Mark began to circulate among Jesus-groups
	The letter to the Hebrews began to circulate among Jesus-groups
80s	Colossians seems to be dated to a point within this decade, written by a disciple of Paul
	Ephesians seems to be dated to a point within this decade, written by a disciple of Paul
	The Gospel of Matthew began to circulate among Jesus-groups
80s–90s	The Gospel of Luke began to circulate among Jesus-groups
	The letter of James seems to be dated to some point within these decades
	The Pastoral letters (1–2 Timothy, Titus) were written by a disciple of Paul (although 2 Timothy, or parts of it, may have been written by Paul)
	First Peter seems to be dated to some point within these decades
90s	The Gospel of John began to circulate in its final form among Jesus-groups
	The Johannine letters (1–3 John) were written soon after (or perhaps just before) the circulation of the Johannine Gospel
	John the Seer wrote Revelation (the Johannine Apocalypse)
	The author of the Gospel of Luke wrote the Acts of the Apostles in this decade or soon afterward
110–130	Jude and 2 Peter seem to be dated to some point within these decades

Timeline of Prominent Events and People in the Vesuvian Context

509 BCE	The founding of the Roman republic
91–89 BCE	The "Social War," in which many Italian towns and cities allied in a federation that fought to gain privileges of closer alignment with Rome (ironically); the Italian alliance was defeated by Rome and forced to capitulate to its overarching rule, ironically (again) opening up closer alignment with Rome as a consequence
80 BCE	The founding of Pompeii as a Roman colony
27 BCE–14 CE	Augustus (formerly Octavius; 63 BCE–14 CE) ruled as emperor of the Roman empire
14–37	Tiberius (42 BCE–37 CE) ruled as emperor of the Roman empire
37–41	Caligula (12–41) ruled as emperor of the Roman empire
41–54	Claudius (10 BCE–54 CE) ruled as emperor of the Roman empire
54–68	Nero (37–68) ruled as emperor of the Roman empire
59	A riot occurred in Pompeii's amphitheater
62/63	A massive earthquake destroyed many structures within the Vesuvian towns (the precise year is impossible to know, but 62 is perhaps slightly preferable and will be used throughout the remainder of this book; see figure 3.8)
69–79	Vespasian (9–79 CE) ruled as emperor of the Roman empire (until June 23, 79)
79–81	Titus (39–81 CE) ruled as emperor of the Roman empire (from June 23, 79, just prior to the eruption of Vesuvius)
79	The eruption of Mount Vesuvius (traditionally dated to August 24–25, but better evidence supports a date later in the autumn, perhaps October 24)
1700s	Excavations of Herculaneum and Pompeii begin sporadically, gaining strong momentum by the end of the eighteenth century
1943	Allied bombers dropped more than 150 bombs on Pompeii, suspecting supporters of Mussolini were hiding in its ruins

PART TWO

Protocols of Popular Devotion

Deities and Temples

4

> When the crowds saw what Paul had done, they shouted in the Lycaonian language, "The gods have come down to us in human form!" ... The priest of Zeus, whose temple was just outside the city, brought oxen and garlands to the gates; he and the crowds wanted to offer sacrifice. When the apostles Barnabas and Paul heard of it, they tore their clothes and rushed out into the crowd, shouting, "Friends, why are you doing this? We are mortals just like you, and we bring you good news, that *you should turn from these worthless things to the living God, who made the heaven and the earth and the sea and all that is in them*."
>
> Acts 14:11–15

These Worthless Things

Speaking to the people of Lystra, the apostle Paul described the temples of the Greco-Roman deities and the sacrifices offered to them as "worthless things." In this, he voiced a viewpoint acceptable to only a small minority of his peers. For the vast majority of his contemporaries, temples were critical components in the smooth running of society. The phrase "these worthless things" probably also included a reference to the deities themselves, in which case Paul voiced a view that would have resonated with an even smaller minority of the population.

To label temples and deities as "worthless" (and to do so in the name of "the living God, who made the heaven and the earth and the sea and all that is in them") would be equivalent today to calling for shutting off all the electrical grids that power the structures of contemporary society. It is little wonder, then, that this narrative shows Paul to be in a position of extreme danger after making his daring pronouncement. The narrator tells us that the people "stoned Paul and dragged him out of the city, supposing that he was dead" (Acts 14:19).

The Temples and Deities in Pompeii and Beyond

Like the Temple of Zeus (or Jupiter) in this narrative, there were many temples beyond the walls of Roman urban centers. Most temples, however, lay within urban walls—usually at the heart of Roman civic centers. Things were no different in Pompeii in this regard. Although one very important temple lay beyond the town's walls (see discussion of the Temple of Bacchus in chapter 8), no fewer than eight temples were dotted around the central forum of the town or sat nearby it (see figure 4.1). The forum toward the southwest of the town (see figure 3.6) was the center of public life in Pompeii (excluding the odd Roman baths dotted here or there beyond the forum and excluding two main complexes east of the town—the amphitheater and the grand palaestra, which was basically a large park). That central forum housed many of Pompeii's public buildings—buildings for devotional worship, for the selling of primary foods, and for the municipal administration of the town. These buildings formed a ribbon around a large rectangular open space where people milled around or moved from one location to another. The forum was the center of the oldest part of the town, and much of the town seems to have grown up around it.

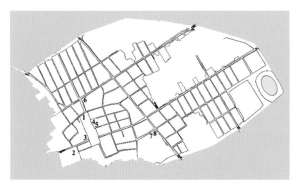

Figure 4.1. The locations of the main Greco-Roman temples of Pompeii in the final years of its existence: 1 = the Capitoline Triad (Jupiter, Juno, Minerva); 2 = Venus; 3 = Apollo; 4 = imperial cult; 5 = emperor Vespasian (imperial cult); 6 = Augustan Fortuna (imperial cult); 7 = Isis; 8 = Aesculapius (or Jupiter Meilichios). The forum is the rectangular space around which temples 1, 3, 4, and 5 are dotted.

Pompeii's temples honored certain deities in particular. Most prominent in the central forum was the temple honoring Jupiter, Juno, and Minerva (temple 1 on figure 4.1)—three deities known as the "Capitoline Triad" because they were worshiped together on Rome's important Capitoline Hill. Also prominent within Pompeii's central forum was a temple honoring Apollo (temple 3), another honoring the imperial family (temple 4), and another honoring emperor Vespasian in particular (temple 5).

Much less prominent was the temple to the Egyptian deity Isis (temple 7). This small temple was tucked away from things, as if to enhance the devotional secrecy of those who were initiated into the mysteries of this popular female deity. It is hard to exaggerate the importance of Isis in Pompeii and elsewhere throughout the Roman world. Her devotees were growing in number by leaps and bounds at precisely the same time that the early Jesus-movement was getting a small foothold in relatively insignificant groups throughout urban centers of the Mediterranean basin. (Chapter 9 will further consider the significance of Isis-devotion in the Vesuvian towns.)

At the southwest pinnacle of the town stood the temple to the female deity Venus (temple 2), who had been selected to serve as Pompeii's primary benefactor and protector. Her temple stood closest to the water, in a position of prominence for those passing by on the sea or arriving from the sea. Except for the Pompeian resident who threatened to break Venus's ribs because he had been unlucky in love (see chapter 1), Pompeians were extremely dedicated to Venus and honored her in many ways. One resident scratched a graffito on the wall announcing Venus to be "the Savior" (*CIL* 4.9867; see also chapter 6), and a fresco

Figure 4.2. The Temple of Jupiter in Pompeii (7.8), which later became the temple to the Capitoline Triad of Roman deities: Jupiter, Juno, and Minerva

on the exterior wall of a shop (9.7.6–7) depicts her with a ruling scepter as she is pulled in a chariot by four elephants. Frescos and graffiti throughout the town show the importance of this deity for the residents of Pompeii.

Honoring the deities in temples and beyond was a crucial part of civic life in the towns and cities of the Roman world. That the deities were essential to the well-being of all that mattered was a key conviction for many people. The deities were numerous, each having his or her primary functions, although those functions often coupled with secondary functions as well. At the heart of the divine world were the twelve deities who purportedly resided at the top of Mount Olympus, around whom the vast resources of Greek mythology revolved.

Inheriting these traditional Olympian deities from Greek mythic narratives, the Romans usually renamed them: Zeus became Jupiter, Poseidon became Neptune, Athena became Minerva, Artemis became Diana, Aphrodite became Venus, Hermes became Mercury, Ares became Mars, Dionysus became Bacchus, and so on (with only Apollo surviving with his original Greek name intact). The number of deities far outstripped the twelve Olympian deities, however. In the Roman world, the deities were limited in number only because of the limits of the human imagination.

Mythologies of these deities did not necessarily depict them as inherently good, gracious, and just. Nor were they shown to be completely knowledgeable, powerful, and

41

benevolent (although Vesuvian graffiti sometimes enhanced their reputation in these categories, as in *CIL* 4.6864: "Best and greatest Jupiter, all-powerful lord!"). Nor were they predominately concerned about overseeing the welfare of humanity (although some were thought to be more intentional in showing favor toward humanity than others). So why was reverence for the deities deeply embedded within Roman culture? Ultimately devotion to the deities derived from the fear that failing

Figure 4.3. A fresco of two women at a temple whose rotunda contains a statue of Venus, with one woman having brought an offering of flowers (from 6.17.41, MANN 8594)

to honor them would incur their wrath and . from the hope that capturing their favor might enhance a person's prospects (see especially chapter 5).

There were, of course, many differing views about the deities. Philosophers and poets of various kinds questioned the validity of many aspects of long-standing Greco-Roman mythologies about the deities. But those mythologies set the overarching context for conversations about the character of the deities. Numerous works of art in the Vesuvian towns (whether in residences, workshops, or public spaces) depict moments in those mythological narratives. Clearly the realm of the deities had captured the imaginations and, no doubt, conversations of the residents of those towns.

Vesuvian residences also illustrate that first-century households could often favor one particular deity, although not to the exclusion of others. The deity Venus was a favorite in Pompeii, as we have seen, and she was frequently called on to enhance prospects in sexual attraction, love, happiness, and commercial enterprise involving sea-faring. Frescos of the deity Mercury adorned some of the shops lining the streets, since he was the deity of commerce (among other things). The high Roman deity, Jupiter, was often depicted in residences to enhance protection within the household. And Dionysus, or Bacchus, was honored in many households, promoting abundant enjoyment (see chapter 8).

There was never any sense that having a favored deity required a person to be devotionally exclusive. Since each deity had his or her own strengths, devotion to the deities was always "complementarian." In Pompeii, for instance, devotion to the town's divine protector, Venus, was completely in keeping with devotion to other deities—Jupiter, Mercury,

Apollo, Juno, Minerva, and all the rest. The deities were like the ancient version of insurance: the more you had, the more secure you were likely to be. Or, to change the analogy, it was like buying into the stock market: the more diverse your portfolio, the less the risk to your finances (generally speaking). For this reason, devotion to the deities was as expansive as it needed to be. And it needed to be expansive in order to engulf all the nooks and crannies of life's complexities. It was even suggested on occasion that the innumerable deities were not, in fact, separate entities in themselves but were collectively the multiple manifestations of the one single divine entity that lay behind them all and permeated all things. This view was not widespread and was usually restricted to discourse among the philosophers, but it was "in the air" nonetheless.

No one would have thought it strange, then, when one Pompeian woman prided herself on being a priestess of both Venus and Ceres—two of the deities whose cults permitted female priestesses (as in the case of "Alleia, daughter of Marcus," in *EE* 8.855; other women who served as priestesses of Venus were Eumachia, Mamia, Holconia, and Isticidia Rufilla, and serving the deity Ceres were Alleia Decimilla, Clodia, Lassia, and Aquvia Quarta—and many others whose names are not mentioned in the surviving Vesuvian realia).

Alongside devotion to the traditional Greco-Roman deities, another form of devotion was springing up everywhere in the civic centers of the first century—that is, reverential worship of the emperor. Augustus (emperor from 27 BCE to 14 CE), Claudius (from 41 to 54), Nero (from 54 to 68), Vespasian (from 69 to 79), Titus (from 79 to 81), Domitian (from 81 to 96)—these emperors were worshiped at one point or another in

Figure 4.4. The high Roman deity, Jupiter, depicted in a statue from Pompeii's Capitoline temple (only the head has survived) (from 7.8.1)

Roman civic centers. If the rise of the Jesus-movement was impressive within the first century, far more widespread was the rise of devotion directed to the emperor—or better, the emperor's divine spirit. (On his deathbed the emperor Vespasian was reputed to have uttered the jocular quip, "O dear, I think I'm becoming a deity"; Suetonius, *Life of Vespasian* 23.) Individual urban centers felt competition to outdo other urban centers in the quality and extent of their emperor devotion. This was because enormous economic and political benefits were attached to those who could demonstrate a pro-Roman sentiment. Those who sidled up to the Roman imperial order were rewarded; the propagation of Roman imperial ideology oiled the machinery of Rome's political interests. It was not necessary for the emperors to advertise their

Figure 4.5. A fresco of Apollo standing next to the stone (covered by a net) that marked the center of the world (and thus the point of universal control; from 6.17.10, MANN 9541)

the modern differentiation of "religion" and "state" within separate spheres of life fails to do justice to the intricate connections between governance and the deities (including the emperor) that characterized the central nexus of power within the Roman world. (We will see more of this in chapters 6 and 7.)

An Ethnic Exception

One ethnic group managed to negotiate things somewhat differently than most of their contemporaries: the Jews or, better perhaps, the Judeans (since their ethnic identity was tied to the land of Judea and to the worship of their deity, whose temple was located there). Whenever local peer pressure promoted emperor worship, Judeans could appear as responsible members of society even without making sacrificial offerings to the emperor in a local imperial temple. This is because Judean priests offered daily sacrifices in the Jerusalem temple (the core of Judean identity) in honor of the Roman emperor—but not in worship of him. These sacrifices enabled Judean identity to be understood as including loyalty to the ruling authority of the day without involving explicit worship of the emperor.

own divinity among the populace; the civic elite did most of the heavy lifting in that regard throughout the cities and towns of the Mediterranean basin. As long as devotion was directed toward the emperor in one fashion or another, people were thought to be exercising their proper duty to the overarching system that had been set in place and legitimated by the deities of Rome. Artifacts and texts from the ancient world repeatedly testify that

This situation helped resolve a point of potential conflict between the Judeans and their polytheistic contemporaries since Judeans, almost uniquely among all people, were known to be exclusive in their devotion to a single deity: YHWH, the covenant deity of the Judean people. Devotional exclusivity had characterized Judean identity for centuries, and the daily sacrifices for the emperor in the Jerusalem temple allowed Judeans both to avoid the stigma of holding back Roman progress and to maintain their long-established devotional exclusivity to their covenant deity.

Figure 4.6. A fresco depicting Solomon on his judgment seat (center of three figures to the right) issuing a wise pronouncement over the fate of a child claimed by two women, one of whom pleads for the child's life (kneeling before Solomon's judgment seat), while the philosophers Plato and Socrates look on in admiration (far left)—a temporal dislocation that seeks to combine the best wise men of Greek and Judean history (from 8.5.24, MANN 113197)

Generally speaking, the exclusivity of Judean devotion was an extremely curious thing in this ancient polytheistic world. To limit devotion to a single deity (putting all your eggs in the basket of only one deity) was seen as limiting one's strategies for survival to a ridiculously meager range of options. Although attitudes toward Judeans ran from admiration (for their ethical wisdom) to aversion (for the practices of Sabbath observance and circumcision), many within the Roman world would have imagined the Judeans to be taking an absurd risk in their devotion to a single deity.

For the most part, the first century witnessed a delicate balancing act whereby a relatively peaceful coexistence between Judean exclusivism and Roman polytheism was generally maintained (perhaps without great support from either side). At times, however, things went wrong. One instance of this occurred in the early 40s, when the emperor known as Caligula (the diminutive nickname of Gaius Julius Caesar Augustus Germanicus) tried to set up a statue of himself within the Jerusalem temple—an attempt to place a wanna-be deity alongside the Judean deity in the sacred space reserved solely for that sovereign deity. The exclusivity of Judean devotion was being challenged directly. As a consequence, thousands of Judeans protested the action, saying they would rather be slaughtered than tolerate this form of blasphemy against their deity. Ultimately Caligula was unsuccessful in his attempt to water down the exclusivist devotion of the Judeans.

The balance was again skewed in the late 60s. For one reason or another, Judeans got caught up in an uprising against Rome, seeking to remove the yoke of subordination to the Roman imperial order and to establish the sole reign of their deity. During the revolt of 66–70 (with the wipe-up operation continuing until 73 or 74), the Roman slaughter of Judeans was relentless. In 70, the temple of the Judean deity was destroyed, and the city of Jerusalem would never again play a central role in the practicalities of Judean devotion. This new fact of life was reinforced once and for all with the defeat of a second major Judean uprising against Rome in 132–135 CE, when the city was decimated and hope for its restoration was decisively crushed. In the aftermath of these two revolts, many would

Figure 4.7. Left: a fresco of the deity Apollo (as a youth) wearing a solar or radiant crown (from 7.2.16, MANN 9449); right: a fresco of Apollo enthroned in the heavens (from 6.7.23, in situ)

have thought that Rome's deities had proved themselves victorious over the Judean deity twice within a seventy-year period.

Challenging the System

A less dramatic but no less controversial form of uprising against the deities of Rome is evident in attitudes expressed by several leaders of the early Jesus-movement in the mid-first century—drawing on Judean resources of devotional exclusivity. Those "apostolic" figures were expressly critical of worshiping Greco-Roman deities, and early Jesus-followers often adopted this apostolic point of view. According to Paul, for instance, residents of the city of Thessalonica had already noticed that Jesus-followers had "turned to God, away from idols, to serve a living and true God" (1 Thessalonians 1:9). This is an astounding claim, for two reasons:

1. Paul was writing to them less than a year after he had initially arrived in Thessalonica to preach his message of Jesus Christ (he probably arrived there in the second half of 49, and he probably wrote them from Corinth in early 50).

2. Turning away from idols would have been seen as a very bold move, perhaps even a ridiculous one, in the first-century world (for reasons that are evident in what we have already seen and from what we will continue to see in further chapters).

A few years after writing to the Thessalonians, Paul elaborated his exhortation to "turn to God, away from idols" in one of his letters to Jesus-followers in Corinth. In 54 or so, he wrote:

We know that no idol in the world really exists, and that there is no God but one.

46

Indeed, even though there may be so-called gods in heaven or on earth—as in fact there are many gods and many lords—yet for us there is one God, the Father, from whom are all things and for whom we exist, and one Lord, Jesus Christ, through whom are all things and through whom we exist. (1 Corinthians 8:4–6)

Paul did not deny that spiritual realities pervade things, whether "in heaven or on earth." What mattered to him was the inventory of the spiritual realities pervading the lives of Jesus-followers. Paul thought that idolatry was a form of enslavement to destructive spiritual forces (Galatians 4:8–9), resulting in the adoption of practices with tragic moral consequences (Romans 1:18–32). Consequently, whereas others *added* deities to their spiritual devotion, Paul and others argued for *abandoning* those other deities.

This is why early Jesus-followers became commonly known as "atheists"—not because they failed to believe in a supreme deity, but because they frequently discredited devotion to any of the recognized deities of the Greco-Roman world. This frequently caused Jesus-devotees to undergo various forms of persecution from their contemporaries. Society, it was thought, ran smoothly when the deities were proper recipients of human piety, and consequently, if some Jesus-followers "turned away" from standard reverential piety, they were wearing down the fabric of a stable and secure society.

For this reason, Jesus-devotees were often seen to be holding back progress and running the risk of bringing the ire of the deities down on society at large. It was the job of the civic authorities to remove such brash and irresponsible "atheism" from the civic arena, in order to preserve the social fabric overseen by the deities and protect the local populations. No doubt this is what Paul referenced when he spoke of the strident opposition that he often encountered: "Three times I have been beaten with rods [and] once I was stoned"—these "danger[s] in the city" and forms of "persecutions" being the initiatives of local populations against the so-called atheism of the early Christian message (2 Corinthians 11:25–26 and 12:10 RSV). Even suprahuman forces could be said to participate in this concerted effort against the preachers of "good news," as Paul suggests in 2 Corinthians 4:4: "The god of this world [= Satan] has blinded the minds of the unbelievers, to keep them from seeing the light of the gospel of the glory of Christ, who is the image of God."

Situations of persecution are evident from the pages of the New Testament itself, across a spectrum of stigmatization and abuse of Jesus-followers. Three scenarios exemplify

Figure 4.8. A fresco on the exterior wall of a Pompeii residence depicting Venus holding a scepter and a ship's rudder—showing her powers of rule and guidance; she is accompanied by her son, the deity Eros, and by two flying Erotes, or cupids of love (from 9.7.1, in situ).

the range of possibilities, with other experiences of ostracism no doubt falling between them as well.

1. The author of 1 Peter spoke of Jesus-followers being "maligned" and "abused" by their non-Christian contemporaries (3:16–17), describing it as "a fiery ordeal that is taking place among you to test you" (4:12; see further passages from 1 Peter in the "Questions to Consider" section for this chapter). Here, social disdain seemingly took the form of shunning Jesus-devotees.

2. The author of Hebrews knew of Jesus-followers who had experienced "the plundering of [their] possessions" (10:34). The taking of someone's possessions was usually orchestrated against those who were deemed to be politically subversive (or at least against those who failed to advocate for the political status quo), and some Jesus-followers seemed to have suffered in this way.

3. The author of Revelation knew of one person who had suffered martyrdom—"Antipas my witness, my faithful one, who was killed among you, where Satan lives [= where the imperial cult thrives]" (2:13).

Public Proclamation

We do not need to imagine that the persecution of Jesus-followers resulted from their denouncing idolatry while standing on public platforms in the central forums of first-century urban centers and shouting above the heads of the crowd. Of course, public proclamation of that kind is suggested by some of the stories about early Jesus-followers (as in the story from Acts 14, recounted at the outset of this chapter). More ordinary forms of discourse must have been the general norm, however—the kind of thing that would transpire in the workshops where early Jesus-followers worked from dawn to dusk. When Paul wrote to new Jesus-devotees in Thessalonica, for instance, the recipients of that letter were manual laborers (1 Thessalonians 4:11), and in that context Paul recalled his labors in a workshop: "You remember our labor and toil, brothers and sisters; we [Paul, Silvanus, and Timothy] worked night and day, so that we might not burden any of you while we proclaimed to you the gospel of God" (2:9; see also 2 Thessalonians 3:8).

This verse helps us imagine Paul articulating his message during his many long hours of labor in a (rented) artisan's workshop—a situation that must have been fairly common among early Jesus-followers. Laborers in workshops would have discussed anything and everything to help pass the time of day while working their craft. Conversations would have included any topic of interest—recent political developments, sporting competitions, sexual couplings, and neighborhood gossip. But during their long working hours, laborers would also have discussed the deities and the mythologies that animated their significance. People like Paul (himself a leatherworker by trade) would have taken any of these opportunities to talk "night and day" about their understanding of the deities in relation to the "good news" they felt commissioned to bring to the Roman world. Paul's rented workshop may well have had frescos of deities and pagan protective devices on its walls. Instead of getting paint and covering them over in disgust, Paul probably used those frescos as conversation starters in his interaction with local people.

Figure 4.9. A small workshop from Herculaneum, with stairs leading up to the sleeping quarters above; Paul would have worked in places somewhat like this as he took his message to cities of the Roman world.

Reconfiguring Temple Imagery

If early Jesus-devotees often polemicized against the Greco-Roman deities and their temples, they generally did not remove the notion of temples from their discourse altogether. Instead, they reinterpreted temples, redefining divine presence in the process. One example of this is evident in the Gospel of John, which identifies Jesus's own body as a [or better, the] temple: "Destroy this temple," Jesus said, "and in three days I will raise it up"—with the narrator informing the audience that Jesus was referring to "the temple of his body" (2:19, 21). Here, divine presence is concentrated in the person of Jesus. In that light, Jesus's dramatic "clearing of the temple" in John's Gospel (2:13–22) looks more like a "replacement" of the Judean temple

than a simple "cleansing" (see the "cleansing" interpretation in Mark 11:15–18; Matthew 21:12–13; Luke 19:45–46).

Elsewhere, divine presence is linked to the temple motif in relation to communities of Jesus's followers rather than to Jesus himself. For instance, when writing to Corinthian Jesus-followers, Paul described Jesus-groups as themselves forming a temple. Here is what he says in 1 Corinthians 3:16–17, where each occurrence of the word "you" appears in its plural form ("you all") in Greek: "Do you not know that you are God's temple and that God's Spirit dwells in you? . . . For God's temple is holy, and you are that temple" (see also 6:19). He makes the same point to the same devotees in a later letter, emphasizing once again the temple's corporate character: "What does the temple of God have in common with idols? Nothing. For we are the temple of the living God" (2 Corinthians 6:16). And as the temple of God, groups of Jesus-devotees enjoyed the presence of God among them—a point Paul added in the same verse, citing scripture from the Hebrew Bible: "As God said, 'I will live in them and walk among them, and I will be their God, and they shall be my people'" (quoting Leviticus 26:12; Jeremiah 32:38; Ezekiel 37:27). The author of Ephesians was similarly convinced that divine presence resides in communities of Jesus-followers. He depicted Jesus-followers as "a holy temple in the Lord" that is being built as "a dwelling place for God" (Ephesians 2:21–22). Evidently Jesus-followers had their temples, but they were not made of bricks and stone, mortar and plaster. Christian temples comprised the flesh and blood of ordinary Jesus-devotees.

There may have been even more to it, however. Temples usually contained within their sanctuaries images of their honored deities.

—those things being "impure thoughts and filthy actions."

This is very much in line with Paul's conviction that groups of Jesus-followers were to display the image of their living deity within "the temple of the living God." That image, however, was not carved in marble and placed on a podium for all to see; instead, it was to be found within Jesus-devotees themselves, who were "being transformed into the same image from one degree of glory to another" (2 Corinthians 3:18). That shared "image" was the image of their deity, Jesus Christ, who was to be recognizable in the lives of Jesus-devotees. Paul seems to have thought that when non-Christians saw transformation in the lives of Jesus-followers, what they were really looking at was the image of the Jesus-followers' deity—the effect of their deity's presence within them, coming alive within the everyday lives of his followers. This image did not display the *physical attributes* of Jesus Christ (as in the case of temple images); instead, it displayed the *character* of Jesus Christ within communities of Jesus-followers.

Paul used any number of metaphors to convey this important notion. In his letter to Jesus-followers in Galatia, for instance, he spoke of Jesus Christ being "formed in" his followers (Galatians 4:19) and of Jesus-devotees being "clothed . . . with Christ" (3:27)—just as he could speak of Jesus Christ coming alive within him personally (2:20). Passersby saw images of temple deities within their temples; so too, within "the temple of the living God" Paul expected that the one whom Jesus called "Father" was working to ensure that Jesus-followers would "be conformed to the image of his Son" (Romans 8:29). Like most temples of the Roman world, every Christian "temple" was to display images of its living deity. Unlike

Figure 4.10. A fresco of the deity Jupiter crowned with a victory wreath, holding a ruling scepter, with his eagle (adopted as the symbol of the Roman army) and a cosmic globe at his feet (from 6.9.6, MANN 9551)

Wherever there was "a holy temple," the normal expectation would be that an image of the temple's deity would be proudly displayed within it. (The main exception to this was, of course, the temple to the deity of Israel in Jerusalem, which had no statue displaying its deity.) According to the philosopher Epictetus (50–135), being in the presence of a deity's image required an elevation of one's morality (*Discourses* 2.8.12–14): "When you are in the presence of an image of god, you do not dare to do any of the things you are now doing" most temples, those images were not carved into static marble; instead, they were embodied within the transformed lives of the deity's followers. Those images were thought to be microcosms of the "new creation" that their deity was empowering within their communities (2 Corinthians 5:17; Galatians 6:15).

This field of temple metaphors finds rich articulation in Revelation—the last book of the New Testament. That book culminates in a vision of the eschatological city of God (Revelation 21–22; compare also Hebrews 13:14: "Here we have no lasting city, but we seek the city which is to come"). The author of Revelation tells us that he "saw no temple in [that] city, for its temple is the Lord God the Almighty and the Lamb" (Revelation 21:22). A city without a temple was unprecedented in the Roman world. In fact, it was an anomaly that made no sense—unless, of course, that city was the ultimate city where the ultimate deity was immediately present. John the Seer (as the author might well be called) thought that a city of that kind could only be called "the holy city, the new Jerusalem" (21:2). It is a city in which the deity proclaimed by the early Jesus-followers "will dwell with them as their God; they will be his people and God himself will be with them" (21:3). It is little wonder that their lord, "seated on the throne," could confidently proclaim, "See, I am making all things new" (21:5).

5 Sacrifice and Sin

> Jesus Christ, the righteous one, . . . is *the atoning sacrifice for our sins,* and not only for ours but also for the sins of the whole world.
>
> 1 John 2:2

Peace with the Deities

We have seen that the deities were usually thought to be essential to the well-being of everything and everyone that mattered in the Roman world. But often what mattered in that world was not so much what the author of 1 John would call "sin" (as in the quotation above), and certainly not "the sins of the whole world." Instead, what really mattered was success—success at every level of existence: personal, neighborhood, civic, regional, national, and international forms of success.

Worshiping the deities was part of that formula for success at all these levels. Consequently, if misfortune struck at any level, it was natural to assume that devotion to the deities had gone wrong in some way. If the deities became offended, it was because people had failed to honor them appropriately. That itself, of course, could be understood in terms of a moral failing; in a sense, the failure to give

deities their rightful deference could be framed in terms of transgressing the expectations of the deities. When the emperor Augustus set out his program for reviving the fortunes of the Roman world, restoring proper piety toward the deities was a main component of his vision. This, he imagined, would relieve the pressures of "sin" within the empire, with the traditional deities of Rome continuing to bless the empire that Augustus oversaw, ensuring its continued success and momentum.

A connection between the deities and personal ethics was not as strong as we might expect, at least when seen in relation to the Judeo-Christian worldview that has influenced so much of the Western world today. For many people, honoring the deities and making offerings to them may have had little to do with rectifying moral failings in their own character—either making restitution for their past failings or preventing their future failings. Honoring the deities was often an exercise in

Figure 5.1. The Temple of Apollo (7.7.32), with its sacrificial altar in the foreground and Mount Vesuvius in the background; a statue of Apollo is situated to the right beyond the edge of this picture.

pragmatic self-advancement; people offered reverence to the deities in order to enhance their prospects. According to Cicero, "Jupiter is called Best and Greatest not because he makes people just or sober or wise, but because he makes them safe, secure, wealthy, and opulent" (*On the Nature of the Gods* 3.87). This statement follows a question Cicero asked: "Did anyone ever give thanks to the deities because he was a good man?" Cicero's answer is negative; the deities are worshiped, he says, because of what they can give to a supplicant. In this way of thinking, if "wealth and opulence" should come to an individual or a neighborhood or a civic center or a region or a nation or the world, it was in accordance with the divine will. Consequently, those who

benefited from divine favor were expected to give thanks to the deities for augmenting their safety and security.

The sense of things was captured in the Latin phrase *do ut des*, "I give [to you] so that you will give [back to me]." The Roman comic playwright Plautus (ca. 255–185 BCE) had one of his characters explain it this way: "The deities put money in the hands of a man to whom they are well disposed. So now I'll attend to the business of sacrificing to them. It's my intention to look out for myself" (*Curculio*, lines 530–32). No doubt Plautus had his character speak in an exaggeratedly crass fashion for humorous effect; but even so, exaggeration is rhetorically effective to the extent that it rings true to its audience. Elsewhere in

53

Figure 5.2. A stylized fresco depicting a pig being brought to slaughter as a sacrifice to a statue of a deity (from the Villa of the Mysteries, in situ; the deity is sometimes said to be Priapus, but it is just as likely to be Bacchus as a mystery deity; see also the statue in figure 8.8)

Plautus's plays, a character captures the sense of piety's utility with these words: "Apollo, I pray that in your benevolence you bestow favor, good health, and good sense on our household, and in your benevolence may you also spare my son" (*The Merchant*, lines 678–79). According to the second-century rhetorician Lucian of Samosata, the popular expectation is that the deities "sell their blessings" to people (*On Sacrifices*, line 2). Piety in the Roman world was a means of improving one's chances for survival, advantage, and advancement.

Underlying all this was the notion of *pax deorum*, or "peace with the deities." Enjoying peace with (and from) the deities was a much better scenario than encountering the *ira deorum*, or "the wrath of the deities." To neglect proper piety was to introduce a breach in the relational fabric connecting the deities and human society, and to inflame the displeasure of the deities. Keeping quiet about the mighty deeds of the deities was itself something punishable. This fundamental "sin" would consequently hold back the momentum toward greater success—whether that was success at personal or corporate levels of existence. The lack of proper piety undermined peace between humans and their deities; the consequences for humans in their relationships with others could be dire if the deities extended their wrath on those whom they deemed deficient in devotion. The author of Acts captures something of this when he

54

depicts the death of Herod Antipas as having come about because "he had not given the glory to God" (Acts 12:23, adding the graphic detail that Herod died because "he was eaten by worms").

Morality and the Deities

By what means, then, were people to know how to live lives that the deities would find acceptable? According to Cicero, it was the philosophers who took pride of place in promoting discourse about how to live a moral life (*On Divination* 2.10–11). And this is what we commonly find in treatises from Greco-Roman philosophers and rhetoricians, who often contributed to the conversation about the deities and personal morality. Many philosophers argued that morality was an important component of living well. For instance, toward the end of the first century, the rhetorician Quintilian (35–100) talked of the need to shape the moral character of children within family structures, which in turn would enhance their effectiveness as adults within society. People were to act justly toward one another. But Quintilian noted that things often went wrong in that regard, with adults practicing deplorable behavior that children simply replicated (*Institutio oratoria* 1.2.8):

> It was we who taught them, they heard it all from us. They see our mistresses, our boy lovers; every dinner party echoes with obscene songs; things are to be seen which it is shameful to name. So first comes the habit, then the nature. The wretched children learn these things before they know these things are wrong. . . . They do not get these vices from schools, they import them [the vices] into them [the schools].

These "wrongs" and "vices" might well have been labeled "sins" by the author of 1 John (whom we referenced at the start of this chapter). But whereas that Christian author embedded his talk of "sins" in the context of transgressing a healthy relationship with the divine, philosophers and rhetoricians like Quintilian were not necessarily bound to follow that same discursive route. For them, enhancing moral virtue and diminishing vices was a pragmatic priority that flowed not so much from what we might call a "religious" commitment but, instead, from wise decision-making informed by thoughtful and sensible reflection about living a good life.

The first-century Stoic philosopher Musonius Rufus (ca. 20–100) stated the matter in this way: "If someone is a good man, would he not be a philosopher too? Yes"—the reason being that "philosophy is the pursuit of nobility of character" (Lecture 8). For Musonius Rufus, the pursuit of justice transpired from philosophical reflection. There is nothing here about devotion to the deities giving the resources for the "nobility of character" and no sense that worshiping the deities enabled someone's character to align with justice. Only by distant extension are the deities involved in that mix. As Musonius Rufus explained in a later context, whereas philosophy enhances one's moral character, this is, in fact, the will of Zeus (or Jupiter):

> His commandment and law is that a human being be just, righteous, kind, self-controlled, magnanimous, above pain and pleasure, and devoid of all envy and treachery. Stated briefly, the law of Zeus orders the human being to be good, and being good is the same thing as being a philosopher. . . . If you pursue philosophy, you will be following Zeus. (Lecture 16)

55

Figure 5.3. A fresco of Iphigenia about to be sacrificed in order to capture the goodwill of the gods and ensure her people's success in a naval battle; Iphigenia appeals to her father, Agamemnon, but he turns away, mourning the necessity of her slaughter but doing nothing to prevent her death for the greater good of his people; at the top right is the deity Artemis (who also stands as a figurine on the pillar next to Agamemnon), who prefers the sacrifice of a deer miraculously brought to her instead, thereby saving Iphigenia's life (from 6.8.3, MANN 9112).

As this quotation illustrates, connections between the deities and ethical living were sometimes made, in one way or another, depending on which philosophy was being espoused. Those connections might not have been robust within the philosophical and rhetorical traditions of the Roman world (at least in comparison with Judeo-Christian ethical discourse), but they were occasionally activated nonetheless. At times, then, the impression emerges that one's inner purity could affect the efficacy of one's ritual practices and sacrificial offerings toward the deities. Another Stoic philosopher made the point this way: "Would you try to win over the gods? Then be a good person" (*Letters from a Stoic* 95.50). The philosopher in question was Seneca (ca. 4 BCE–65 CE), the advisor to emperor

Nero (who himself was not known for virtuous character).

In this way a person's moral character and social success may have met at the sacrificial altars of Greco-Roman temples: the more a person demonstrated inner goodness, the more success a person might have. The connection may have often been thin, but it was possible to make it nonetheless. The deities were not generally known for providing the necessary and sufficient resources for inner personal transformation. Such resources were usually thought to emerge from a person's own will, derived from thoughtful "philosophical" reflection (or, perhaps, from good common sense). But again, there were exceptions. For instance, Seneca insisted (on the basis of his Stoic philosophy) not only that "God is near you . . . [and] is with you . . . [and] is within you" but also that "no one can be good without the help of a deity" (*Letters from a Stoic* 41.1–2).

Sacrificing to the Deities

The peace of the deities required sacrifice, and sacrifices were front and center in the temples of every urban center of the ancient world. Generally, these involved the slaughter of an animal on sacrificial altars—usually, the bigger the animal, the better. The apostle Paul offers us a glimpse into this world when he notes that "those who are employed in the temple service get their food from the temple, and those who serve at the altar share in what is sacrificed on the altar" (1 Corinthians 9:13). Sometimes offerings of grain, wine, or oil were made to the deities on the same altars. These sacrifices and offerings were considered gifts given to the deities to ensure their continuing favor and to avoid their punishing wrath.

Figure 5.4 shows a marble depiction of a sacrifice in progress, from Pompeii's Temple of Vespasian. There are different ways of interpreting some aspects of the scene, but one interpretation will be set out here, with material in parentheses introducing other possible interpretations.

On the right of the scene, a bull is being led to the slaughter by a temple slave who carries a mallet (in another interpretation, it is an axe). The priest stands to the left of the altar, with his long toga draped over his head and his right arm outstretched, holding a sacrificial bowl. A flute player stands behind the altar and next to the priest (facing to our right); he is enriching the sacredness of the moment with music. Other attendants also stand behind the priest, including a young boy at the far left of the scene, who is holding temple vessels for the sacrifice. To the right of the flute player stands a man who is looking directly at the priest, and who seems to be the suppliant, the one who is offering the sacrifice to the deity. The priest's sacrificial bowl contains a mixture of sacred flour and salt that the priest will soon pour between the horns of the bull, marking it as an acceptable offering to the deity (in another interpretation, it is a libation or liquid offering to the deity). The bull's headdress and ornamental garb will soon be removed. A prayer will then be offered, and the sacrifice itself will take place. The bull will be hit on the head with the heavy mallet, stunning him and causing him to fall to his knees; then, as the bull's head is lifted high by an attendant, his throat will be slit across the neck. (In another interpretation, the animal is simply slaughtered with an axe.) The carcass will then be dismembered, and the internal organs will be inspected to ensure that they are perfect. Some of the meat will be placed on an altar fire, with the deity consuming it as it burns. Other parts of the meat will

Figure 5.4. A marble carving depicting a bull to be sacrificed, being led to a priest by a temple slave (displayed at Pompeii's Temple of Vespasian, 7.9.2; see also figure 7.8)

end up in the market to be sold, or distributed to the priests for their use, or given to dining associations connected with the temple.

One important temple in Pompeii where such sacrifices were performed was the temple honoring the deity Aesculapius (which has often been referred to as the Temple of Jupiter Meilichios, or "Jupiter, Sweet as Honey"). Here, sacrifices were offered to Aesculapius as petitions for the enhancement of one's health. According to popular Greek mythology, the father of Aesculapius (or Asclepius, as the Greeks knew him) was Apollo, who impregnated a human female who gave birth to the semi-divine Aesculapius. But Aesculapius was later fully divinized by the deities, becoming known as a compassionate deity who excelled in healing those who honored him. Many ancients believed that Aesculapius worked his cures on their behalf through "dream therapy." Some claimed to have met the deity in their sleep. His priests would apply potions and medicines to the person's body, with temple dogs licking the afflicted parts of their bodies to remove the pus. Meanwhile, those who sought healing from Aesculapius were thought to benefit from a diet of white pepper and onions, while reducing liquid intake.

These measures supplemented the sacrifice to Aesculapius, who was petitioned for healing through his kind compassion.

The Epicurean Alternative

Although sacrifice was big business in the ancient world, not everyone was convinced of its efficacy for gaining the favor of the deities. Many people adopted an Epicurean worldview, drawing on the perspective of the Greek philosopher Epicurus (341–270 BCE). The Epicureans were not atheists, but they did not believe that the deities had any interest in the running of human society or the created order. There were far too many faults in the world (wars, famines, diseases, death) to imagine that supreme beings of a higher order were somehow involved in (or even interested in) the running of this world. According to Epicurean thought, the deities lived in a realm completely separated from the world of humanity, being blissfully complete in their happiness and, as such, being models for human relationships and happiness. Epicureans thought it right to honor the deities, but only because the deities belonged to a higher order of being that was worthy of respect. Accordingly, Epicureans offered sacrifices to these higher beings simply because it was proper decorum to do so—not because of fear that the deities might retaliate if sacrifices were neglected. Epicureans placed no stock in pleading with the deities; that was thought to be useless and ineffective. Because the deities extended neither beneficence nor wrath toward humans, the anxious pursuit to preserve "the peace of the deities" was fruitless. The will of the deities has no bearing on human life in the present, past, or future. Neither is there life beyond death for human beings. A later poet said much the same thing:

Figure 5.5. The Temple of Aesculapius (sometimes identified as the Temple of Jupiter Meilichios, at 8.7.25)

"No hell below us, above us only sky" (John Lennon, "Imagine"). Or in the words of Lucretius (an Epicurean poet of the first century BCE whose full name was Titus Lucretius Carus), the deities are "far separate, far removed from our affairs"; because the deities are "free from every sorrow, every danger" and are "strong in their own powers," they are "needing nothing from us," and consequently "they are not won by gifts nor touched by anger" (Lucretius, *On the Nature of Things* 1.46–49). Sacrifices, in other words, have nothing to do with winning the favor of the deities or avoiding their wrath.

Lucretius noted that "deep in every home were aching hearts and torments of the mind, all hapless, self-inflicted without pause, and sorrows breeding furious laments" (*On the Nature of Things* 6.14–16). The Epicurean alternative was to lead an undisturbed life informed by three convictions:

1. It is good to pursue pleasure (properly interpreted as leading a balanced life of virtue).
2. It is good to avoid pain, stress, and fear.

59

Figure 5.6. A mosaic depicting philosophers deep in thought (from the Villa of T. Siminius Stephanus, to the north of Pompeii's Vesuvian Gate, MANN 124545); the artist who crafted this mosaic did not place a scroll in the hands of the philosopher at the far left, whom most of the others are looking at intently (perhaps the scroll's omission was intentional for humorous effect).

3. This short life ends at death and goes no further.

Epicureanism was clearly present within the Vesuvian towns. On the outskirts of Herculaneum, for instance, a grand villa was discovered that, when excavated, was shown to have a considerable library containing more than eighteen hundred scrolls of texts. Although these scrolls have proven to be extremely difficult to decipher and more may still be excavated from the villa, the majority of them seem to be copies of texts originally written by Philodemus, a popular Epicurean philosopher. (A copy of Lucretius's Epicurean poem *On the Nature of Things* has also been found there, along with copies of at least three books of Epicurus's *On Nature* [Books 2, 11, and 25].) In Pompeii, a school operated by a man named Potitus (at 9.8.2) seems to have specialized in teaching philosophy to boys, and all indications are that the philosophy of choice within that school was Epicureanism. (We even know the names of some of the boys, including the fact that they were beaten for not learning their lessons well enough; *CIL* 4.5207–11 and 4.9089–94.) And of the many quotations of great literature that appeared in graffiti on the walls of Pompeii, the Epicurean Lucretius was the fourth most cited (at seven citations, coming just behind eight citations of Ovid's reflections on love and nine citations of Propertius's love poems, but far behind the extremely popular epic the *Aeneid* by Virgil, at thirty-six citations). Evidently Epicureanism had a strong foothold within the Vesuvian towns.

Contrasting Views

The early Christian message had very little in common with the Epicurean outlook on life (although both sought to relieve the fear of death). It ran against the grain of Epicureanism to acknowledge anyone as "God with us" (Matthew 1:23). It ran against the grain of Epicureanism for a deity to say to his followers, "Wherever two or three come together in my name, there I am with them" (18:20, my translation), or again, "I am with you always" (28:20). For Epicureans, deities simply don't do that sort of thing. Neither do they do what is said of the Word of God in the prologue of John's Gospel: "And the Word became flesh and lived among us" (John 1:14). A first-century Epicurean might have agreed that "no one has ever seen God" in personified form (1:18), but the same Epicurean would have found that claim to drift into unproductive territory with the subsequent affirmation that "it is God the only Son (who

is close to the Father's heart) who has made the Father known." Christian apostolic voices were not asserting that a celestial deity had visited the realm of creation from outside its sphere; instead, they proclaimed their deity to be intrinsic to the whole of the created order. In the words of John 1 (again), "All things came into being through him, and without him not one thing came into being" (1:3; see also Colossians 1:15–20, among many other passages).

One early Christian apostle heartily endorsed (a parodied form of) Epicureanism, but only with a significant proviso that intentionally undermined his endorsement. According to the apostle Paul, if the good news about the resurrection of Jesus Christ is not true, then everyone should adopt an aberrant form of Epicureanism, living by the unsophisticated slogan, "Let us eat and drink, for tomorrow we die" (1 Corinthians 15:32, perhaps a caricature of popularized Epicureanism but one drawn from the Greek version of Isaiah 22:13). Since Paul firmly believed in the resurrection of Jesus Christ, he advocated a different way: Since tomorrow we die, let us do all things in service of God today, in our hope of the resurrection. To this we can contrast the attitude of a rich man whom Jesus described as saying to himself, "You have plenty of grain laid up for many years, so take life easy; eat, drink and be merry" (Luke 12:19 NIV).

According to Paul, the resurrection of the crucified Messiah was a momentous event of divine invasion into history—an event that transforms the lives of all who get caught up within it through the power of a deity who is (in contrast to Epicurean beliefs) actively involved in this world. The lives of Jesus-devotees were to look completely different from (Paul's negative caricature of) Epicureanism. So Paul

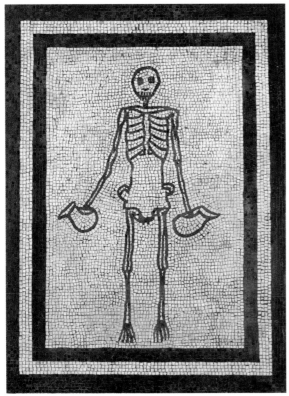

Figure 5.7. A floor mosaic from Pompeii depicting the Epicurean philosophy that we are all dead people whose only goal should be the pursuit of pleasure (represented here by wine pitchers held by the skeleton; from 6.17.19–26, MANN 9978)

urged them in this way: "Let us live honorably as in the day, not in reveling and drunkenness, not in debauchery and licentiousness. . . . Instead, put on the Lord Jesus Christ, and make no provision for the flesh, to gratify its desires" (Romans 13:13–14). For Paul, the lives of Jesus-followers were to be places of holiness, footholds for the power of their lord within this world.

Reconfiguring Sacrificial Imagery

In a world where sacrifices were embedded within every aspect of life, early Jesus-followers were encouraged to think of their own lives as sacrifices to their deity. For instance, Paul wrote: "I appeal to you therefore, brothers and sisters, by the mercies of God, to present your bodies as a living sacrifice, holy and acceptable to God—a genuine form of worship" (Romans 12:1). The ordinary lives of Jesus-devotees were to be thought of as sacrificial offerings. We saw in chapter 4 that Paul identified Jesus-followers as "the temple of the living God" (2 Corinthians 6:16); exploring the temple imagery further, he depicted their lives as the "holy and acceptable" sacrifice within the temple. He even depicted himself as an "altar-servant of Jesus Christ to the nations in priestly service of the good news of God," in the hope that "the nations might become an acceptable offering" to God (Romans 15:16).

Paul added further depth to the sacrificial metaphors by identifying Jesus Christ as "our paschal lamb" who "has been sacrificed" (1 Corinthians 5:7). The imagery of the Passover lamb derives from the account in the Hebrew Bible in which the people of Israel were released from their Egyptian slavery. The tenth of ten plagues was the visitation of death upon the eldest sons of Egypt, but the Hebrew people were protected from this plague by placing the blood of an unblemished lamb above their doorways (see especially Exodus 12). The lamb for each household was "the Passover sacrifice to the Lord," with the explanation that Israel's deity had "passed over the houses of the Israelites in Egypt" and "spared [their] houses" (12:27).

In the Roman world of insecurities, anxieties, stresses, and fears, the portrait of Jesus Christ as "our paschal lamb" would have induced a sense of protective security for those who understood the significance of the imagery. But in the context of 1 Corinthians 5,

Paul used it to shock his Corinthian audience out of their ethical complacency, since they were upholding within their community a man who was engaging in "sexual immorality . . . of a kind that is not found even among pagans"—in particular, "a man is living with his father's wife" (5:1). This is probably not a case of incest, with the son having sexual relations with his mother; instead, the "father's wife" was probably a later spouse to the father, after the death (or divorce) of the son's mother. It is generally thought that the father must already have died when this behavior was going on, but that might not have been the case. Paul noted, for instance, that the son's behavior was shameful even among "pagans," and there is little reason to think that a son having sex with a later wife of his deceased father would have been much of a problem in the Roman world. It is possible, then, that the father was still alive, with the son's behavior being seen as an abhorrent offense against the moral fabric of the structures of the household. But whatever the situation, Paul applied a powerful sacrificial metaphor as part of his forceful rhetoric to remove the man from their midst, since his sin was polluting the whole community of Jesus-followers (5:1–13). The people of the unblemished paschal lamb were not to be complicit in the blemishes of sinfulness. Such blemishes only compromised the protective security of their powerful deity.

Other New Testament authors also employed sacrificial terms to depict Jesus Christ. The author of Ephesians spoke of Christ as "a fragrant offering and sacrifice to God" (5:2). The author of 1 Peter spoke of him as a "lamb without blemish or defect" (1:19). The author of Revelation likened him to "a lamb looking as if it had been slain" and who

Figure 5.8. A fresco depicting King Pelias (middle) in the process of making a sacrifice when he spots Jason (bottom right), who will later overthrow him (from 9.5.18, MANN 111436)

rises in triumph (5:6 NIV). But it is the author of Hebrews who developed sacrificial imagery most fully. Just as Paul mixed metaphors when depicting Jesus-devotees as the temple of their deity and as the sacrifice to their deity, so too the author of Hebrews mixed metaphors when depicting Jesus as the high priest who offers the sacrifice and as the sacrifice himself. The text of Hebrews is imbued with the combination of these images (and others, as well). For instance, with regard to priestly imagery, the author depicted Jesus Christ as "a merciful and faithful high priest in service to God" who makes "atonement for the sins of the people" because he is the "great high priest who has ascended into heaven" (2:17 and 4:14). To that priestly imagery, the same author fused other imagery regarding Jesus Christ as sacrifice (10:10, 12, 14):

> We have been made holy through the sacrifice of the body of Jesus Christ once for all. . . . When this priest had offered for all time one sacrifice for sins, he sat down at the right hand of God, . . . for by one sacrifice he has made perfect forever those who are being made holy.

For the author of Hebrews, there is still more to be sacrificed, but not in the Jerusalem temple or, by extension, on pagan altars. Instead, "through Jesus, . . . let us continually offer to God a sacrifice of praise—the fruit of lips that openly profess his name" (13:15 NIV; see also 1 Peter 2:5, where Jesus-followers are "to be a holy priesthood" who "offer spiritual sacrifices to God through Jesus Christ," and 4:8, where it is said that the "constant love" shown by Jesus-followers "covers a multitude of sins"). Once again, sacrifice is refocused away from the Jerusalem temple and, by implication, away from the plethora of temples that were dotted around the Mediterranean basin. For the author of Hebrews, legitimate sacrifices were the exclusive possession of Jesus Christ and his followers, who "have an altar" of an altogether different kind in "the city that is to come" (13:10 and 14).

We have seen how apostolic voices explored metaphors of sacrifice in relation to Jesus Christ and his followers. Perhaps the impetus for this notable exploration of sacrificial metaphors is partially explained by the fact that some Jesus-devotees expressed their devotion in exclusive terms, shunning the worship of other deities. Without recourse to blood sacrifices, this stripe of Jesus-devotion would have been notably exceptional—both strangely eccentric and bizarrely deviant. Devising sacrificial metaphors in Christian discourse may have been the natural impulse to this novel situation in which exclusivist Jesus-followers found themselves. Having lost access to sacrifices of one kind, early Jesus-followers often refreshed the discourse of sacrificial imagery through metaphors imaginatively applied to their own deity and their own lives.

Rethinking Sacrificial Practices

Beyond reconfiguring sacrificial imagery, early Jesus-followers needed also to rethink the practicalities of sacrificial practices in relation to everyday realities. For instance, toward the end of the first century, some Jesus-followers in Thyatira were eating meat that had earlier been sacrificed to idols in pagan temples (Revelation 2:20). Was this an acceptable practice? Eating sacrificial meat was not uncommon in the ancient world. Some of the meat from temple sacrifices supplemented meal situations, being sold in the local meat market or used in temple banquets associated with the temples (see figure 5.9). Could Jesus-followers eat that meat without compromising their faithfulness to their "paschal lamb"?

That issue arose among some Jesus-followers in Corinth, as we know from 1 Corinthians 8–10 (and the complexity of the issue requires it to be considered also in chapter 17, although in relation to a slightly different aspect of the issue). In 1 Corinthians 8–10, Paul held the view that meat previously offered in temple sacrifices was not defiled meat, since all food is part of the good creation of his deity and since idols are non-existent (8:4–8). Consequently, Paul affirmed that it is acceptable to "eat whatever is sold in the meat market without raising any question on the ground of conscience,"

Figure 5.9. The macellum of Pompeii (7.9.7/8), where much of the meat from temple sacrifices ended up for sale to the public (notice the twelve supports placed in a circle, which would have held an awning protecting sellers and buyers from the sun and rain)

doing so on the basis that "the earth and its fullness are the Lord's" (10:25–26; see also 8:8). But Paul also knew that this could cause difficulties for some who did not share his perspective. Consequently, for the sake of those people who were bothered by his perspective on the matter, Paul also maintained that meat originating from a sacrificial context might need to be avoided by Jesus-followers, lest the faith of others should be unnecessarily problematized (8:9–13).

Sacrifices were ubiquitous in temples throughout the urban centers of the Roman world. They provided early Jesus-followers with metaphorical resources for articulating their own theological discourse, while at the same time being problematic in relation to the practical aspects of life. These focal points of Roman society forced early Jesus-devotees to pivot in one direction or another in the process of teasing out their understanding of what following Jesus Christ entailed in a world immersed in devotion to the deities. Devotion to the deities must have rung hollow for some people, especially the Epicureans, who deemed the deities to be wholly uninterested and uninvolved in human affairs. Many Jesus-followers found the traditional deities to be unworthy of devotion because the one true deity was now known in Christ Jesus, placing the sacrificial systems of the Roman world in a new light altogether. To many people in the first century, that conviction contributed to the sense that Jesus-devotion was potentially a perilous cancer on the infrastructure of Roman society. But reconfiguring the realm of the divine is also what gave the early Jesus-movement much of its venturous spirit to conceptualize the world in fresh ways and to enter into new forms of relationality.

6

Peace and Security

On that day, when evening had come, he said to them, "Let us go across to the other side." And leaving the crowd behind, they took him with them in the boat, just as he was. . . . A great windstorm arose, and the waves beat into the boat, so that the boat was already being swamped. But he . . . rebuked the wind, and said to the sea, *"Peace! Be still!"* Then the wind ceased, and there was complete calm. He said to them, "Why are you afraid? Have you still no faith?" And they were filled with great awe and said to one another, "Who then is this, that even the wind and the sea obey him?"

Mark 4:35–41

From Chaos to Peace

Chaos, followed by the suppression of chaos and the enactment of peace—this pattern, inherent in the story of Jesus stilling the storm, follows the general pattern of the Roman imperial narrative. In a popular version of that story, social chaos had engulfed much of the world until the imposition of Roman imperial rule under emperor Augustus and his successors (dating from 27 BCE onward). According to imperial propaganda, this blessed time was the time of the *Pax Romana*, "the peace of Rome" (or more elaborately, the peace brought by and overseen by Rome). It was a peace that was bringing the nations together in concord. It was a time of plenty, when abundance was

being brought to the whole world through the management of efficient social structures. It was a time of justice, when right relationships were being established among the inhabitants of the empire. If the time of the Roman republic (roughly 509 to 27 BCE) laid the foundations for the Roman imperial order, it was only with the establishment of the imperial order that the blessings of the Roman project could finally become manifest. If history had been driving to a culminating moment, that moment was the founding of the Roman imperial order.

According to popular propaganda and sentiment, the deities of Rome had overseen this process of implementing Roman rule.

In Pompeii, one of those special deities was Venus—the deity of love, fertility, and fruitfulness, who was also closely involved with Roman rule. When Pompeii was established as a Roman colony in 80 BCE, Venus (or "Pompeian Venus," as she is called in some graffiti; *CIL* 4.26, 4.538, 4.2457, 4.4007) was chosen as the deity to oversee the town's place within the Roman project. Venus could be depicted as "the mother of the Roman race" (Lucretius, *On the Nature of Things* 1.1, although he sought to redefine that claim quite significantly) because she was the divine mother of Aeneas, the heroic ancestor of the Romans. It is not surprising, then, that the Roman emperor Nero and his wife, Poppaea, had sent gifts "to the most holy Venus" in Pompeii (*AE* [1985], 283–84). These were gifts to the divine mother to whom the Roman people could trace their origins, and no doubt the gifts helped bolster the legitimacy of Nero's reign within the Vesuvian town.

The conviction that the Roman project was in capable hands with Venus may play a subtle role in a fresco from a Pompeian residence (1.13.9). It depicts Venus sitting in the back of a ship, capably guiding the ship and those within it across the sea in safety (see figure 6.1; compare the narrative portrait of Jesus in the boat in Mark 4:35–41 [quoted above], Matthew 8:23–27 and 14:22–33, and Luke 8:22–25). The fresco was accompanied by a Greek inscription declaring Venus "the Savior" (*CIL* 4.9867, where Venus is referred to by her Greek name, Aphrodite). The impression is that everything is good in this Roman town, with deities like Venus linked to the Roman project of eradicating chaos and establishing order. In his praise of Venus, the philosopher Lucretius said something similar about peace overcoming the seas in relation to her reign: "For you

Figure 6.1. A faded fresco of the deity Venus as she safely guides a ship through stormy seas (notice the twisted sail, blown in a tempest; from 1.13.9, MANN 20697)

the seas' horizons smile, and sky, all peaceful now, shines clear with light outpoured" (*On the Nature of Things* 1.1, although Lucretius held a highly redefined sense of how Venus is to be understood).

Affirming the Roman Project in the Vesuvian Towns (and Beyond)

Celebrations of the Roman project are found throughout the Vesuvian towns. Nowhere is this more evident than in the huge building in Pompeii's main forum that was funded by

Figure 6.2. The statue of Eumachia stands at the back of her magnificent building in Pompeii's forum (7.9.1).

Concordia to the imperial (Augustan) family. Making the connection between the Roman deities and the imperial family explicit, the statue of the deity Concordia Augusta was fashioned in the likeness of Livia, the wife of emperor Augustus and the mother of his imperial successor, Tiberius.

This building (which isn't worth a picture, since there isn't much left of it other than bare walls) was probably used for a number of purposes, although we cannot be sure what those purposes were. Regardless of what went on inside the building, what Eumachia advertised on the outside of the building is most telling. Both the small entrance at the back of the building and the large entrance at the front were adorned with inscriptions honoring "Augustan Concord and Piety" (see figure 6.3). The word "piety" connoted giving due respect to all who are worthy—whether the worthy ones were deities or human contemporaries. The word "concord" involved the establishment of harmonious relationships between different urban centers that, in reality, were frequently in competition with one another. Civic concord between urban centers was the key to the expansion of the Roman empire. One Roman rhetorician made the point this way: "If we maintain concord in the state, we shall measure the empire's vastness by the rising and the setting of the sun" (*Rhetorica ad Herennium* 4.33.44; the author's name remains unknown to us). We can see, then, that Eumachia's inscriptions at both entries into her building advertised the establishment of beneficial relationships with the deities and with other urban centers in the promotion of the Roman imperial agenda.

The claim that the Roman imperial reign had inaugurated an era of abundant peace, beneficial concord, and lasting security was

a leading Pompeian woman, Eumachia, and her son. (Her husband had been one of the two main civic leaders of the town in the year 2–3.) The huge building she paid to have built (at 7.9.1) advertised the imperial narrative in several ways, including statues and inscriptions dedicated to Rome's "founding fathers" (i.e., Romulus and Aeneas) and to the female deity Concordia Augusta—linking the deity advertised by the reconstruction of the seaside architecture of Herculaneum. That quaint maritime town was extensively renovated during the Augustan period in a manner that was in complete alignment with Roman imperial ideologies of peace and prosperity. The town's waterfront profile was originally dominated by the outline of a military garrison. This advertisement of strength and impregnability may well have benefited the seaside town of Herculaneum in a time prior to Augustus (when, for instance, pirates roamed the seas looking for weaknesses to exploit both on the waters and on the coastline), but, as propaganda had it, those difficult times faded from view with the rise of the Roman imperial order. And so, during the reign of Augustus himself, Herculaneum's waterfront profile was transformed under the direction of an influential local resident, Nonius Balbus, a strong supporter and friend of emperor Augustus (see figure 6.4). In that transformation, the town's military appearance was replaced with the outline of opulence, as rich houses were set along the seaside frontage in a display of luxury. The dogma of the day claimed that the age of insecurity and chaos had given way to the age of peace and prosperity, and this claim was evidenced in the waterfront profile of the Augustan town. No longer advertising strategic defense, Herculaneum was marketed as a prosperous town with residences, luxuries, and enterprise, in alignment with the Augustan ideology of the day (see figure 6.5).

A few decades after the death of Nonius Balbus of Herculaneum and Eumachia of Pompeii, an incident took place that ran completely contrary to the official imperial ideology. At a sporting event in Pompeii's amphitheater in 59, a group of local thugs began a skirmish with residents of Nuceria, a town

Figure 6.3. The inscription at the front of Eumachia's building (7.9.1), advertising "Augustan Concord and Piety" (Latin: [*Conc*]*ordiae Augusta*[*e Pietati*])

Figure 6.4. The statue of Nonius Balbus placed at the waterfront of Herculaneum in honor of his renovation of the town in compliance with the Roman imperial ideology of peace and security

Figure 6.5. Part of the seafront of Herculaneum after its extensive renovations by Nonius Balbus, who wanted to advertise peace and prosperity to those passing the town by sea

near Pompeii. Things quickly got out of hand, and the whole event turned into an uproar, with violence erupting and some people losing their lives (see figure 6.6). More injuries and deaths were inflicted on the residents of Nuceria than on the residents of Pompeii, but the people of Pompeii suffered their own form of defeat. This is because the event was brought to the attention of the senate in Rome, which decreed that Pompeii could not hold events of this kind for the following ten years (as reported by Tacitus, *Annals* 14.17).

The senate handed down such a harsh sentence because it needed to make an example out of Pompeii, as a deterrent to other urban centers. Quite simply, the riot was dangerous because it embodied an ethos that ran against the grain of official propaganda about the peace and concord that had taken hold since the inauguration of Roman imperial reign.

The ethos of the senate's edict is captured well in the words of the Roman historian Marcus Velleius Paterculus (19 BCE–31 CE), who propagated the imperial mythology in words intended to bolster the emperor Tiberius. Velleius Paterculus depicted urban centers throughout the world as having been set right through imperial reign of the Roman emperors Augustus and Tiberius. Here is an excerpt of this sycophant's exuberant

70

Figure 6.6. Painting of the riot of 59 in Pompeii's amphitheater, with groups beating each other (from 1.3.23 [a residence that may have housed gladiators], MANN 112222)

acclamation (*Compendium of Roman History* 2.126.1–4).

> Credit has been restored in the forum, strife has been banished from the forum, . . . discord [has been removed] from the senate-house; justice, equity, and industry, long buried in oblivion, have been restored to the state; the magistrates have regained their authority, the senate its majesty, the courts their dignity; rioting in the theatre has been suppressed; all citizens have either been impressed with the wish to do right, or have been forced to do so by necessity.

Pretty impressive! But, he continued with more praise of the Roman imperial order:

> Righteousness is now honored, evil is punished; the humble man respects the great but does not fear him; the great has precedence over the lowly but does not despise him. When was the price of grain more reasonable, or when were the blessings of peace greater? The *pax Augusta*, which has spread to the regions of the east and of the west and to the bounds of the north and of the south, preserves every corner of the world safe from the fear of brigandage.

Who couldn't help but be impressed by that? Who wouldn't want to get on board with such a positive phenomenon of "blessing"? But there is still more:

> The cities of Asia have been restored; the provinces have been freed from the oppression of their magistrates. Honor ever awaits the worthy; for the wicked punishment is slow but sure; fair play has now precedence over influence, and merit over ambition, for the best of emperors teaches his citizens to

71

do right by doing it, and though he is greatest among us in authority, he is still greater in the example which he sets.

Buying into the public discourse about the new era of the Roman imperial order, many people sought to align themselves publicly with Rome and its rule. Oaths of allegiance to Roman rule were not uncommon. One example captures an extreme form of fervent devotion to the Roman imperial family. This oath of zeal was sworn by civic and business leaders in the Roman province of Paphlagonia in the year 3 BCE (*OGIS* 532):

> I swear by Zeus, Earth, Sun, all the gods [and] goddesses, and by Augustus himself that I will be loyal to Caesar Augustus and his children and descendants for all the time of my life, in word, deed and thought, considering as friends whomever they [i.e., the imperial family] consider so, and reckoning as enemies whomever they themselves judge to be so.

Those who took this oath to the imperial family did so with utter seriousness, seeing things in a "life and death" scenario:

> I swear that in their interests I shall spare neither body nor soul nor life nor children, but in every way for those things that pertain to them I shall endure every danger; and that if I see or hear anything hostile to them being either said or planned or carried out, I will report this and shall be the enemy of the person who is saying or planning or doing any of these things. And whomever they themselves [i.e., the imperial family] may judge to be their enemies, these people I will pursue and defend them against, by land and sea, by sword and steel.

If those who took this oath failed to kill enemies of the emperor "by sword and steel,"

they would kill their whole family instead, as indicated by the final section of the oath:

> But if I do anything contrary to this oath or do not conform to the letter with the oath I swore, I bring down on myself and my body, soul and life, and on my children and all my family and all that belongs to me utter and total destruction down to my every last connection and all my descendants, and may neither the earth nor the sea receive the bodies of my family and descendants nor bear fruit for them.

We do not know whether the commitments expressed in the oath were acted on in reality or whether they were simply extreme rhetorical exaggerations. Either way, this oath expressed a sentiment that early Jesus-followers would come up against repeatedly: if you were in any way hesitant about the Roman project, you were part of the problem to be removed. There were some pockets of resistance to this sentiment (and some Pompeian examples form part of that slim database), but for the most part they seem not to have been very vocal, unsurprisingly.

"Disturbing Our City"

Against this mythic backdrop of the grandeur of society under Roman imperial reign, the emergence of Jesus-devotion was frequently viewed as dangerous to the fabric of the Roman world. The Gospel of John offers an inkling of this. In one episode of that narrative, prominent Judean leaders notice that many people are becoming interested in Jesus because of his astounding power (in particular, resurrecting the dead man Lazarus); extrapolating what might happen if things continue along that trajectory, the leaders recognize the political dangers, saying, "If we let him go on like this, everyone will believe in him, and the Romans will come and destroy both our holy place and our nation" (John 11:48). The story captures the sense that the power of Jesus Christ might work along lines that potentially threaten traditional forms of power.

Similarly, the story of the emergence of Christianity in the Acts of the Apostles is often immersed in folds of political intrigue. Was there a danger in following a deity who was remembered to have said, "I came to bring fire to the earth. . . . Do you think that I have come to bring peace to the earth? No, I tell you, but rather division" (Luke 12:49, 51)? (See also Matthew 10:34–36, discussed further in chapter 16.) The ancient reader would have listened with intent when hearing stories about Christian leaders in urban centers of the Roman world. In Philippi, for instance, local residents accused those Christian leaders of "disturbing [their] city"; a crowd joined together "in attacking them"; the magistrates of the city had them "stripped of their clothing" and ordered that they "be beaten with rods" (Acts 16:20, 22). Were Christian leaders upsetting the status quo? By "advocating customs that [were] not lawful for . . . Romans to adopt or observe" (16:21), were Christian leaders introducing chaos into Roman urban centers?

Much the same is evident in the Acts narrative recounting how Paul brought his message of "good news" to Thessalonica. In that city, a group of people "formed a mob and set the city in an uproar" when they heard Paul's message (Acts 17:5). They announced to the city authorities that "these people who have been turning the world upside down have come here also and . . . are all acting contrary to the decrees of the emperor, saying that there

is another king named Jesus" (17:6–7; compare also John 19:12, where Jesus is said to be worthy of crucifixion since "anyone who claims to be a king sets himself against the emperor"). The ancient hearer of this story is not surprised to learn that "the people and the city officials were disturbed when they heard this" (17:8). Were Jesus-followers pulling apart the threads of society's fabric? This scenario of suspicion and animosity interweaves with Paul's own words to the same Thessalonian Jesus-followers (1 Thessalonians 2:2): "Although we had already suffered and been shamefully mistreated at Philippi, . . . we had courage in our God to declare to you the gospel of God in spite of great opposition."

The author of Acts used these incidents in his narrative to demonstrate that the early Jesus-movement was not, in fact, inherently chaotic and did not necessarily stir up trouble within Roman society. Despite accusations that Paul was "a troublemaker, stirring up riots . . . all over the world" (24:5 NIV), the author of Acts allowed Paul's self-defense to be heard in simple terms: "I have done nothing wrong . . . against Caesar" (25:8 NIV). Of course, the same author seems convinced that people sometimes do not like the truth that they need to hear, so for him there was some sense in which Christianity was rightly "turning the world upside down." But his narrative seems to suggest that ugly mob scenes such as the ones that transpired in Philippi and Thessalonica were not the *inevitable* result of the emergence of Jesus-devotion, except in those situations when others inelegantly sought to remove the divine presence from their societies. One civic magistrate from Ephesus articulated this view precisely when he calmed the angry crowd with these words: "We [Ephesians] are in danger of being charged with rioting today, since there is no cause that we can give to justify this commotion" against Jesus-followers (19:40). For the author of Acts, the profound challenges that the "good news" posed were not to foster anarchic impulses or chaotic confusion within society.

Questioning the Roman Project in the Vesuvian Towns

The propaganda of the mythic grandeur of the Roman imperial order was often very different from the reality felt by people on the ground. It goes without saying that things were not as splendid as the advocates of the Roman imperial order sometimes made them out to be. We get occasional inklings of this in Pompeii itself. For instance, one prominent interpretation of the riot in Pompeii's amphitheater suggests that it was initiated by a local Pompeian group that gloried in the pre-Roman days of the town, judging indigenous identity to be more cherished than Roman identity. We will never know for certain, but it makes sense of some of the most important pieces of the puzzle (which cannot be fruitfully considered here).

Another tantalizing Pompeian artifact that might be considered in this light is a graffito from the exterior wall of the residence at 9.13.5. In order to understand that graffito, we need to understand how it riffs on what was the most popular epic of the first century—the *Aeneid*. The epic's author, Virgil, constructed a narrative demonstrating how the establishment of Rome fulfilled the wishes of the deities. The opening phrase of that epic reads: "I sing of arms and a man" (*arma virumque cano*). This phrase references both

1. the military might (or "arms") that resulted in Rome's ascendency as the lead-

ing world power of the Greco-Roman world, and

2. the epic's main character, Aeneas (the "man"), whose story demonstrates the divine legitimacy of Roman rule.

In this epic narrative of the founding of the Roman empire, Aeneas ensures that the mighty Trojan people, having fled from defeat in Troy, subsequently resettle in Italy, where they will eventually come to dominate the world through Roman rule. This popular epic (which the emperor Augustus encouraged Virgil to write) linked the heritage of the emperor Augustus to the great hero Aeneas (whose mother was the deity Venus), giving the emperor the imprimatur of the Roman deities. Archaeologists have found about three dozen quotations of this epic in Pompeian graffiti—a dozen of them referencing the epic's opening line, acting as a sound bite that encapsulates the ideology of the whole epic.

One reference to the first line of the *Aeneid* is the graffito found on the external wall of a fullery (at 9.13.5)—a laundry in which garments were cleaned and prepared to be worn again. Knowing that the owl was the mascot of the fullers (or laundry workers), we can see the graffito as a parody of the opening line of Virgil's *Aeneid*: "I sing of launderers and an owl, not arms and a man" (*fullones ululamque cano, non arma virumque*; CIL 4.9131). In this graffito, the great Roman hero Aeneas is replaced with laundry workers, and the military "arms" that prepared the way for Roman dominance are replaced by an owl.

Most graffiti that cite the opening line of the *Aeneid* must have been written in support of the pro-Roman sentiment of the epic; this little graffito is different, however, articulating a different sentiment altogether. The politically offensive word in the fullery graffito is the little word "not"—as in the phrase "*not* arms and a man." If the person who wrote this graffito had intended to make a politically innocuous statement, he could simply have written the first phrase and left it at that: "I sing of launders and an owl." Or he could have written "and" where instead he wrote "not." Or he could have composed a list containing arms, a man, launderers, and an owl. Any of those possibilities would not have involved a negation of the pro-Roman story. But he did not choose any of those options. This graffito does not extend the legitimacy of the Roman imperial order to include a special focus on the humble, down-to-earth stories of everyday workers in the fullery. The singer's song is intentionally not placed within the song about the grandeur of Roman rule. Instead, the macro-narrative of Roman power and authority is set aside, with the micro-narrative of the laundry workers existing as the only story to which the inscriber was committed. This was someone who preferred not to place his identity within the grand narratives of Roman imperial propaganda; instead, he preferred to understand his life story within the simple narrative of localized launderers and their mascot, the owl. That preference is virtually harmless when restricted to a single voice, but it could prove subversive if it were replicated more widely. A casual attitude toward the legitimacy of Rome was not something the supporters of the system would have appreciated. Intriguingly, this graffito was etched into a public wall just below a fresco of Aeneas, adding a further twist to the political awkwardness of the graffito. (For another Pompeian example of the subversion of the story of Aeneas, see chapter 11.)

Also of interest for its political relevance is another graffito found on an exterior wall in

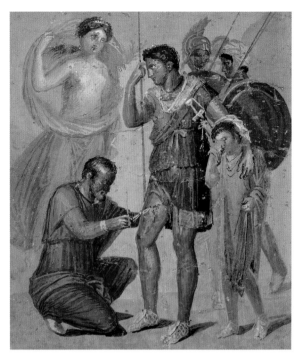

Figure 6.7. A fresco of the wounded hero Aeneas being treated by the physician Lapix; Aeneas leans on his son Ascanius while his divine mother, Venus, looks on with compassion (from 7.1.47, MANN 9009).

Pompeii (near 6.8.5). Like the graffito that is built on the opening line of the *Aeneid*, this graffito may be built on a famous dramatic scene in one of Cicero's works from about 70 BCE (*In Verrem* 2.5.162). In Cicero's scene, a Roman citizen is violently and unjustly tortured. Despite his sufferings, he does not cry out in pain. Instead, he repeats only one phrase in the hope of bringing his torment to an end: "I am a Roman citizen." But his pronouncement does nothing to change the course of his persecution, and he ends up dying on a Roman cross, with justice having misfired in this instance.

The graphic graffito on an external Pompeii wall (*CIL* 4.1261) may be twisting the various components of this story (e.g., themes of citizenship, silence, and crying out) until they play new roles in a disturbing sexual metaphor that ultimately seeks to undermine the legitimacy of Roman rule. Using sexually explicit language, the graffito compares Roman rule to sexual predation, with Roman citizens in a subjugated role. These coerced citizens, who are collectively depicted as females, keep silent when violated, except to cry out with "respectful moans." In this narrative, Rome takes its pleasures from the people, whose moans give the oppressor what it wants to hear. This graffito could, in theory, be interpreted as a statement of support for Rome (on the assumption that the citizens are willing participants in Rome's initiatives), but this is unlikely. Since Cicero's original scene included condemnation against the perpetration of injustice, the author of this graffito probably imagined that, despite their "respectful moans," the citizens were not willing participants in the Roman project: instead, citizens were violated and forced into submission. In this interpretation, the effect of Roman rule on the people is being likened to a tragic and atrocious rape. History teaches us that in situations where power is abusively overbearing and resistance is futile, it is not unusual for the oppressed to feel that, in order to survive, they must give in to the oppressor, while saying what the oppressor wants to hear—and all this, despite the absence of genuine consent.

If this graffito is suggestive of this sentiment of resigned animosity, it must be seen as ingenious in its subversiveness. This is because, as noted above, the graffito itself can actually be heard as an affirmation of Roman rule, even if it can also signal a protest against Roman rule. This double dimension of the graffito should not be surprising. People who consider themselves oppressed by empire sometimes choose not to articulate their discontent explicitly; instead, they

prefer to keep a low profile and articulate their sentiments through encoded discourse seemingly devoid of explicit articulation. Is this graffito an instance of that kind of thing? If pressed, the graffito composer could argue that all he/she meant to say is that the citizens are enjoying the penetration of Rome. If pressed, he/she could argue that the link to Cicero's famous scene is spuriously attributed to his/her otherwise innocent expression of political support for Rome. In other moments, a surreptitious look when alluding to Cicero's story takes the graffito's significance in the other direction. Here, the fogginess of the link to Cicero acts as a tool of self-protection. That link is effective in moments when a subversive posture can be fostered, just as the same link can disappear from view in the very moment when a subversive posture would compromise one's strategies for survival or advancement.

Uneasy Neighbors

At times, Christian discourse also followed lines that were not necessarily politically innocuous. For instance, in his letter to the Jesus-followers in Rome (written about 57), Paul spoke of peace and prosperity in a way that bypassed the Roman imperial narrative altogether. Instead of creation benefiting from abundance through the Roman imperial reign, Paul spoke of creation being in "bondage to decay," of creation's subjection "to futility," and of its "groaning in labor pains" even "right up to the present time." Paul claimed that creation "waits with eager longing" for divine peace and prosperity (in a sense) to take hold once and for all through the initiatives of the deity he proclaimed (8:19–23). Whereas Nonius Balbus wanted to advertise that Roman peace

Figure 6.8. A fresco depicting the cosmic sovereignty of Rome (symbolized by the eagle of Rome, a globe, a thunderbolt of Jupiter, and a scepter; from the House of the Ephebus, 1.7.11, in situ)

and prosperity had already established themselves within Herculaneum through the divinely ordained initiatives of Augustus, Paul maintained that divine abundance overflows throughout the whole of creation through "the one man, Jesus Christ" (5:17). These two forms of discourse diverge dramatically in the direction of their rhetoric.

Perhaps because his discourse could be seen as flowing against the grain of Roman imperial rhetoric, Paul added further advice later in his letter. In Romans 13, Paul urged Jesus-devotees to "be subject to the governing authorities" and to "pay to all what is due them—taxes to whom taxes are due, revenue to whom revenue is due, respect to whom

Figure 6.9. A fresco depicting the power of Rome (symbolized by the instruments of war of the Roman Mars; from the House of the Ephebus, 1.7.11, in situ)

respect is due, honor to whom honor is due" (13:1, 7). Paul wanted it to be recognized that going against the grain of Roman political ideology and mythology did not necessarily mean rising up against the establishment. But even if believers are to submit to the establishment, Paul also let it be known that the ruling authorities are authorized not by the deities of Rome, as in the Roman imperial narrative, but by a higher power, "for there is no authority except from God" (13:1). When functioning as instruments of justice (and only then), the Roman authorities are to be seen as a "servant" of the deity whom Paul proclaimed (13:4, 6), not the culmination of history that the Roman deities had overseen.

A subtle supplanting of the Roman narrative is in play here. In Pompeii, a graffito writer seems to have abandoned his commitment to the macro-narrative of Rome in favor of the simple micro-narrative of the launderers; in his letter to Jesus-followers in Rome, Paul allowed the macro-narrative of his deity to replace the macro-narrative that ultimately legitimized the Roman empire. Even in his most conservative moment, then, Paul allowed some discourse to run against the grain of the Roman imperial order.

A second example comes from Paul's first letter to Jesus-followers in Thessalonica—probably his earliest extant letter. Paul knew that Jesus-followers in that city were undergoing persecution (not unlike that described in the narrative of Acts 17, quoted above; see 1 Thessalonians 1:6; 3:3–4; 2 Thessalonians 1:4). In that context of persecution, Paul spoke against those whose allegiances were shaped by the motto, "There is peace and security" (1 Thessalonians 5:3). For Paul, those people had placed their faith in the wrong master-narrative, since the real narrative of salvation centers not on the *Pax Romana* but on "our Lord Jesus Christ, who died for us, so that . . . we may live with him" (5:9–10). It is the deity proclaimed by Paul who "calls you into his own kingdom and glory" (2:12). When push comes to shove, even Paul, the relatively conservative Roman citizen, was compelled to put the ideology of the Roman imperial order in its place; to adopt that ideology as the ultimate macro-narrative is to promote "darkness" in this world, in contrast to the light of the good news that Paul preached (5:4–8). No wonder Paul felt it important to assert that, for Jesus-followers, "our citizenship is in heaven, and it is *from there* that we are expecting a savior, the Lord Jesus Christ" (Philippians 3:20).

We have dropped various probes into the discourse of the early Jesus-movement and of Roman imperial ideology. Further probes could add further data but would not change the results too much. We would continue to find the ideologies of early Jesus-devotion and of the Roman imperial order to be uneasy neighbors, sometimes snarling sweetly at each other, sometimes not so sweetly. One example of a "not so sweet" relationship is evidenced in the Johannine apocalypse, Revelation. But proper consideration of that text requires the exploration of other issues as well—issues that are addressed in the next chapter of this book.

Genius and Emperor

7

The grace of the Lord Jesus Christ be with *the spirit that is among you all.*

Philippians 4:23

Spiritual Identities

The verse that starts this chapter is usually translated "The grace of the Lord Jesus Christ be with your spirit," and the phrase "your spirit" is sometimes understood to mean "the spirit of each one of you individually." But Paul probably meant something different in these final words to the Philippian Jesus-followers. With the word "your" being plural and the word "spirit" being singular, he seems to be referencing the singular "spirit" or ethos that Jesus-followers shared corporately among themselves, something that transpired within their gatherings. So the phrase is translated here as "the spirit that is among you all." We might call this "spirit" the "personified character" or the "spiritual identity" of the community as a single entity. Although we do not think in these terms very often in the twenty-first century, it was very common in the ancient world to imagine that entities had spiritual representations, projections of their true inner essence and identity. In Latin, these were often called the *genius* (male) or *juno* (female) of the entity.

This view of things is found throughout the Vesuvian towns, and in any number of spheres of life. As we will see, it informed inscriptions and legal documents, it motivated the construction of temples, and it was graphically displayed on devotional shrines or in mosaics in residential entryways. The same ancient view also informed the practice of emperor worship in the Roman imperial world.

Juno and *Genius*

One place where this view of things is evidenced is in the tombs, located beyond the gates of Pompeii. Many tombs benefited from the addition of tubes that opened above the surface but went down into the ground where the ashes of the deceased had been placed. At certain times, people sent food down those

79

tubes to nourish the spirits of deceased household members. At one tomb, for instance, a tube was installed to allow nutrients to be fed into the tomb for the benefit of "the *juno* of Melissaea Amyce" (*CIL* 10.1009, at tomb HGW04e/f); elsewhere, another tube was installed to benefit "the *juno* of Tyche, [the slave] of Julia Augusta" (*CIL* 10.1023, at tomb HGW16).

This was a common practice in the tombs of Pompeii. Of course, any nutrients fed through these tubes were not benefiting deceased bodies (which, after all, would most likely have been cremated); instead, the nutrients benefited a person's non-corporeal spirit. The female *juno* or the male *genius* was a person's generative power and spiritual life force, which existed regardless of a person's physical existence within a body. In this regard, a person's essential identity was greater than the sum of his/her physicality, encompassing more than mere materiality. The spiritual *juno* or *genius* was related to but separate from a physical body. Feeding the *juno* or *genius* of a person after that person's death may not simply have been a loving gesture extended by the deceased person's relatives or friends. Since spiritual entities were powerful, such feedings were probably a form of household insurance, encouraging the *juno* or *genius* to look favorably on the households to which they had been attached prior to their deaths.

Instead of the female *juno*, more frequently we see the male *genius* emerging from the Vesuvian remains (which is unsurprising in a male-dominated society). In one residence (9.1.20), two freedmen set a marble plaque within the household shrine with the words, "To the *genius* of our Marcus and to the *lares*" (*CIL* 10.861). Since the *lares* were the spiritual guardians of that particular resi-

dence, this shrine featured devotion to two types of spiritual forces that were thought to protect the household—guardian spirits of the place (the *lares*) and the life force of the householder (his *genius*). A portrait bust in another Pompeii residence is dedicated "to the *genius* of our Lucius"—complete with blemishes of his physical appearance (*CIL* 10.860; see figure 7.1).

Household shrines often depicted the householder's *genius* in visual form. These were not necessarily portraits of the householder himself, although they may have approximated his general appearance. The shrines were access

Figure 7.1. The bust of Lucius, dedicated to his *genius* (from the House of Jucundus at 5.1.26)

points to the spiritual world, and the figures depicted in them were predominately spiritual figures. So, for instance, the shrine in the Pompeian residence at 1.14.6 (see figure 7.2) displayed in its center cubicle an image of the householder's *genius* holding a cornucopia, or horn of plenty. On the bottom of the shrine are images of the river deity Sarnus (who oversaw the harbor activity), men weighing produce, men transporting goods to and from the harbor, and men loading produce onto boats. Presumably the householder who resided in this house operated a sea-faring business of some kind, and his *genius* was expected to oversee the success of the business, in conjunction with Sarnus—as long as offerings were made in this household shrine.

Another residence displays a typical fresco shrine (see figure 7.3). The fresco incorporates several components in its depiction of both physical and spiritual realities involved in a household sacrifice. An altar is the centerpiece of the display's upper register. To the right of the altar, the *genius* of the householder holds the cornucopia, while overseeing the sacrifice. Large figures on the outer flanks of the fresco represent the *lares*, the spiritual forces that protect the place in which the household resides. Miniaturized figures within the fresco are three human players in the ordeal: the person who will soon sacrifice a pig (second from the left), a priestly assistant (second from the right), and a flute player (to the left of the altar, perhaps taller than the other human characters to give an aesthetic balance to the fresco). On the lower register, the protective spirits of the place (or the *lares*) are represented by two snakes. Although they are non-corporeal beings, the protective spirits nonetheless partake of the nutrients provided by a physical sacrificial offering.

Figure 7.2. The shrine at 1.14.6, with the *genius* of the householder (center) and the householder's business dealings overseen by the river deity Sarnus (below)

Other Spiritual Life Forces

If humans and places have a spiritual component to their identity, so too do animals, or so many thought in the Greco-Roman world. This is attested in mosaics of dogs at entrances into some Pompeian residences (e.g., 1.7.1; 5.1.26; 6.8.5; see figure 7.4). One mosaic even

Figure 7.3. A fresco shrine depicting the material and spiritual realities involved in a sacrifice (from 7.6.38, MANN 8905)

comes with the Latin warning "Beware of the dog." These mosaics were not meant to depict the appearance of the guard dog on duty within the house. Instead, these mosaics signaled that the residence was under the protection of a canine spirit—a spirit that was powerful, loyal, and potentially fierce against malicious intruders. Posted at residential entrances, these mosaics advertised the canine *anima*, or life force, that the householder called up to protect the premises, with an ominous threat against any who would seek to harm the household. The same is true for residences depicting a wild boar or a wounded bear at their entryways (7.2.26; 7.2.45). Neither of those animals was physically present within the residences, of course; instead, their fierce spiritual counterparts were on duty as

essential components in the security system of those residences.

People in the ancient world also imagined that places had their own spiritual aspect. Whether it be at the level of residences or neighborhoods or urban centers or regions or nations—each distinct place within these levels of society was thought to have its own atmosphere, its own ethos, its own character that transcended its physical features and components. One household was recognized to have a different ambiance from another nearby it; one neighborhood had a different character from another nearby it; one regional territory had a different feel from another nearby it. People in the first century thought that a full explanation for these differences needed to reference the different life forces that

Figure 7.4. Floor mosaics advertising the residence's protection by the canine spirit (left: from 6.14.20, in situ; right: from 1.7.1, in situ)

animated those distinct places. That spiritual dimension operated in tandem with the material dimension of the place. If the spirit of the place was not tended to, the material dimension of the place would suffer as a consequence. If the spirit of the place was healthy, good things came to its material dimension.

This "spirituality of space" is evidenced repeatedly in the material remains of the Vesuvian towns, with snakes representing the benign spirit of the place (seen already in figure 7.3). Snakes also frequently appear on frescos at neighborhood shrines, where the spirit of the neighborhood is appeased through sacrificial offerings (see figure 7.5). One inscription from Pompeii, for instance, refers to a gift given to the neighborhood *lares* by the presidents of the neighborhood association (*CIL* 10.927).

Beyond residences and neighborhoods, one of Pompeii's temples takes to another level this connection between the material and spiritual aspects of a place. It was a temple paid for by an important Pompeian woman of the early first century. Her name was Mamia, and she

was honored after her death by the construction of a magnificent tomb "by a decree of the town council" (*CIL* 10.998; see figure 7.6). During her life, the "public priestess" Mamia paid for the construction of a temple on what had been "her own land" and "at her own expense"—a temple dedicated to "the *genius* of the colony" (*CIL* 10.816). (Archaeologists originally thought the inscription honored "the *genius* of Augustus," but more recent arguments suggest that "the *genius* of the

Figure 7.5. A neighborhood shrine from Herculaneum (in an obvious state of disrepair) depicting two snakes (on either side of the altar) that represent the neighborhood's protective spirit

83

Figure 7.6. The "seat memorial" of Mamia (HGW04), funded by the town council in return for her public benefaction in service of the *genius* of the colony; the three pillars in the center of the picture are not part of her memorial but belong to a tomb behind hers.

colony" may be the preferred reading. It is not clear where this temple was erected.) Residents of Pompeii would have imagined this temple to attend to the spiritual identity of the local area, with the hope of increasing prosperity within the region. Similar dedications to the *genius* of the colony appear in the nearby urban centers of Puteoli (*CIL* 10.1562–68, 10.1574, 10.1591) and Nola (*CIL* 10.1236).

Spiritual Identities in Christian Texts

In all these ways, we can see how the ancient mindset often imagined material realities to have spiritual aspects that represented them

and helped to protect them. With these things in mind, Paul's comment in Philippians 4:23 regarding "the spirit that is among you all" seems perfectly at home in its first-century context. When Philippian Jesus-followers met for worship, they were not just an ad hoc convergence of separate individuals; they became a single entity, "the body of Christ." Paul could exhort them to "stand firm in one spirit" (1:27). Even the senate of Rome was thought to have a *genius*, and so did the Roman people—both were single entities composed of many individuals with a single *genius*. In the same way, believers in Philippi could be thought to share a single corporate spirit when they gathered for worship. Paul called on divine grace to infuse the community's corporate ethos, thereby protecting and enriching their corporate life and their common assembly.

Much the same is evident in other Pauline letters. In Philemon, the word "you" sometimes appears in plural form, and this is true of the blessing at the very end of the letter: "May the grace of the Lord Jesus Christ be with your spirit" (Philemon 25). The sentence is precisely the same as the sentence from Philippians 4:23, cited at the beginning of this chapter. Once again, although the word "your" is plural, the word "spirit" is singular, referring to the single spirit that was fostered among them all—or, in a sense, their corporate *genius*, "the spirit that is among you all" (see also Galatians 6:18). This corporate spirit seems to be what the author of Ephesians was referencing with the phrase, "be renewed in the spirit of your minds" (4:23).

Paul can be understood as referencing the corporate *genius* at several other points in his letters. In 1 Corinthians he asked, "What human being knows what is truly human except the human spirit?" (2:11). Paul could say to the Corinthian Jesus-groups, "Though I am absent [from you] in the body, I am present in spirit" (5:3). Later, he noted that unmarried women benefit from being undistracted by household matters and thus are able to "be holy in body and spirit" (7:34). Later still, he characterized the phenomenon of "speaking in tongues" as a form of prayer language of "the [human] spirit" that does not include the human mind (see especially chapter 8). Toward the end of the same letter, Paul declared Jesus Christ to have become a "life-giving spirit" (15:45) and spoke of his own spirit having been refreshed by the fellowship provided by Stephanus and his household (16:17–18). So

too in Romans he claimed to have served his deity "with [his] spirit" by announcing the good news (1:9). Some people among his intended audience might have heard this as a reference to his *genius*, which animated his concrete efforts. If so, they might also have been interested to hear in the same sentence that Paul remembered them "always in [his] prayers"—since those prayers would have been empowered by a faithful *genius* that fostered an effective ministry (empowered by the divine Spirit; see chapter 18).

This view of things also helps explain other aspects of early Christian discourse. For instance, John, the author of Revelation, presents himself as a seer of realities in the transcendent world beyond the material world. His authority derives from the fact that he "was in the spirit on the Lord's day" when the voice of the Lord addressed him "like a trumpet" (1:10). It was then that John was commanded, "Write in a book what you see and send it to the seven churches, to Ephesus, to Smyrna, to Pergamum, to Thyatira, to Sardis, to Philadelphia, and to Laodicea" (1:11). Those churches are addressed in Revelation 2–3, with the sovereign Lord critiquing the spiritual health of the various communities of Jesus-followers. In each instance, however, it is not the church itself that is addressed. Instead, the address is spoken directly "to the angel" of the various churches: "to the angel of the church in Ephesus" (2:1); "to the angel of the church in Smyrna" (2:8); and so on (see also 2:12, 18; 3:1, 7, 14). In each instance, the critique (through one who is "in the spirit") is addressed to the spiritual projection of the inner realities of the church's physical gatherings. The angels are the spiritual embodiment of the individual churches, the representations of those churches projected onto the screen of the heavens and captured in the figure of distinct angels.

This also helps us understand a peculiar episode in Mark's Gospel (see also Matthew 14:1–11). When Herod Antipas (the pro-Roman ruler of Galilee whose family had connections with the imperial household of Rome) heard that Jesus was becoming tremendously popular, he interpreted Jesus's popularity with these words: "John, whom I beheaded, has been raised" (Mark 6:16). We might think that Herod had taken leave of his senses to imagine that John the Baptist, who had been killed perhaps only a few months earlier, had been physically resurrected in the person of Jesus, who must have been in his late twenties at this point in the story and whose life had overlapped with John's for some time. But Herod was not a fool. Suspecting that John the Baptist had been raised, Herod was imagining that John's spirit had come to reside within Jesus, so that it now empowered Jesus's

Figure 7.7. A winged *genius* from the Villa of Fannius Synistor in Boscoreale, a few miles north of Pompeii

ministry. According to Mark's Gospel, this is what some people were, in fact, saying: John the Baptist had been raised "and for this reason these [miraculous] powers [were] at work in him" (6:14). Still others imagined that the spirit of one of Israel's ancient prophets was empowering Jesus (6:15; see also 8:27–28).

There is an ominous note in Herod's view that the spirit of John was now empowering Jesus's ministry. Herod, we are told, "feared John, knowing that he was a righteous and holy man" (Mark 6:20). To murder a righteous man (see 6:17–29) was not necessarily the end of the dead man's influence, for one had to be on guard against the return of the righteous man's spirit. This is why Herod's comment is not an insignificant observation but, instead, would have carried an ominous note for ancient audiences of the narrative. Herod was signaling that Jesus posed a threat to Herod's political ambition, with the spirit of John the Baptist now on the loose, enraged and more to be feared than when John was alive. People in urban centers of the first century would have readily understood the political intrigue of this episode, being immersed in a world in which people have a *genius* or *juno* that transcends their material existence.

The Emperor and His *Genius*

This is where we need to consider a most important human figure: the Roman emperor. In one way, the emperors were no different from everyone else. Between the date of their birth and the date of their death, they loved, lusted, hated, manipulated, schemed, partied, suffered, won, lost, strove—these being ordinary traits of human life. And like every other man, each emperor had a *genius*. (People in Pompeii sometimes took oaths that affirmed the truthfulness of their legal testimony "by the *genius* of Imperator Augustus and his children"; see VAR Tab. 16–17, 23–24.) But from the late first century BCE onward, it was fashionable to think that the *genius* of the emperor was worthy of worship. This was not the worship of a human being (for example, Augustus or Nero or Domitian). It was the worship of the potent life force that infused the emperor, the force that was the conduit of the will of Rome's deities. If the

Figure 7.8. Pompeii's temple honoring the divine emperor Vespasian after his death (7.9.2)

genius of the householder could receive sacrifices to ensure the protection and benefits of the household, so too the *genius* of the emperor could receive sacrificial offerings to ensure the protection and benefits of the empire, in accordance with the will of the deities. (In fact, it is possible that the *genii* in some household shrines depict the emperor's *genius* instead of the householder's *genius*.) We cannot be certain that everyone in the Roman provinces understood imperial worship to involve the worship of a living emperor's *genius* rather than the worship of the living emperor himself, and some evidence suggests that at times the distinction may have been lost. (Of course, when an emperor died, the distinction no longer applied.)

Whether they always understood the distinction or not, the people of Pompeii were strong advocates of the imperial cult. This is clear from the people's priorities in the final two decades of the town's life. In 62 (or perhaps 63, since ancient sources differ with regard to the specific year), the temples of Pompeii were devastated by a severe earthquake, but by the time of the eruption in 79, most of the temples to the traditional Greco-Roman deities (e.g., the Temple of Apollo, the Temple of Venus, and the Temple of Jupiter, Juno, and Mercury) were still far from being fully restored and were either not yet functioning (as in the case of Venus) or had only a low-grade functionality. By contrast, the temples that were fully restored and functioning were those associated with the imperial cult and the mystery deities (on which, see chapters 8 and 9). At some point in the 70s (probably even in the final months of Pompeii's existence), a prominent Pompeian resident and Roman citizen donated funds to establish a temple to emperor Vespasian, a temple sitting prominently within Pompeii's forum district (see figure 7.8 and figure 5.4—noting that the bull, which is central in figure 5.4, was the expected sacrificial animal in offerings to the imperial *genius*).

Jesus-Followers and the Emperor

If Pompeians were eager to participate in the worship of the emperor's *genius*, they must have imagined that they were contributing to the health of the empire in the process. Some Jesus-devotees sought to find a way to allow for "honoring" the emperor without worshiping him (for example, 1 Peter 2:17; see also Romans 13:1–7; 1 Timothy 2:1–2; Titus 3:1). Some probably heard validation for this approach in Jesus's (somewhat ambiguous) pronouncement, "Give to the emperor the things that are the emperor's, and to God the things that are God's" (Mark 12:17; also Matthew 22:21 and Luke 20:25).

One Christian voice took the lead in denouncing not only the worship of the emperor but the whole of the system within which imperial worship was embedded. In the view of this man, emperor worship was only one part of a much larger cancer that was spreading infectious disease throughout the whole world. The prophetic voice that articulated this way of looking at the world belonged to John, the author of Revelation. Probably written (or finally assembled) in the 90s (during the reign of emperor Domitian), that apocalyptic text purports to reveal the future victory of the deity who will prove to be sovereign by eradicating deeply entrenched evil and establishing "a new heaven and a new earth" in which that deity's sovereignty will permeate all reality (as revealed especially in Revelation 21–22). Along the way, John immerses the reader in a narrative that is deeply entrenched in political critique.

John's sights are set on the power that is concentrated on the "seven hills" (Revelation 17:9), and in the ancient world it was common knowledge that Rome was built on seven hills. What kind of power was concentrated in the halls of Rome? If the Roman imperial ideology advertised Rome as the embodiment of the deities' will for humanity, John unmasks it as an entity that received its power from the dragon, who is "the Devil and Satan, the deceiver of the whole world" (12:9). The potent force driving the Roman program is not the benevolent *genius* of the emperor, which is in harmony with the will of the divine. Instead, the spiritual power that emboldens the forward movement of the Roman program is the fraudulent satanic charlatan who leads the whole world away from aligning itself with the divine will. (For a similar critique, see 2 Thessalonians 2:1–12.)

This depiction of the satanic force embedding itself within the Roman system appears especially in Revelation 12–13. The reader is first introduced to a mythological dragon who tries to destroy Jesus Christ, his forebears, and his followers (Revelation 12). Being unsuccessful in that, the dragon hands his power to the beast, giving the beast "his power and his throne and great authority" (13:2). In all this, the author demonizes the Roman program; the beast is shown to empower the whole of the Roman imperial complex. While it is sometimes difficult to interpret the first-century symbolism of Revelation, John's severe critique of interwoven aspects of the Roman imperial order is visible despite the apocalyptic veneer of his discourse. Three aspects of the Roman program are given prominence:

1. Rome's military might, as represented by the "power" that the dragon gave the beast, with the people proclaiming in amazement, "Who can fight against it?" (13:4)

2. The worship of the Roman emperor (or his *genius*), as represented by the "throne"

that the dragon gave the beast, with "all the inhabitants of the earth" worshiping a beast that emerges from the whole power complex of the dragon (13:8; this is further illustrated in 13:12 and 14:11)

3. Rome's imperial reign over all the nations, as represented by the "authority over every tribe and people and language and nation" that the dragon gave the beast (13:7)

And as we will see in chapter 14, even the economic systems of the Roman world did not evade the author's devastating critique.

One feature in this political critique is the fascinating reference to "the name of the beast or the number of its name" (Revelation 13:17). The audience of John's Revelation is exhorted in this way: "Let anyone with understanding calculate the number of the beast, for it is the number of a person" (13:18). The number of the person is famously said to be 666.

Some graffiti from Pompeii help set the context for understanding what is involved in "calculating the number of the beast." Someone from Pompeii wrote on a wall, "I love her whose number is 545" (*CIL* 4.4861). Someone else referred to his "lady," stating that "the number of her honorable name is 1035" (*CIL* 4.4839, although the graffito is difficult to read, so the number might be 45). In the ancient world, letters were often given numerical values, especially in Greek and Hebrew. So people could refer to others on the basis of the numerical value of their name. When this is applied to the number 666, it is probable that the number cryptically refers to the emperor Nero. When the name "Nero Caesar" is transliterated into Hebrew characters and those characters are given their numerical values,

Figure 7.9. A statue from Herculaneum depicting emperor Augustus in garb reminiscent of the young divine Jupiter

the number 666 emerges. As most interpreters agree, the number 666 references Nero, the emperor who dramatically embodied the "bestial" character of Roman reign and delighted in the worship he received from many even while he was alive. (There is another textual tradition that lists the value as 616 instead of 666, and curiously, that number also corresponds to a version of Nero's name.)

A contemporary of John also offered a negative critique of Nero using the value of his name as the basis for the critique. In the year 59, Nero orchestrated the murder of his mother, Agrippina. According to the Roman historian Suetonius (*Nero* 39.2), not long after Agrippina's death someone inscribed the Greek phrase "he killed his own mother" on a wall, next to the name "Nero" in Greek.

Intriguingly, the letters of the sentence add up to 1005, precisely the same value as Nero's own name (when valued according to the system used for Greek letters). For this person, when the emperor's name is placed alongside this sentence, there is a certain appropriate balance to it, with numerical equivalence helping to reveal the murderous character of the emperor.

Those who supported the Roman imperial order often advertised it as authenticated and empowered by the deities, a force for good that suppressed chaos, brought goodness and plenty to all, and inaugurated peace and security for the nations that submitted themselves to it (as seen in chapter 6). The narrative of Revelation, however, attempts to unmask the Roman imperial order as being animated by a different spiritual order altogether, empowered by satanic forces—forces that ultimately are bestial and chaotic, and forces that cannot stand before the sovereign power of divine justice. This, ultimately, is not a world away from Paul's own brief formula at the very end of Romans: "The God of peace will soon crush Satan under your feet" (Romans 16:20 NIV). But it runs directly against the grain of the Roman imperial ideology, in which the *genius* of the emperor is the conduit through which the prayers and sacrifices of the people of the empire pass to the deities of Rome, and the conduit through which the blessings of Rome's deities pass, for the benefit of the people of the empire. In John's estimate, a narrative of that kind is "haughty and blasphemous" (Revelation 13:5) and "deceives the inhabitants of earth" (13:14).

Mysteries
and Knowledge

8

> I did not come proclaiming the mystery of God to you in lofty words or wisdom.... We speak *God's wisdom, secret and hidden,* which God decreed before the ages for our glory.... Think of us in this way, as servants of Christ and *stewards of God's mysteries.*
>
> 1 Corinthians 2:1, 7; 4:1

Mysteries of the Deities

It was extraordinary to claim (as Paul did in 1 Corinthians 2:1) to know the mystery of the divine will, which had been hidden for ages. Similar claims appear in other letters of Paul (see, for instance, Romans 16:25–27), coming to the fore especially in Ephesians and Colossians (see Ephesians 1:9; 3:5, 9, 18–19; Colossians 1:26; 2:2; 4:3). Assertions of this kind cohere with Jesus's statement to his disciples, "To you it has been given to know the secrets of the kingdom of God" (Luke 8:10; see also Matthew 13:11; Mark 4:11). Or when Simon Peter confessed that Jesus is "the Messiah, the Son of the living God," Jesus is depicted as stating, "Flesh and blood has not revealed this to you, but my Father in heaven" (Matthew 16:16–17). In fact, Jesus is remembered to have "rejoiced in the Holy Spirit" when praying to his Father, because his Father had "hidden these things from the wise and the intelligent and . . . revealed them to infants," for this was the Father's "gracious will" (Luke 10:21).

If the claim to know the secret mysteries of the deity who created all things was extraordinary, it was not without precedent in the Greco-Roman world. In fact, at the same time that Christianity was getting a foothold, other forms of devotion that also promised insights into the mysteries of the deities were spreading like wildfire. These "mystery religions" were precisely that—forms of devotion dedicated to the worship of certain deities whose devotees were given knowledge of esoteric mysteries that were to enhance their lives.

91

Deities of Mystery

Scholars sometimes differentiate between two somewhat distinct forms of devotion:

1. devotion to the traditional Greco-Roman deities (Jupiter, Juno, Mercury, Venus, Apollo, and the like) and
2. devotion to the mystery deities (such as the initiation cults associated with the deities Demeter/Ceres, Dionysus/Bacchus, Cybele, Isis, Sabazius, and Mithras).

Of course, these two forms of devotion overlapped significantly. Whatever differences there might have been between traditional and mystery forms of devotion were largely a matter of degree rather than kind. The form of devotion that sprang up around mystery deities was in some ways only an intensification of aspects of devotion already offered to traditional deities. Even the schematization that differentiates "traditional" from "mystery" deities does not work all that well in some regards, since (1) the mystery deities Demeter and Dionysus, for instance, were themselves included among the Olympian deities of traditional Greek mythology, and (2) other Olympian deities (Apollo and Artemis) were deities of oracular revelations of mysteries, wisdom, and insight. Moreover, mystery devotion was usually motivated by the same interest as more traditional forms of devotion—to enhance everyday life by improving the situations people found themselves in. The phenomenon of *do ut des* ("I give in order that you might give," noted in chapter 5) pertains as much to mystery devotion as to more traditional forms of devotion. People expected their lives to be improved as they accessed the special knowledge granted to them by the mystery deities.

And yet, even with these caveats in place, the forms of devotion that sprang up around mystery deities were sometimes subtly different from devotion toward non-mystery deities, enough to merit postulating a soft distinction between them. The basis of that soft distinction is a sense of heightened intimacy in people's relationship with the mystery deities. The people who devoted themselves to one or more of the mystery deities seem to have expected those deities to take a personal interest in their well-being, to an extent that outstripped more traditional forms of devotion. Devotion to the mystery deities seems to have fostered solutions to the quest for personal meaning in a way that was less evident in more traditional forms of devotion. Traditionally, deities were known to prop up structures of society (as noted in chapter 6), but they were not always reputed to offer relational intimacy with their devotees. Mystery deities were somewhat different in that regard. Providing their devotees with beneficial resources (such as augmenting their understanding of the world, their identity, and their sense of worth), the mystery deities were thought to be more intimately involved with the lives of their devotees—as in the case of Dionysus/Bacchus, of whom it was said that "no god is more near" than he (Ovid, *Metamorphoses* 3.658–59). Of course, a person did not abandon the practice of honoring other deities just because he or she adopted the practice of honoring a mystery deity or two. But it seems that many people who practiced a mystery religion found that it went deeper into the heart of things than more traditional practices of devotion.

This sense of intimacy with divine beings fostered other expectations—in particular, the expectation that devotees of mystery deities would have powerful religious experiences. Those experiences might involve transcending the constraints of this world in order to be in touch with the fundamental forces of creation, or even a personal encounter with the deities themselves. A second-century account articulates in first-person voice what an experience of that kind might have been like (Apuleius, *The Golden Ass* 11.23, my translation):

> I have come up to death's very boundary and placed my foot on the entrance to Proserpina's domain [i.e., the underworld]. I have traveled through the fundamental elements of the world and returned again. In the depths of night, I have gazed on the shining sun in dazzling white light. I came face-to-face with the deities below and the deities above, and in unmediated intimacy I worshiped them.

Honoring the mystery deities often involved undergoing progressive stages of initiation, enabling devotees to proceed "further up and further in" through a series of ranks within a group of like-minded devotees (and increasing people's stature within that group as they climbed the ladder of knowledge and prominence).

For some, that process of progressive initiation also resulted in a change of character. We see this view articulated by the first-century-BCE Roman philosopher Cicero. At one point in his work *On the Laws* (2.14.36), a character articulates his attachment to the advantages that come from worshiping a mystery deity:

> Nothing is better than those mysteries. For by means of them we have been transformed from a rough and savage way of life to the state of humanity, and have been civilized.

Figure 8.1. A fresco of the mystery deity Bacchus (or Dionysus), wearing apparel (a garb of grapes) appropriate to his role as the bringer of good times (literally, the deity of wine and celebration); he stands next to Mount Vesuvius, with the snake (the benevolent spirit of the place) enjoying a sacrificial offering made to it on a shrine; here, then, Bacchus is depicted as the life-giving benefactor of Vesuvian fruitful harvests and enjoyment (from 9.8.3/6, MANN 112286).

> Just as they are called initiations, so in actual fact we have learned from them the fundamentals of life, and have grasped the basis not only for living with joy but also for dying with a better hope.

Evidently in some instances mystery devotion was characterized as transforming the devotee from a savage person to a civilized person who has learned the fundamentals of life.

The historian Diodorus Siculus (who wrote between 60 and 30 BCE) said something similar about the ethical transformation within a particular branch of mystery devotion—devotion to the great deities of Samothrace, whose mysteries and initiation rites attracted a significant number of devotees in the Roman age (*Library of History*, Book 5, 49.1–6).

> Now the details of the initiatory rite are guarded among the matters not to be divulged, and are communicated to the initiates alone; but the fame has traveled wide of how these gods appear to mankind and bring unexpected aid to those initiates of theirs who call upon them in the midst of perils. The claim is also made that men who have taken part in the mysteries become more pious and more just and better in every respect than they were before.

Evidently some forms of devotion to a mystery deity (but certainly not all) were thought to result in the development of a person's moral character.

The development of character in this life was sometimes thought to qualify a person for the "better hope" beyond this life. The philosopher and biographer Plutarch (46–120) made this connection, for instance, noting that many people "think that some sort of initiations and purifications will help" them since, having been "purified," they "will go on playing and dancing" in the afterlife "in places full of brightness, pure air, and light" (*Non posse suaviter vivi secundum* 1105b). Is this what Cicero's character was referencing when referring to mystery devotees "dying with a better hope"? We will see something of this in chapter 9. For now, it is enough to note that being "transformed" into a "purified" person (or a person of moral character) was usually the terrain traversed by philosophical insight about what makes for fruitful human living, not so much by traditional forms of devotion to the deities. Evidently, then, something significant ("the fundamentals of life") and exciting ("nothing is better") was happening in the realm of devotion to the deities of mystery.

These "mystery religions" tended to reach the parts of the human person that others did not reach. For instance, when his daughter died, Plutarch noted that one thing that helped him cope with the sorrow was "the mystic formulas" of a mystery deity. Plutarch found that those mystic formulas granted a certain comforting "knowledge"—a knowledge that those "who are participants share with each other" (*Consolatio ad uxorem* 611D). Those formulas reinforced for him the notion that the soul is "imperishable" and comparable to "a captive bird" that is "entangled in the passions and fortunes of this world"; for Plutarch, the worst condition of life is for the soul to become "stale in its memories of the other world" and to "cling tenaciously to this [world]" (*Consolatio ad uxorem* 611E). Evidently Plutarch's experiences of mystery devotion granted him the elevated knowledge of how to conceive of his place within the arrangement of the eternal realities, with the soul being eternal and living beyond death. From this, we can see how certain aspects of mystery devotion held great attraction and served a significant existential function beyond other forms of devotion. This is significant since Plutarch, himself an important philosopher of the Roman age, was testifying to the existential power of a form of mystery devotion, rather than a philosophical idea per se. Moreover, Plutarch's claim that mystery devotion reveals something significant about the soul correlates well with some forms of mystery devotion evidenced within Pompeii (especially Pompeii's "Villa of the Mysteries," as noted below).

Mystery Deities in Pompeii

Things said in literary texts do not always correspond with the archaeological record; sometimes the two offer different kinds of data, which don't necessarily overlap easily. In this case, however, some Pompeian artifacts correspond significantly with some of the discourse of Cicero, Diodorus Siculus, and Plutarch that we have just noted. As mentioned in chapter 7, between the time of the earthquake of 62 and the volcanic eruption in 79, most of the temples to traditional deities remained "unfit for purpose," but the temples servicing mystery deities and the imperial cult were fully functioning. (In fact, Pompeii's civic leaders seem to have prioritized all sorts of other initiatives ahead of the restoration of the traditional temples—including the building of the Central Baths, the repairing of the water supply, and the restoration of the macellum and the Eumachia building.) This Pompeian data suggests, then, that mystery devotion often held greater interest among the populace and served more personal interests than traditional forms of honoring the deities.

Of the various cults to the mystery deities, two were especially popular in the Vesuvian towns:

1. The cult of Dionysus, known to the Romans as Bacchus, the deity of wine and "the good life"
2. The cult of a female deity from Egypt, Isis, the deity who enriches life in the present and sends her devotees on their way to life beyond death

The Pompeians saw these two mystery deities as overlapping in what they offered. This is illustrated by the fact that a limestone bust of Bacchus (in stately Egyptian headdress) was found in the main ceremonial space of the Isis temple. So too, a full statue of Bacchus stood in a niche around the back of that temple's ceremonial space (see figure 8.2).

The mystery deities Bacchus and Isis deserve close attention, since they both help to illustrate certain attractions that may, in turn, help us to understand some of the attractions of the early Jesus-movement. In order to do justice to each form of mystery devotion, this chapter will consider the cult of Bacchus, and the cult of Isis will be showcased in the next chapter. (Groups of Sabazius-devotees were based in a few Pompeian houses [2.1.12,

Figure 8.2. A statue of the young Bacchus, which stood within the grounds of the Temple of Isis (8.7.28)

95

1.13.9], but Sabazius-devotion seems not to have had the same stretch of influence in the Vesuvian towns as these other two mystery cults—although Sabazius-devotion may originally have overlapped with Dionysus/Bacchus-devotion.)

Devotion to Bacchus (Dionysus) in Pompeii

In 1943, the Allies dropped more than 150 bombs on Pompeii with the hope of flushing out supporters of the Italian dictator Mussolini (see figure 3.9). In that raid, a stray bomb landed less than a mile south of Pompeii and uncovered a previously unknown temple to Bacchus, which had overlooked the local Sarno River prior to the eruption of Vesuvius. Evidently, devotion to this deity, which was widespread in Pompeii, had a focal point in that small temple.

Figure 8.3. Amphorae for the storage of wine, from a wine shop in Herculaneum (from 5.6, in situ)

It does not take a PhD in rocket science to understand the appeal of the Dionysian or Bacchic cult. As the deity of grape harvests and wine (among other things), Bacchus was honored in Pompeii to help ensure profitable harvests and, consequently, profitable businesses in the local area. It is little wonder, then, that depictions of Bacchus are more plentiful in Pompeii than depictions of Venus, Pompeii's own patron deity. Paintings of Bacchus appear in numerous Pompeian houses, and small figures of him were commonly placed in shrines of Pompeian households. Few Vesuvian residents would have shunned the idea of having a good party, and to have a good party it was suitable to honor Bacchus in one way or another. This relatively superficial form of Bacchic devotion might have been attractive simply as a means of intensifying a household's reputation for hosting festive social events.

But at times Bacchic devotion was taken to quite another level, with the deity's mysteries residing at the heart of it all. Again, it is not hard to see the attraction of this form of devotion for small groups. Meeting to enjoy the Bacchic mysteries, groups would celebrate in a fashion that usually involved drunkenness, perhaps punctuated by ecstatic frenzy interpreted as spiritual enlightenment. Sometimes this went hand in hand with "sexual debauchery" (in which case, there may not have been a lot of "moral transformation" going on, at least in the Judeo-Christian sense of that term). With the assistance of wine, the devotees of Bacchus considered themselves to be entering into mystical union with the deity, perhaps precisely through such apparently liberating acts of self-release that broke the boundaries of usual decorum and were powered by a brute animalistic drive. Bacchus

was thought to induce madness in his devotees during their celebrations, with wine helping to liberate the mind from the constraints
normally placed on it and freeing the spirit
to encounter the deity. These activities were
seen as enabling Bacchus-devotees to enter
progressively further into the revelation of his
mysteries and to tap into the primal forces and
primordial powers that flowed through him.

The Vesuvian material remains testify to
the presence of these two (related) forms of
Bacchic devotion—with Bacchus-devotion
being thought to augment frivolity at dinner
parties and, at times, to foster mystical union
with him and his power. This archaeological
evidence falls in line with the impressions offered by the Roman historian Livy (59 BCE to
17 CE). On the one hand, Livy knew of Bacchic devotion that involved "the open practice
of his rites and the public advertisement of his
trade" (*History of Rome* 39.8). Livy had no
objection to that form of devotion, which is
probably what we see most often in the Pompeian depictions of Bacchus, who brings good
harvests to the fields and enhanced dinner
parties. The other form of Bacchus-devotion,
on the other hand, revolved around Bacchus
as a "hierophant" or a revealer of sacred
knowledge in "secret ceremonies performed
at night," which involved "the pleasures of
drinking and feasting." Livy noted that "when
wine had inflamed their feelings, and night
and the mingling of the sexes and of different ages had extinguished all power of moral
judgement, all sorts of corruption began to be
practiced." Livy even gave specific examples of
these wine-induced frenzies (39.13):

> From the time when the rites were held pro-
> miscuously, with men and women mixed
> together, and when the license offered by

Figure 8.4. A bronze figurine of Silenus, a cohort of Bacchus, sitting on a wineskin made of the carcass of a dead animal, with legs tied to prevent leakage, while the wine flows freely from the animal's open neck (from the Villa of the Papyri in Herculaneum)

> darkness had been added, no sort of crime,
> no kind of immorality, was left unattempted.
> There were more obscenities practiced be-
> tween men than between men and women.
> Anyone refusing to submit to outrage or re-
> luctant to commit crimes was slaughtered
> as a sacrificial victim. To regard nothing as
> forbidden was among these people the sum-
> mit of religious achievement.

Although not all formations of the Bacchic
mystery cult looked like this, the secret ceremonies that transpired around the revealer
of the deep mysteries were frequently characterized in terms similar to Livy's depiction.

Pompeii's Villa of the Mysteries

In a villa on Pompeii's outskirts, now referred to as the Villa of the Mysteries, we get a glimpse of Bacchus-devotion unlike anything else from the ancient world. In a deeply recessed section of the villa, the walls of a large room had been used as the canvas on which to depict beautiful frescos. In those frescos, several human figures (mostly female) have been joined by Bacchus, featured on the center panel of the fresco, together with Silenus, his tutor, who frequently accompanied him in a state of drunkenness. The various components of the fresco are commonly interpreted as depicting distinct stages in a Bacchic ceremony. Scholars have detected bridal themes in some of the female adornments. Might the fresco capture an initiation ceremony that authenticated the initiate's identity as a bride,

legitimately prepared for marriage? If so, was the Bacchic ceremony some form of preparation for a woman to enter into her role as a married matriarch? Or was it enlisting her as a spiritual bride of Bacchus himself? Or is something else going on? We might guess, but we will never know for sure. Nonetheless, some interpretations of the fresco are worth articulating here.

One section of the room's frescos depicts a variety of people busy doing things (see figure 8.5). A young boy is reading from a scroll, overseen by a woman behind him (perhaps a priestess), who also holds a scroll; perhaps this alludes to a liturgical element in the celebrations. Toward the middle of this section of the fresco, a woman holds a tray of what seem to be food items, perhaps alluding to a ritual meal. Toward the right of this section of the

Figure 8.5. Part of the fresco depicting what seem to be different elements in a Bacchic celebration (from the Villa of the Mysteries, in situ)

Figure 8.6. Two women in the process of Bacchic ecstasy, one naked and dancing in circles (right) and one bending over in order to be scourged with a whip by a spiritual being, as depicted on the adjacent wall (from the Villa of the Mysteries, in situ)

fresco, a woman lifts a veil or towel with her left hand while another woman pours liquid over her right hand, perhaps alluding to a purification ritual of some kind.

In another part of the fresco (see figure 8.6), a naked woman dances in circles while clanging cymbals together with her hands—probably working herself up into a spiritual frenzy through the spinning motion. Meanwhile, to her left, a kneeling woman leans into another woman's lap in the moment just before a whip lands on her exposed back. Her back is being scourged by a figure who appears on the adjacent wall of the shared corner (with her whip swinging from the right side of the front panel to the right panel itself). Being a winged figure, the figure doing the scourging is a spiritual being, perhaps suggesting that, if whipping was literally carried out at some point in the ceremony, the human who performed that task was merely the agent of

spiritual forces—a task probably associated with purifying the soul through physical discipline and preparing it for its spiritual release from the body.

The centerpiece of the fresco (now with significant damage; see figure 8.7) features a reclining Bacchus, who oversees the celebratory proceedings in a drunken stupor, supported by his human wife, Ariadne (or perhaps by the deity Venus). To Bacchus's left, a young man gazes into an empty wine goblet (held for him by Silenus), being astounded at what he sees therein. To his right, a woman is about to see something that has been hidden by a veil up to this point. The best guess is that the man and woman are being shown the mysteries of Bacchus because of their participation in his ceremonies of revealed mysteries. Bacchic art frequently depicts a woman unveiling a phallus (see also figure 8.8). Evidently the women who sought release from their bodies

Figure 8.7. The centerpiece of the Bacchic frescos, featuring a drunken Bacchus (leaning against Ariadne, his wife) and the revelation of mysteries on either side of him (from the Villa of the Mysteries, in situ)

(through spinning and flagellation, techniques commonly used by those seeking to release the spirit from the body) were preparing themselves to encounter Bacchus and benefit from the revelation of his mysteries.

Figure 8.8. Depicted in colored marble, a woman in spiritual rapture unveils a phallus in a Bacchic celebration (MANN 9979; experts disagree as to whether this marble was found in 7.4.31/51 or 7.2.38).

Negotiating Mystery Devotion in Early Christianity

With this quick sketch in view, we can see how some people who heard about Jesus-devotion may have imagined it to be similar to some forms of Bacchic devotion. We have already noted Paul's emphasis on the revelation of the divine mysteries. In his view, communities of Jesus-followers are endowed with "the Spirit [who] searches all things, even the deep things of God" (1 Corinthians 2:10 NIV). Later, when the Corinthians felt the need to have leaders with impressive resumes of spiritual experiences, Paul was forced to boast about an incident fourteen years earlier when he was caught up to the third heaven—"whether in the body or out of the body, I don't know, only God knows" (2 Corinthians 12:2–3); in the context of "paradise" (as he calls it), he "heard things that are not to be told, that no mortal is permitted to repeat" (12:4). A statement like this could easily have been interpreted

100

as the articulation of a profound experience conferred by a mystery deity—one of those deities that captured so many people's interests in Paul's day (although in this regard the experience also overlaps with the descriptions in Judean apocalypses of journeys of apocalyptic ascent into higher regions of reality).

Note also what Paul says when advising the Corinthians about how to manage the spiritual gift of speaking in tongues. This seems to have been an instance in which spiritual ecstasy resulted in utterances of linguistic gibberish within the corporate gatherings. Some Corinthian Jesus-devotees were "eager for spiritual gifts" (1 Corinthians 14:12). Although Paul did not want them to dwell too much on "speaking in tongues," he nonetheless recognized that "those who speak in a tongue . . . are speaking mysteries in the Spirit" (14:2), perhaps with "tongues . . . of angels" (13:1). But he tried to dissuade the Corinthians from thinking that tongues were spiritual pyrotechnics that propelled the individual into a mystical hysteria, like an out-of-body experience of mystical frenzy. For Paul, these spiritual utterances needed to be deciphered into ordinary language, being articulated in known words that benefited the group as a whole—these became words of prophecy that helped interpret the group's corporate life in relation to the deity they worshiped (1 Corinthians 14).

It wasn't simply ordinary language that Paul wanted Jesus-devotees to use; he also wanted them to use their minds. In Bacchic celebrations, initiates sought release for their souls as they explored the boundaries of ecstasy. In the process, Bacchus was thought to inspire wine-induced forms of temporary madness in his devotees, as they lost themselves in an overwhelming swell of primordial energies. Paul shunned any appearance

of induced madness within communities of Jesus-devotion. He worried that spiritual speech might get out of hand, leaving Jesus-groups looking chaotic and unruly. In that situation, others would say, "You are out of your mind" (1 Corinthians 14:23)—perhaps a subtle reference to the madness induced in Bacchic celebrations. For Paul, the sober use of the mind was essential in discerning the deep things of the Spirit. In Paul's view, speaking in tongues is prayer language that leaves the intellect untouched: "For if I pray in a tongue, my spirit [or *genius*?] prays but my mind is unproductive" (14:14). Paul did not want the "mind" to be bypassed in favor of the "spirit." He says it this way:

> What should I do then? I will pray with the spirit, but I will pray with the mind also; I will sing praise with the spirit, but I will sing praise with the mind also. . . . In the assembly of believers, I would rather speak five words with my mind, in order to instruct others also, than ten thousand words in a [spiritual] tongue. (14:15, 19)

Also pertinent here is Paul's discussion of women in 1 Corinthians 11. It is likely that what provoked his discourse about the necessity of women wearing head-coverings in that chapter was an interest among Corinthian Christian women to rise above their gender and find their true spiritual androgyny in Christ. Perhaps they had heard Jesus's saying recorded in Mark 12:25: "For when they rise from the dead, they neither marry nor are given in marriage, but they are like angels in heaven." Were angelic beings male and female, or were they androgynous? According to Plutarch, his experience of mystery devotion taught him that our identity outstrips our physical bodies (male and female). Were

101

Corinthian women finding redemption (from their oppression in a male-dominated world) in the new mysteries revealed to them in Corinthian groups of Jesus-devotion? In a context where ideas of this sort were being considered, Paul was eager to reintroduce femaleness as an essential ingredient in the identity of Corinthian Christian women (1 Corinthians 11:2–16).

As a bit of an aside (but not unrelatedly), it is helpful to remember the extent to which the first century was immersed in patriarchal structures of society. To give just one example of this, seven hundred years before the turn of the Common Era, the Greek poet Hesiod collected myths regarding the origins of the Greek deities in his poem *Theogony*. In that famous extended poem, Hesiod includes a myth regarding the creation of woman/women. In this account, the deity Zeus was angered when he saw that Prometheus had stolen fire from Mount Olympus and given it to men (there being no women in existence at this point in the myth). Out of his anger at Prometheus's benevolent gesture toward men, Zeus "made an evil thing for men as the price of fire"—that "evil thing" being woman. Although "wonderful to see," woman is nonetheless "the beautiful evil" and "the price for the blessing" of fire. From the one evil woman come all other women, "the deadly race . . . who live among mortal men to their great trouble," doing nothing to offset poverty, but only soaking up men's wealth. In these ways, "Zeus who thunders on high made women to be an evil to mortal men, with a nature to do evil" (Hesiod, *Theogony* 561–612).

Clearly this myth did not match the tone of all discourse about women. Moreover, some women found ways to rise to social prominence as valued members of society—even in Pompeii, as we have already seen (in chapters 6 and 7) and will see again. Nonetheless, this myth was included within the cultural discourse about female gender and helped to support the patriarchal structures of that society. Mythology cannot tell us about the experience of real people on the ground, but it can alert us to ideological assumptions that those mythological narratives may have helped to foster within society. Is it any surprise, then, that women sometimes wondered whether their gender might be an impediment to their inner spiritual identity, something that their inner self might even be able to escape?

Perhaps this is what we catch glimpses of in Corinthian communities of Jesus-followers. Rather than denouncing entrenched myths of the sort perpetuated by Hesiod, some women may simply have sought release from the oppressive force of those myths by renouncing their identity as women. Whatever we think of Paul's specific arguments about headship in 1 Corinthians 11, his attempt to restore the contribution of "women as women" within the devotional practices of early Christianity offered women an alternative way to understand their identity in Christ rather than seeking to escape from their gender in worship contexts.

The same interest in delving into their spiritual identities over against their physicality might have caused some Corinthian Jesus-devotees to consider the merits of asceticism (see Paul's comments in 1 Corinthians 7). Maybe sexual relations should be shunned for those who are spiritual (7:1); maybe Jesus-devotees should not get married (7:8–9); maybe spouses should divorce each other (7:10–11). Could these notions have been part of an expectation among some Corinthian

Figure 8.9. A fresco of Bacchus (with his wine goblet) being escorted in a procession through the urban streets by an entourage of his followers, one of whom is a spinning, naked woman, who perhaps is advertising spiritual release as a Bacchic benefit for women (from 5.4.a, in situ)

Jesus-followers that it was good to transcend the body in order to enrich the spirit?

We have already seen that Paul did not imagine Jesus-devotion as bypassing the human mind within communities of Jesus-devotion. In fact, he emphasized the need for exercising the mind: "Be transformed by the renewing of your minds" (Romans 12:2); "Take every thought captive to obey Christ" (2 Corinthians 10:5). Part of that process involved recognizing and appreciating all that is good within the created order: "Whatever is true, whatever is honorable, whatever is just, whatever is pure, whatever is pleasing, whatever is commendable, if there is any excellence and if there is anything worthy of praise, think about these things" (Philippians 4:8). The mysteries of Paul's deity did not draw his devotees into some non-corporeal realm where wine-induced madness released them from their

Figure 8.10. A fresco showing Silenus (Bacchus's companion) holding up a drunken Bacchus (from the Villa of the Mysteries, in situ)

minds were to be transformed and renewed. The author of 1 Timothy followed this same stream of thought. Referencing "the mystery of faith" (1 Timothy 3:9, which is unpacked further in 3:16), this author ensured that the divine mystery was not detached from a notion of the goodness of creation: "For everything created by God is good, and nothing is to be rejected, provided it is received with thanksgiving" (4:4). Because the Judeo-Christian deity was the creator of all creation, wherever truth and goodness could be found within that good creation, those true and good things originated in and were sustained by the sovereign deity of creation, who was making all mysteries known in Christ.

For Paul, one other aspect was also essential in this process: "If I have prophetic powers, and understand all mysteries and all knowledge, . . . but do not have love, I am nothing" (1 Corinthians 13:2). Here, it isn't simply the mind that Paul emphasized; it was the mind enmeshed within an all-encompassing narrative of self-giving love. For Paul, the ultimate mystery was revealed in the self-giving of the deity of ultimate power; as Jesus-devotees immersed themselves in that mystery, they experienced the transformation of "mind renewal" in Christ Jesus. This narrative of the transforming power of the self-giving deity is what Paul referenced in his gospel of "the mystery of God" (2:1).

ordinary lives; instead, Paul imagined that all the good things of the created order were resources of refreshment on tap for those whose

Death and Life

9

Do you not know that all of us who have been baptized into Christ Jesus were baptized into his death? Therefore we have been buried with him by baptism into death, so that, just as Christ was raised from the dead by the glory of the Father, *so we too might walk in newness of life.* For if we have been united with him in a death like his, we will certainly be united with him in a resurrection like his. . . . *If we have died with Christ, we believe that we will also live with him.*

Romans 6:3–5, 8

The Story of Isis and Osiris

The mythologies surrounding the mystery deities captured the interests of many people in the first century and beyond. One of those mythologies was the story of Isis and Osiris—one of Egypt's most long-standing and influential stories. By the first century, the mythology of these Egyptian deities had captured the enthusiastic imagination of many residents in the Vesuvian towns and of many others throughout the Mediterranean basin. If ancient mystery devotion is often beyond the reach of our field of vision (because of the very nature of the "mysteries" that were often kept secret by their advocates), we nonetheless know quite a lot about devotion to these Egyptian deities, Isis and Osiris. This is because Isis-devotion was given extended attention (albeit with a few indulgent elaborations) in the works of two important Roman writers: (1) the prolific Roman essayist Plutarch (46–120 CE) in the late first century (in particular, his philosophical treatise *Moralia*, Book 5, titled *Isis and Osiris*) and (2) the Roman rhetorician Apuleius (125–180 CE) in the late second century (in particular, his novel *The Golden Ass*, or the *Metamorphoses*). Moreover, there are extensive references to the Isis mythology in literature and portraiture far and wide within the Greco-Roman world.

From these resources, it is evident that several versions of the Isis story circulated in the ancient world. In its most basic form, however, the general story went something like this. The rightful king of Egypt, Osiris, was murdered by his brother, Seth, who usurped the throne and discarded Osiris's body (either throwing it into the Nile encased in a coffin or dismembering it and having the parts sent to different areas of Egypt). But Osiris's wife, Isis, searching far and wide and suffering in sorrow the whole time, eventually gathered her husband's body (or body parts) and reanimated it (or them), bringing his body to life again (although more a pseudo-life, almost what might today be called "an undead"). Isis then became pregnant by Osiris, who became the deity of the underworld. Their offspring, Horus, reclaimed the imperial throne, restored the rightful line of reign, and overthrew injustice within the land.

This story has deep roots in Egyptian folklore, going back at least two millennia prior to the Common Era in its most basic form. Its appeal is unsurprising, not least since it encompasses the themes of suffer-ing, triumph, and the enhancement of life— themes placed within the broader context of the battle between good and evil. In the Vesuvian towns, both Isis and Osiris were considered important deities, but it was Isis who was the deity of choice in these urban centers. Again, this is unsurprising. She was a deity who offered her devotees relief from their suffering (since she herself had suffered, as retellings of her story pointed out); consequently, many of her ancient devotees thought that she could help relieve physical illnesses through healings. But Isis did not simply offer her devotees an enhanced life in the present. She also offered them access to some form of life beyond death. (This aspect of Isis-devotion may have been relatively new within the first century, but it seems to have been gaining a foothold in that period nonetheless.) Around the same time that small Jesus-groups were appearing in pockets of the Roman world, the Isis myth was increasingly explored in relation to its potential benefits for life both here-and-now and in the murky realm beyond.

Figure 9.1. Isis gathers a wooden coffin holding Osiris's body from the Nile River before restoring him to (a form of) life (from the Temple of Isis at 8.7.28, MANN 8929).

Isis-Devotion in Pompeii and Beyond

In the first century BCE, political leaders in Rome were suspicious of the Isis cult, wondering whether it might introduce unstable elements into traditional forms of devotion. But suspicion increasingly gave way to embrace. (For instance, an Egyptian coin from the early 70s CE displays the emperor Vespasian on one side and the deity Isis on the other.) And within Pompeii itself, evidence for the popularity of Isis-devotion comes from various data.

1. In the aftermath of the earthquake of 62, some private homes decorated their walls with celebrations of Isis-devotion. Nowhere is this clearer than in the House of the Golden Cupids (at 6.16.7/38), where a fresco shrine to Isis is incorporated at a key focal point in the central peristyle of the residence (see figure 9.3).

2. From political campaign advertisements, we know that Isis-followers seem to have had a sense of corporate identity in Pompeii, with "the worshipers of Isis" calling on the townspeople to vote for particular politicians (*CIL* 4.787, 4.1011).

3. As noted in earlier chapters, in the period between the earthquake of 62 and the eruption of 79, the traditional temples had not received much attention by way of repair and restoration; by contrast, the Temple of Isis was rebuilt and fully functioning, probably as much as a decade before the eruption and with the support of the civic authorities. (Note also that the Temple of Bacchus/Dionysus was fully functioning at the time of the eruption.)

Figure 9.2. Osiris on a throne, between two cobra snakes, beside a sycamore with a serpent; in the original fresco, Isis was to the left of Osiris and sitting on a superior throne (from the Temple of Isis, 8.7.28, MANN 8927).

These indicators testify that Isis-devotion had infiltrated deeply into the political and cultural arena of Pompeii.

Four things about Pompeii's Temple of Isis are notable.

Figure 9.3. A damaged fresco of Isis and Osiris, each shaking a devotional sistrum rattle (from 6.16.7, in situ)

107

1. Whereas most temples permitted ease of physical and visual access into the temple precincts, the Temple of Isis had only a single doorway entrance and high walls all around the temple precinct—both of these architectural features evidently enhancing the sense of privacy in relation to the activities of this mystery cult.

2. Next to the temple's altar was a housing for a subterranean reservoir of water drawn (allegedly) from the holy Nile River. This was an important feature, since water rituals were a part of Isis celebrations, water being the source of life (as the Nile River rose to life in floodwaters every spring).

3. In the back of the temple precinct was a large hall, used for banquets and initiation purposes.

4. The temple included a small selection of apartment rooms and a kitchen, allowing the priests of Isis to live on-site (probably only when they were on duty).

Drawing on what we know of Isis ceremonies elsewhere, we can expect that the Isis temple of Pompeii hosted two daily services. The morning service began just before sunrise, when worshipers would have gathered at the temple. While rattling their sistrums to add drama to the moment, Isis-devotees would have been shown an image of their deity. As the sun rose, they would have offered prayers of thanks for its rebirth. The afternoon service featured a celebration of water. A special ceremony recalling the restoration of Osiris's dismembered body by Isis's power was held in mid-November. This important ceremony might have been the main occasion for initiating new members into the cult.

If Isis could facilitate a form of life after death, some people in the Roman world did not believe in such a thing. One graffito on a tomb near Rome gives good testimony to this common lack of belief in an afterlife: "I didn't exist, I existed, I don't exist, I don't care" (*CIL* 5.2283, although the final phrase might be translated "I don't have any more cares"). The same sentiment appears in a graffito in the interior of the House of the Centenary in Pompeii (9.8.3): "Once you are dead, you are nothing" (*CIL* 4.5279).

Figure 9.4. The Temple of Isis (8.7.28); left: the sacrificial altar and, behind it, the storage facility for the ceremonial water; right: the main temple, with the altar on the left

But a good number of people in the Roman age did believe in an afterlife—at least an afterlife of some kind, even if the concept was not well defined. In an inscription on a Pompeii tomb, a rising star of Pompeian society (a man named Publius Vesonius Phileros, who is discussed further in chapter 13) denounced a former friend (a man named Marcus Orfellius Faustus) by appealing to "the gods of the underworld" and urging them not to "receive the man who lied about our dealings" (*AE* [1964], 160). Evidently Vesonius Phileros believed in the possibility of life in an "underworld existence" after death, and he used his tomb inscription to identify someone whom the deities of that world should consider an illegitimate candidate for that blessing. The sentiment is not much different from the graffito noted already in chapter 1, in which it is hoped that "those who veto love die twice" (*CIL* 4.4091)—which might mean that they should die in both the physical realm and the spiritual realm beyond.

The many devotees of Isis would have agreed with Vesonius Phileros's conviction about the afterlife. For instance, a first-century liturgy of initiation into the Isis cult (whether the first century BCE or CE is hard to tell) includes these words, spoken by Isis: "I conquer Fate; Fate listens to me" (*RICIS* 302/0204). Probably the word "Fate" includes a reference to "death," over which Isis has power. (Compare Cicero's comment about mystery devotees "dying with a better hope" and Plutarch's comment about mystery devotees imagining that they will be "playing and dancing" in the afterlife "in places full of brightness, pure air, and light"—both referenced in chapter 8.) This same conviction is evidenced in Apuleius's explanation of the attractions of Isis-devotion in the late second century. Here,

Figure 9.5. A fresco of a priest of Isis offering a sacrifice before the sarcophagus of Osiris (from the Temple of Isis, 8.7.28, MANN 8570)

Isis speaks directly to Lucius, the main character in the novel, who has just become one of her devotees (*The Golden Ass* 11.6):

You shall live blessed. You shall live gloriously under my guidance; and when you have travelled your full length of time and you go down into death, there also, on that hidden side of earth, you shall dwell in the Elysian Fields and frequently adore me for my favors. For you will see me shining on in the midst of the darkness of Acheron and reigning in the Stygian depths. So if you are found to merit my love by your dedicated obedience, your devotion, and your constant chastity, then you will discover that it is within my power to prolong your life beyond the limit set to it by Fate.

Isis had the power to control Fate to the advantage of her devotees. That incredible claim matches the motifs of Isis's sovereignty as depicted in Pompeian art and architecture. One fresco from the House of Philocalus (at 9.3.15) depicts Isis Fortuna standing with her

Figure 9.6. A fresco depicting the deity Isis (specifically, Isis Fortuna) holding the horn of plenty (in her left hand) and a sistrum rattle (in her right hand), with a rudder (illustrating her power to guide situations), and with her foot on an astral globe (from 9.3.15, MANN 8836)

of plenty held nearby her gaze. This "globe motif" appears elsewhere in Pompeii, sometimes with particular reference to Isis (also in 1.3.25, 8.5.39, 9.3.7), sometimes without reference to Isis, but always in reference to the deities. One Vesuvian fresco depicts a muse of Apollo holding a beautifully translucent globe, evidently depicting the astral mysteries that determine the course of the world (see figure 9.7). When the deities are depicted with an astral globe in Pompeian frescos, they are almost always the oldest Olympian deities of ancient Greece (Apollo at 6.7.2 and 6.7.23; Zeus/Jupiter at 6.9.6 at the Suburban baths, where he is represented by his eagle; Hera/Juno at 9.5.6; Urania, the daughter of Zeus, at 6.17.42 and 8.3.12) or the deity Fortuna, who brought good fortune in numerous guises (at 1.2.20, 6.9.6, 6.11.9, 7.10.3, 8.4.3, and 9.7.7). In the same way, many Pompeians, evidently fascinated by the power of Isis (specifically Isis Fortuna), depicted her as exercising sovereignty (or at least sharing in the exercise of sovereignty) over the whole world.

This conviction also morphs into depictions of Isis seated on a throne (see the description to figure 9.2). This aspect of her sovereignty was emphasized on the upper pediment of Pompeii's Temple of Isis—the pediment being the most important space for interpreting the significance of the ritual practices that went on within the temple space below it. In the center of the pediment, standing above all the proceedings of the cult, was the enthroned Isis. The scene also depicts her devotees, prostrate and worshiping the sovereign Isis as they rattle their sistrums with one hand and hold some kind of figure in the other (the figure being either the Ankh, which was the Egyptian symbol of life, or Isis herself—see figure 9.8).

foot on an astral globe (perhaps containing the four elements of creation: earth, wind, fire, water) while holding a horn of plenty in her hand (see figure 9.6). These artistic elements seem to illustrate Isis's benign sovereignty and power over the created order. A fresco in the house of Julia Felix (2.4.6) shows Isis seated on a great throne and beneficently overseeing the world—these themes again illustrated by the combination of an astral globe and a horn

Figure 9.7. A fresco of Urania, one of the muses of Apollo, who holds for him an astral globe, symbolizing knowledge of the mysteries of the astronomical elements that determine the course of the world (from the Moregine villa near Pompeii)

With such explicit expressions of Isis's exalted sovereignty being articulated in the Vesuvian towns and throughout the Mediterranean basin, it is easy to understand how some people identified Isis as the one who can rightly say of herself, "I am all that has been, and is, and shall be, and my robe no mortal has yet uncovered" (as noted by Plutarch, *Isis and Osiris* 9; compare the deity proclaimed in Revelation 1:4 and 1:8, "who is, and who was, and who is to come"). Isis could be thought to encompass everything, with her deity outstripping all human attempts to discern her immutable essence. A few decades after Pompeii's destruction, Plutarch described Isis as a "kindly nurse and provider for all things" who "fills our earth here with all things fair and good" (*Isis and Osiris* 34 and 78). Plutarch was convinced that "the effort to arrive at the Truth" is nothing more than "a longing for the divine," and that longing finds its fulfillment in the worship of Isis, "a goddess exceptionally wise and a lover of wisdom"; through worship of Isis "we shall comprehend reality if, in a reasonable and devout frame of mind, we pass within the portals of her shrines" (*Isis and Osiris* 2). Again, the Isis-devotees of Pompeii would presumably have agreed. Like Plutarch, many Pompeians may have conceived of her as the one who "discloses the divine mysteries to those who truly and justly have the name of 'bearers of the sacred vessels' and 'wearers of the sacred robes'" (*Isis and Osiris* 3). Through Isis comes

Figure 9.8. A drawing of the upper pediment of the Temple of Isis (8.7.28), depicting an enthroned Isis being worshiped (see credits)

111

Figure 9.9. A fresco from Herculaneum depicting an Isis temple ceremony in progress (MANN 8924)

the comprehension of reality and of one's place within it.

Life and Beyond

For several centuries beyond the first century CE, Isis-devotion and Jesus-devotion were often locked in a process of mutual self-definition and identity formation. The same might well have been happening even as the first manifestations of Jesus-devotion began to infiltrate the Roman world. If we substitute the word "his" with the word "her," Isis-followers could easily have borrowed these words from 2 Peter: "His divine power has given us everything needed for life" (1:3).

112

In the Gospel of John, Jesus is remembered in a way that could easily have been heard to include a polemical edge in relation to Isis-devotion. Although "no one has ever seen God" (compare Isis's claim "My robe no mortal has yet uncovered"), it is "God the Son, who is close to the Father's heart, who has revealed God's inner heart" (1:18). The same prologue (1:1–18) states that "all things came into being through him," specifically noting that "what came into being in him was life" (1:3–4) and, later, "grace and truth came through Jesus Christ" (1:17). These claims operate as one of the main lenses for interpreting the Gospel of John. Little wonder, then, that this narrative has Jesus declare, "I give [my followers] eternal life, and they will never perish" (10:28); "I am the Way, the Truth, and the Life" (14:6); "I am the resurrection and the life; those who believe in me, even though they die, will live" (11:25). Isis may not have said words of precisely this order, but many people hearing these words in the first century would have made a mental note, "Compare Isis."

So too, when the same Gospel states that Jesus gives his followers "life . . . to the fullest extent" (John 10:10, my translation), a first-century audience might hear a thinly veiled contrast with other divine life-bringers, since the Greek behind this phrase suggests something that is not only extraordinary and remarkable (as was true for all mystery deities) but also exceptional and incomparable. The story of the raising of the dead man Lazarus from his tomb dramatically demonstrates this Gospel's claim, as encapsulated in the simple words, "the dead man came out" of the tomb (11:44). It is little wonder, then, that in a summary of the main features of Jesus's "public ministry," the short outline of John 12:44–50

culminates with Jesus's claim that he has done everything in order to offer "eternal life" to his followers (12:50).

The Gospel of John elaborates these claims further. First, this Gospel makes it clear that Jesus both lays down his life freely and takes it up again after death. Unlike Osiris, who needed to be given life by Isis, Jesus notes in this Gospel, "I have authority [or "power"] to lay it [my life] down and authority [or "power"] to take it up again" (10:18 NIV). Nowhere else in the New Testament is Jesus said to resurrect himself; the normal pattern was to speak of Jesus having been raised ("by God") rather than raising himself. Perhaps John's Gospel steps out from the norm of early Christian discourse in order to polemicize against the Isis narrative, in which Osiris is restored to (a form of) life by Isis.

Second, this Gospel explores life in relation to the imagery of water, a key component of Isis celebrations. "The water that I will give will become in them [i.e., Jesus-followers] a spring of water gushing up to eternal life" (John 4:14); so "let the one who believes in me drink; as the scripture has said, 'Out of his heart [the believer's heart? Jesus's heart?] shall flow rivers of living water'" (7:38). By contrast, a funerary inscription dating to the last decade of the first century (the same decade as the circulation of the Johannine Gospel) speaks of death not as a time of thirsting in the underworld but as the time when devotees of Isis and Osiris come to enjoy "the refreshing water" of the afterlife (*RICIS* 501/0164). For the Johannine author, those refreshing waters can be found only in Jesus Christ. As if to drive the point home, he narrates that the crucified body of Jesus was pierced by a spear, with water (together with blood) immediately flowing from his side (19:34)—an occurrence not mentioned

113

in the other three canonical Gospels (and notice the narrator's emphasis of this narrative detail in 19:35). Truth, living water, eternal life, the revelation of the divine identity—devotees of Isis may well have been surprised to hear these familiar themes being applied in combination to a deity other than Isis.

Certain passages from the Pauline corpus may also have resonated with Isis-devotees. Jesus-followers were told that they would be "filled with the knowledge of God's will in all spiritual wisdom and understanding" as they "bear fruit in every good work" and "grow in the knowledge of God," being "made strong with all the strength that comes from his glorious power" (Colossians 1:9–11). According to Paul, that power resided in the message he proclaimed. Although that "good news" might be "foolishness to those who are perishing," Paul insisted that "to us who are being saved it is the power of God" (1 Corinthians 1:18), or "the power of God for salvation" (Romans 1:16). Stripping the message to its core, Paul explains things simply: "The end is eternal life" (6:22)—a notion that Isis-devotees would easily have understood, although in this case it is "eternal life through Jesus Christ our Lord" (5:21; see also 2:7; 6:23; 2 Corinthians 4:17; Galatians 6:8; 1 Timothy 1:16; 6:12; Titus 1:2; 3:7). The author of 2 Timothy claimed that grace "has now been revealed through the appearing of our Savior Christ Jesus, who abolished death and brought life and immortality to light" (1:10). Paul stated the matter quite simply in 1 Corinthians: "Death has been swallowed up in victory" (15:54).

The Sovereign and Suffering Deity

Life after death was, then, a motif shared by (some?) devotees of Isis and by devotees of Jesus Christ. But for early Jesus-followers, the resurrection of Jesus did not simply open the possibility of eternal life; it also proved the sovereignty of the deity who raised Jesus Christ from the dead. This comes to succinct expression in a number of Pauline texts: "God put this power to work in Christ when he raised him from the dead and seated him at his right hand in the heavenly places, far above all rule and authority and power and dominion" (Ephesians 1:20–21); "He was crucified in weakness, but lives by the power of God . . . [and] we will live with him by the power of God" (2 Corinthians 13:4; see also Romans 6:14; Philippians 3:10–11, 21; Colossians 2:12). The power of life emanating from the throne of a deity who was above all other claimants—convictions of this kind would not have been foreign to worshipers of Isis.

One other trait characterized both Jesus and Isis. The Egyptian deity was often cherished because, as narratives of her story recounted, she had suffered sorrow at the loss of a loved one, making her sympathetic to the needs of human beings, who inevitably experienced the same kind of loss themselves. The Gospel of John traverses similar ground, depicting a deity who had himself experienced the "troubled heart," as he himself declared (12:27; see also 11:38; 13:21). And when a beloved friend of his died and all the people around him were weeping at their loss, the narrative notes that Jesus himself "was greatly disturbed in spirit and deeply moved" when he saw them weeping, so that he too wept along with them (11:33–35). This is a deity who, like Isis, was "acquainted with grief" (Isaiah 53:3 RSV) and could sympathize with the sorrows of his devotees. Because this deity experienced sorrow and yet was victorious over death, he can instruct his devotees, "Do not let your hearts be troubled" (John 14:1).

The theme of the deity's suffering took on a novel form in the theology of the apostle Paul. He put a spin on the motif of life after death in a manner that had some semblance to mystery devotion while also going beyond it in terms of the explicitness of its imagery. In one passage, for instance, he wrote: "I want to know Christ and the power of his resurrection and the sharing of his sufferings by becoming like him in his death, if somehow I may attain the resurrection from the dead" (Philippians 3:10–11). Paul had come to see the death of Jesus as the point of transference, the portal, from the present form of life into a new realm of life. He elaborated that notion in fuller terms in his letter to Jesus-followers in Rome, as noted at the outset of this chapter (6:3–5, 8).

But one of his most glaring claims appears in what is probably one of his earliest letters: "I have been crucified with Christ. It is no longer I who live, but it is Christ who lives in me" (Galatians 2:20, although in some translations this appears as 2:19–20). Both the death and the new life of Paul's deity had so engulfed Paul's own life that he could claim to be dead in Christ, who had come alive in him. Similarly, the audience of Colossians heard that they had "put off the body of the flesh"; they had been "buried with him" and been "raised with him through faith in the power of God, who raised him from the dead"; and in this way they had been made "alive with him"— the one who "is seated at the right hand of God" in sovereignty (Colossians 2:11–13; 3:1). For Paul, the death of Jesus Christ became the means to new life.

The Oddity of Resurrection

With all the commonalities between the deities of Isis-followers and of Jesus-followers, it is

Figure 9.10. The statue of Isis (who holds the key to the Nile) that resided in the Temple of Isis (8.7.28); the statue was originally decorated in rich colors.

hardly surprising that at times Jesus-followers interpreted their devotion in ways that coincided with the worldview of mystery devotion. This seems to have happened, for instance, when some Jesus-devotees in Corinth imagined that the resurrection of their physical bodies was not something they needed to expect. Paul addressed the matter in 1 Corinthians 15 but replicated their view of things earlier in the letter with the sarcastic commendation: "Already you have all you want! Already you have become rich . . . [and] have become kings!" (4:8). Evidently the Corinthians imagined that since their deity had already been raised to life, and since they had already been joined with him, they too must already be joined with him in the newness of life in the Spirit. After all, Paul himself proclaimed Jesus Christ to be "a life-giving spirit" (15:45). What need was there for a resurrected body—especially if those bodies were deemed to be products of the inferior created world? (See the Corinthian view articulated by Paul in 15:35; compare also the view of Hymenaeus and Philetus in 2 Timothy 2:17–18.) Why would anyone want to exist in some kind of a restored body beyond death? The Corinthians had already experienced resurrection power, and some of them did not feel the need to return to a physical body after their death, since they expected that they would be enjoying the spiritual life of their lord—or as Paul expressed things later in Romans, their co-crucifixion with Christ had taken place "so that the body of sin might be destroyed" (Romans 6:6), the same body that Paul calls "this body of death" (7:24).

Perhaps the Corinthian Jesus-followers imagined they were simply following through on a Pauline idea, asserting something like his later pronouncement that "we will certainly be united with him in a resurrection like his" (Romans 6:5). Jesus's resurrection, they imagined, could not have involved bodiliness; it must have been a "resurrection" of the spirit, a release from bodiliness altogether. And they, as participants in his death, must already have been raised spiritually into the power of his

spiritual resurrection. If Christ has been exalted "to the right hand of God" (8:34; Colossians 3:1; Ephesians 1:20), leaving behind the physical body that walked the paths of Galilee and Judea and being exalted as "the heavenly man" (as Paul called Jesus Christ in 1 Corinthians 15:49) and the empowered Lord, why would anyone imagine the need for a bodily resurrection?

It all made sense, but only on the assumption that salvation entailed being set free from the material world and emerging into the world of pure spirit. That view of things was not usually foregrounded in Judean (or Jewish) theological reflection, precisely because it undersold the created order, which had been set in motion by its creator. For this reason, non-Judean sectors of the Roman world may not have understood much about the Judeo-Christian concept of resurrection, even if belief in the existence of spirits beyond death was widespread.

We see this lack of comprehension reflected in Acts 17 in the story of the Athenian philosophers, who mistakenly understood Paul to be "the proclaimer of [two] foreign deities"— Jesus and Anastasis, with *anastasis* being the Greek word for "resurrection" (17:18). Since *anastasis* is a feminine word, these Athenians might even have imagined a partnership of a female deity (Anastasis) and a male deity (Jesus)—rather like Isis and Osiris. If so, the counterpart to Isis would be "Resurrection," and the counterpart to Osiris (who was "resurrected") would be Jesus.

Going beyond Cults of the Soul

Corinthian Jesus-followers may have done better than the Athenian philosophers in their understanding of resurrection, but theirs was far from satisfactory, in Paul's view. It threatened one of Paul's core convictions—that the one who raised Jesus Christ to new life is the same deity who created the world. This is why Paul could say that the one who has acted in Christ is in the process of setting creation "free from its bondage to decay" (Romans 8:21). In short, the deity proclaimed by the early Jesus-followers was not to be seen as offering a spiritual release from creation; instead, that deity was to be seen to be in the process of restoring the whole of creation. In 1 Corinthians 15, Paul granted that the resurrection body will not be a reanimation of the present body, with all its frailties. But neither is resurrection simply something that applies to the human spirit (which, for Paul, was a non sequitur). Just as Jesus Christ was raised in bodily form (15:3–8), so too his devotees will be raised in bodily form. Paul granted that the form of the resurrection body will be different from any earlier form of bodiliness, according to the will of the creator (15:38), but he insisted that "if there is a physical body [and there is], then there is also a spiritual body" (15:44). That claim would most likely have been derided among a good number of people in the Roman period. If there was life beyond the death of our bodies, it certainly did not involve the soul having to continue to be embodied (even in a transformed body); instead, it involved the freedom of the soul to transcend out of its current embodied state.

Ultimately, however, Paul's claim about the "spiritual body" was not simply an analysis of the components of human identity beyond death; his claim was motivated by his theological convictions concerning creation and its creator. For Paul, eternal life through Jesus Christ was empowered by a deity who is not only sovereign but also the sole creator—the one who created physical materiality and created it as "good." This notion that the creator has engraved goodness within creation is deeply embedded within the creation account of Jewish scripture: "God saw everything that he had made, and indeed, it was very good" (Genesis 1:31; see also 1:4, 10, 12, 18, 21, 25). For Paul, the created order was not some second-rate or regrettable initiative undertaken by a deity who had not thought it all through; nor was creation simply a temporary staging for humans who will later leave it all behind and enter the pure world of the spirit. Instead, knowing that his deity was the creator, Paul affirmed two interconnected notions:

1. The deity he proclaimed was sovereign over all (including any other claimants to sovereignty).
2. Salvation did not bypass the created order (as if human spirits could exist without bodies) but included the created order (so that human spirits are raised ultimately within bodies—albeit spiritual bodies).

The Corinthians seem to have accepted the first affirmation, but some of them had not seen the corollary of the second as a necessary complement to the first. In essence, Paul's discourse regarding the resurrection in 1 Corinthians 15 is a lesson in the nuances of Judeo-Christian creational theology. In Christ, the true deity is not neglectfully abandoning creation; in Christ, that deity is demonstrating divine commitment to the whole of the good creation. In a sense, the true deity wants creation back from those forces that would steal creation away and collapse it into chaos— forces identified as "cosmos-grabbers" in Ephesians 6:12. As the second-century theologian

Irenaeus noted, Paul was countering people in Corinth whose theological deficit lay in the view "that the handiwork of God is not saved" (*Against Heresies* 5.9.1).

We see Paul making the same two affirmations elsewhere in his letters. In a single sentence of Philippians, for instance, he affirmed that the sovereign creator "will transform the body of our humiliation that it may be conformed to the body of his glory, by the power that also enables him to make all things subject to himself" (Philippians 3:21). For Paul, a properly aligned creation theology put everything into perspective, undermining the claims of all other deities and affirming a different narrative of "the afterlife." The "good news" was not simply to spawn a cult in which a deity was thought to offer life to individuals after death; it was a narrative in which individuals were getting caught up in the life-giving power of the creator deity in the process of rectifying the cosmos and restoring it on a cosmic scale, overturning the devastating effects of malignant suprahuman forces on the whole of the created order.

At the heart of all this is an affirmation of divine supremacy. More than a century after Paul wrote his letters, Apuleius affirmed what many followers of Isis might already have affirmed in Paul's day regarding the supremacy of Isis. In his work *The Golden Ass*, Apuleius had Isis speak these words of self-identification (11.5):

[I am] the mother of the universe, the queen of all the elements, the original offspring of eternity, the loftiest of the gods, the queen of the shades, the foremost of heavenly beings, the single form of gods and goddesses alike. I control by my will the dazzling summits of the sky, the wholesome breezes of the sea, the despairing silences of the dead below.

In Apuleius's narrative, Isis contends that "the whole world worships my power under an abundance of images, a variety of rituals, and an array of names" (for instance, Venus, Minerva, Diana, Ceres, Juno, and more). Paul would have countered these claims to divine sovereignty at every point. In 1 Corinthians, he made the point this way:

Even though there may be so-called gods in heaven or on earth, . . . yet for us there is one God, the Father, from whom are all things and for whom we exist, and one Lord, Jesus Christ, through whom are all things and through whom we exist. (1 Corinthians 8:5–6)

Or as the author of Revelation would later say, "Fear God and give him glory, for the hour of his judgment has come; and worship him who made heaven and earth, the sea and the springs of water" (Revelation 14:7). For these authors, Jesus-devotion was not simply one cult among other cults of the day—say, a Christ-cult. Instead, the "good news" was intricately and organically rooted in the power of the sovereign creator, who was bringing life to the cosmic order through the "one Lord, Jesus Christ through whom are all things and through whom we exist."

PART THREE

Protocols of Social Prominence

Prominence and Character

10

> As for those who in the present age are rich, command them not to be haughty, or to set their hopes on riches that are uncertain, but rather on God who richly provides us with everything to enjoy. *They are to do good, to be rich in good works, generous, and ready to share.* In this way, they will be storing up a treasure for themselves as a strong foundation for the future age, *so that they may take hold of the only true life.*
>
> 1 Timothy 6:17–19

Social Prestige in the Public Arena

Doing things with beneficial impact, being rich in good works, being generous—people who were able to undertake initiatives of this sort were highly regarded in the Roman age (all other things being equal). Being "rich in good works" was the essential oil for the machinery of society, especially as those who had enormous financial reserves used them to benefit the processes of public life.

Of course, most people who were "rich in good works" did not give of their reserves simply out of the goodness of their heart. Their initiatives were part of a balanced relationship of reciprocity, with their initiatives bringing them social prestige in one form or another, which could attract further economic resources. When those people who were most prominently placed undertook initiatives of beneficial impact for society, they in return received a beneficial boost to their own prominence in status. In short, their "good works" were part of a "win-win" situation, in which the giver received something in return.

Often, the pinnacle of social prominence was being elected to public office. In Pompeii, elections for various positions in local government were held every year in March, with the winners of those elections starting their civic duties on the first day of July. Various officers were elected in this way:

- Two junior magistrates were elected to a one-year position as *aediles*, who

121

Figure 10.1. A fresco probably depicting a politician (dressed in a toga and seated prominently in a chair) distributing bread to eligible voters on the street (from 7.3.30, MANN 9071)

oversaw the maintenance of the streets and the public buildings.

- Two senior magistracies were also up for election, for a three-year term. These *duoviri* (literally, "the two men"; sometimes *duumviri*) chaired the urban council meetings and were responsible to ensure that the decrees of the council were fulfilled.

- Once every five years another magistrate was elected, the *quinquennial* (literally, "the five-yearly"), whose job was to update the list of citizens in the town and the list of magistrates on the town council.

These magistrates were the men of real prominence in the town. In return for their efforts and initiatives, they would receive benefits in any number of ways. Most tangibly, they were granted the most prominent

Figure 10.2. The bases of the two statues in honor of Gaius Cuspius Pansa, erected at different parts of Pompeii's forum by the town council (see also figure 10.5)

Figure 10.3. A possible location for the tomb paid for by the local council in honor of Aulus Umbricius Scaurus (HGW17); the marble inscription honoring Scaurus actually belonged to the adjacent tomb (HGW16), because during the eruption it had tumbled to the ground between HGW16 and HGW17 and archaeologists decided to fit it to HGW17, even though it would fit much better on HGW16.

seats in the town's amphitheater and theaters. Being seen in the middle of all the proceedings was an exceptional honor. They might also be granted a public statue in the forum—as in the case of four local politicians in the course of Pompeii's history: Quintus Sallustius, Gaius Cuspius Pansa (two forum statues; see figure 10.2), Marcus Lucretius Decidianus Rufus (again, two forum statues for him), and Aulus Umbricius Scaurus. A marble inscription on a tomb testifies that Scaurus (a member of a prominent family who made their money producing fish sauce) was also granted a public tomb that was paid for by the town council (see figure 10.3). It was people of social prominence such as this (or even greater prominence) that the author of Acts wants his readers to have in mind when he speaks of "some of the officials of the province" befriending Paul and seeking to save his life from the machinations of the thronging masses who were in uproar against him (Acts 19:31 NIV).

Campaigning for Influence

As today, campaigning was a highly visible enterprise. Political campaign advertisements were painted on the external walls of residences and workshops. This enabled people to express publicly their view about which candidate was most suitable for office. Typically, endorsements of this kind (about 2,800 having been found on Pompeian walls) were rather basic, with the endorser simply asking others to vote for the preferred candidate. Occasionally an endorsement was more elaborate, as in this example: "Birius, together with Biria, ask you to elect Gnaeus Helvius Sabinus aedile, a good man, worthy of public office: Onomastus, vote for him eagerly" (*CIL* 4.9885). Sometimes the endorsements came from groups of people, whether they be "all the worshipers of Isis" (*CIL* 4.787, 4.1011) or even people of relatively low station, such as "all the fruit-vendors" (*CIL* 4.202), "all the mule drivers" (*CIL* 4.97; similarly 4.134), or "the onion-sellers" (*CIL* 4.99). In one telling graffito, "the destitute" along with another group whose identity is unclear (*unguentari*, perfumers; or perhaps *proletari*, the laborers) urged their fellow residents to elect "Modestus for aedile" (*CIL* 4.9932a)—a rare instance of people beyond the normal echelons of political power nonetheless exercising their corporate voice to elect a candidate in whom they had placed their hopes.

Women also took the initiative to express their support for particular candidates (as we noted in chapter 2, when discussing the case of Zmyrina). This is intriguing because women were not able to vote—a legal impediment that did not stop some women from expressing their political views. Campaign advertisements were put up by female supporters of particular candidates, and these supporters included women

named Asellina (4.7873, as noted in chapter 2), Maria (*CIL* 4.7866), Statia and Petronia (*CIL* 4.3678), Caprasia (*CIL* 4.171), "Appuleia, along with her neighbor Mustius the fuller and Narcissus" (*CIL* 4.3527), and various others. One proud grandmother even took the initiative to sponsor her favorite political candidate: "Taedia Secunda, his grandmother, asks and demands that you make Lucius Popidius Secundus an aedile" (*CIL* 4.7469).

Only in rare instances does an endorsement give a suggestion as to what the populace might expect from a candidate's future term in office. For instance:

- "Genialis asks for Bruttius Balbus as duumvir. He will preserve the treasury" (*CIL* 4.3702).
- "Marcus Casellius Marcellus is a good aedile and a great giver of [gladiatorial] games" (*CIL* 4.4999).
- "I ask that you elect Gaius Julius Polybius as aedile. He bakes good bread" (*CIL* 4.429).
- "The holy ordo elects and asks that you elect Marcus Epidius Sabinus, most worthy young man, *duovir* for administering justice. Greetings to Clemens, the holy judge" (*CIL* 4.7579).
- "All the fruit-vendors, in agreement with Helvius Vestalis, ask you to elect Marcus Holconius Priscus, *duovir* for administering justice" (*CIL* 4.202; see also 4.7242 in figure 10.4).

Preserving the treasury, giving games, distributing bread, administering justice—these are the sorts of thing that endorsers occasionally lauded in their candidates of choice.

Also relatively rare are endorsements that register comments about the character of

Figure 10.4. A full election notice on an exterior wall of a residence (*CIL* 4.7242 at 1.7.13, in support of Gaius Gavius Rufus and Marcus Holconius Priscus)

the candidate. Only occasionally do we find candidates who are said to be "honorable," "honest," "very deserving," "excellent," or a "man of integrity." Two men are notable in this regard:

Figure 10.5. The campaign notice articulating the merits of Gaius Cuspius Pansa (*CIL* 4.7201, at the entrance of 1.7.1; see also figure 10.2)

- "If integrity is thought to be of any use, this man Lucretius Fronto is worthy of great honor" (*CIL* 4.6626).
- "Gaius Cuspius Pansa for aedile: If any honor should be given to one living modestly, fitting honor ought to be given to this young man" (*CIL* 4.7201; see figure 10.5; the monuments in figure 10.2 were erected to honor this same politician).

Along this trajectory of character we can place the advice found in 1 Timothy 6:17–19 (listed at the start of this chapter). The author of that text instructs that "those who in the present age are rich" should not be "haughty." Being people of character involves setting one's hopes not "on riches that are uncertain" but "on God who richly provides us with everything to enjoy"—which is part of what

125

Figure 10.6. A statue base from Pompeii's forum commemorating "Marcus Claudius Marcellus, son of Gaius, patron" (*CIL* 10.832; Marcellus was the nephew and son-in-law of emperor Augustus)

it means to "take hold of the only true life." The same author notes that corporate leaders (in this case, leaders of a group of churches) should be "above reproach," which includes being "temperate, sensible, respectable, hospitable, an apt teacher, not a drunkard, not violent but gentle, not quarrelsome, and not a lover of money" (3:2–3). A similar list appears in Titus, where an ecclesiastical leader is to be "blameless," which includes being "hospitable, a lover of goodness, prudent, upright, devout, and self-controlled" instead of being "arrogant or quick-tempered or addicted to wine or violent or greedy for gain" (1:7–8). These calls for ecclesiastical leaders to be people of character tap into the common-sense notion, articulated by Cicero, that "the leading men in society have always dictated its character; whenever there has been a transformation of morals and manners among the social leaders, the same transformation has followed among the people" (*On the Laws* 3.31). As the Vesuvian electoral notices and the author of the Pastoral letters both suggest,

what some people wanted in their leaders was a character of "integrity."

Whether residents of the Vesuvian towns got what they wanted probably depended on who they were and how they might have defined "integrity." In the satirical novel *The Satyricon*, the Roman novelist Petronius has one character curse the civic magistrates for operating on the principle of being mutually beneficial to one another, at the expense of the people: "You scratch my back and I'll scratch yours," they say to one another, with the result that "the little people come off badly; for the jaws of the upper classes are always keeping carnival" (*Satyricon* 44).

It did not take a satirist to see what was obvious to all—that the political realm was a vehicle for potential promotion in power and prestige. The Epicurean poet Lucretius from the first century BCE (who was mentioned in chapters 5 and 6) saw nothing good in all this. He saw it as embodying the worst aspect of humanity—that being their competitiveness: "Behold, see them: contending with their wits, fighting for precedence, struggling night and day with unending effort, climbing, clawing their way up the pinnacles of wealth and power" (*On the Nature of Things* 2.11–13). Lucretius saw all of this as futile and destructive to a wholesome life: "O miserable minds of men! O blind hearts! In what darkness, among how many perils, you pass your short lives!" (*On the Nature of Things* 2.14–16). But critiques of this sort may have had little impact. Even Lucretius's literary patron, Gaius Memmius, to whom Lucretius's poem was dedicated, spent the years immediately after Lucretius's death (in 55 BCE) seeking to expand his influence and prominence in the political arena—an attempt that ended in failure and exile.

It should not be surprising, then, that a cut-throat atmosphere could easily infuse political campaigns. These were not necessarily moments of great decorum or upstanding character. At times, there was little more than name-calling and derision. In Pompeii, for instance, we have evidence of what seem to be negative campaign advertisements. These were usually pitched not so much in terms that denigrated the candidate himself but, instead, in terms that denigrated those who supported him. For instance, in one inscription, those who endorsed a political candidate were said to be "all the run-away slaves" (*CIL* 4.7389)—clearly a fictionalized group someone conjured up in this graffito in order to denigrate a candidate. Other graffiti carry on in the same fashion, as perhaps in this graffito: "The dice-throwers [gamblers?] ask for Gnaeus Helvius Sabinus" (*CIL* 4.3485). One candidate by the name of Marcus Cerrinius Vatia came under par-

ticular attack through the denigration of his sponsors:

- "All the late-drinkers ask that you elect M. Cerrinius Vatia as aedile" (*CIL* 4.581).
- "Macerio and all the sleepers ask that you elect Vatia as aedile" (*CIL* 4.575).
- "The petty thieves ask that you elect Vatia as aedile" (*CIL* 4.576).

We don't know whether the smear campaign against Vatia was successful or not.

Occasionally we hear both sides regarding the worth of a political candidate. One man named Thalamus advertised his patron Publius Paquius Proculus, who was running for the position of "duumvir with judicial power" (*CIL*

Figure 10.7. Political candidates would have addressed the residents of Pompeii from this speaker's podium in the center of the forum.

Figure 10.8. A political cartoon, etched onto a wall of the Villa of the Mysteries (in situ) and not much bigger than a small coin, with the words "This is Rufus" etched above, helping the observer to appreciate the comic deprecation of this prominent man wearing a toga and wreath

4.933). Others joined Thalamus, calling themselves "all the Pompeians" and asking others to "elect Paquius Proculus as *duovir* for administering justice. He is worthy of the state" (*CIL* 4.1122). Evidently, Proculus won the election, as suggested by a single graffito that denounces his character and the character of the populace who elected him to office: "The bleating sheep have elected Proculus aedile. Yet this office required the dignity of an honest man and respect for the function" (for this translation, see credits). Apparently not "all the Pompeians" were enamored with Paquius Proculus. Unlike Thalamus, someone thought him unworthy of his elected position.

Competition and Collaboration in Jesus-Groups

At times, groups of Jesus-followers could act in ways that were not all that far from the political campaigning evident in Pompeii.

Some in Corinth decided that it would be good to endorse particular leaders over others (see 1 Corinthians 3–4). Self-identifying with different leaders, the Corinthian devotees of Jesus Christ began to form bases of support for one leader in preference over others. "I am of Apollos," some Jesus-followers claimed, declaring their allegiance to an impressive Christian leader from Alexandria in Egypt, who had immaculate knowledge of the scriptures and could speak eloquently (Acts 18:24). Others advertised that they were "of Cephas," another name for Simon Peter, declaring their allegiance to an apostle who had been a close associate of Jesus. Still others enlisted themselves as being "of Paul," preferring the apostle who had taken the lead in establishing communities of Jesus-devotion among the gentiles.

These different preferences within Corinthian communities were not expressed in the context of political campaigns, of course, but they began to take on competitive dimensions of a similar kind. This, at least, was Paul's take on the matter. As ever, he saw beyond the specific issue at hand, linking it to a more fundamental issue—the human propensity for self-promotion at the expense of others. He articulated his point in these terms:

> For as long as there is jealousy and quarreling among you, are you not of the flesh, and behaving according to human inclinations? For when one says, "I belong to Paul," and another, "I belong to Apollos," are you not merely human? (1 Corinthians 3:3–4)

Things may not have become overtly snide among the Corinthians, as in the Pompeii graffito that declared a prominent magistrate as having been born "between a beet and a cabbage" (*CIL* 4.4533, found on the wall of the atrium of 6.14.37). But because things regularly became ugly in competitive contexts, Paul worried about the corporate health of the Corinthians. He tended to see an unhealthy competitive spirit as fundamental to the human problem (as in the quotation from 3:3–4 above; see further in chapter 13). Consequently, he highlighted the dangers inherent within the Corinthians' desire to align themselves with respective Christian leaders over against others and doing so in terms not unlike the campaigning of prominent civic leaders.

Paul went on to place a different spin on things altogether. Instead of framing things in terms of competition, Paul preferred to frame them in terms of collaboration. He argued that the various strengths of individual Christian leaders worked together for the benefit of Corinthian Jesus-groups. This was not to be a contest of allegiance to one leader over another; instead, it was to be a combining of strengths offered by each of the leaders, in a community that was ultimately being built up by divine power.

> I planted, Apollos watered, but God gave the growth. So neither the one who plants nor the one who waters is anything, but only God who gives the growth. The one who plants and the one who waters have a common purpose. . . . So let no one boast about human leaders . . . so that none of you will be puffed up in favor of one against another. (1 Corinthians 3:6–8, 21; 4:6)

Paul wanted the Corinthian Jesus-followers to see what they had in common and to unite around that denominator. "Were you baptized into the name of Paul?" (1:13). Or Apollos? Or Cephas? No. Instead of aligning themselves in Pompeian style as "all the Apollos supporters" or "all the Cephas supporters" or "all the Paul supporters," Paul simply advised, "Let the one who boasts, boast in the Lord" (1 Corinthians 1:31; see also Jeremiah 9:24). What united Jesus-followers was their mutual share in "the mind of Christ" (1 Corinthians 2:16). In Paul's view, having the mind of Christ emerges from the unifying message of the cross—a message that strikes at the heart of all accumulations of power that rely on status or prestige. The self-giving act of Christ was to establish the ethos of relationality within the corporate body of Christ.

On the assumption that self-giving love would be "genuine" within the ethos of Jesus-groups (Romans 12:9), Paul urged his Jesus-followers not only to "love one another with mutual affection" but also to "lead the way in showing honor to each other" (12:10, sometimes translated "outdo one another in showing honor"). This was not simply the showing of honor to socially prominent people within their groups but the showing of honor to all members of the body of Christ. To ensure that this form of "leading the way" did not simply promote the interests of those who were already socially prominent, Paul spoke of the need to recognize that each and every Jesus-follower is tasked with contributing essential resources to the body of Christ (12:3–8). His corporate vision highlighted the value of all people working practically together, sharing their giftings within the body of Christ. Paul imagined the body of Christ to be the epitome of the abundant community (whose resources were supplied by an abundant Spirit), where all members had important contributions to make, regardless of their socio-economic profile.

The idea of working together toward a goal that is collectively prized was not invented by Paul, of course, but it was fundamental to his vision of the spirited community of

Jesus-followers. In the body of Christ, it was not simply the socially prominent who were expected to resource the community; even those with few economic resources were to be recognized as bringing other essential resources to the Jesus-group that they belonged to locally. Whereas the economically secure could be seen as tasked with the responsibility of supporting that group financially, others were being tasked by the Spirit of Christ to offer resources of another kind altogether— perhaps encouragement or prophecy or compassion or wisdom or discernment or some skill gifted to them by the Spirit. Those who were unable to gift the community economically were to be seen as gifting the community through whatever non-economic resources the Spirit was inevitably bringing to life in them.

In this way, Paul ensured that those who held minimal forms of status within the Roman world were nonetheless recognized as crucial members of the "new creation" in which "everything old has passed away" and "everything has become new" (2 Corinthians 5:17; see also Galatians 6:15). Within communities of novelty, even those who were low on the socio-economic scale of the Roman world were to be recognized as gifted to make resourceful contributions to local communities of Jesus-groups. Avoiding unhealthy competition and enacting self-giving concern for each member, those communities of character were to fully harness the diverse resources of all their members, as they leaned into new forms of relationality within the new creation.

Money and Influence **11**

What then is my reward? Just this: *that in my proclamation I may make the gospel free of charge,* so as not to make full use of my rights in the gospel.

1 Corinthians 9:18

Money and Politics

Everyone knew that money came with strings attached. This was made clear in a number of ways throughout the Vesuvian towns, even from the earliest days after the founding of Pompeii as a Roman colony. In the so-called "Social War" of 91–89 BCE, certain urban centers in the Samnite region of Campania (south of Rome's direct rule) banded together to assert their mutual muscle in a confrontation with Rome (the nuances of which are complicated and not necessary to reconstruct here). Roman force eventually won the day, of course. In 89 BCE, Pompeii fell in submission to Rome. In 80 BCE, Rome officially colonized Pompeii, incorporating it into Rome's direct sphere of influence. At that point, the local Samnite population was minimized with respect to their socio-political status and their numerical percentage within the local population. Rome achieved this by inserting a large cadre of former military personnel into Pompeii. These pro-Roman residents, perhaps as many as four thousand of them and their families, were probably rewarded for their services to Rome, being given houses conscripted from the local Pompeian people. It was at this time that the predominant language of Pompeian inscriptions shifted from Oscan (the language of the Samnite people) to Latin (the official language of Rome). And it was at this time that Latin inscriptions in Pompeii started to make it clear (if it wasn't already) that money came with strings attached.

This is evident, for instance, from official inscriptions that announced the prominence of Quinctius Valgus and Marcus Porcius— Pompeii's earliest mayors, or *duoviri*. Two inscriptions set up in Pompeii's huge amphitheater (or *spectacula*) announced that Quinctius Valgus and Marcus Porcius erected the amphitheater "at their own expense"—doing so "for the sake of the colony's honor" and

131

Figure 11.1. Coins found fused together in a wicker basket in Herculaneum

dedicating the amphitheater "to the colonists to use forever" (*CIL* 10.852; see figure 11.2). The costs involved for the construction of the amphitheater must have been huge. But the enormous funds donated by these *duoviri* were linked to Pompeii's new identity as a colony of Rome. Marcus Porcius appears as bene-

Figure 11.2. An inscription (broken off on left side) established in Pompeii's amphitheater (2.6), advertising the benefaction of Quinctius Valgus and Marcus Porcius and highlighting Pompeii's status as a colony of Rome

factor of another gift to Pompeii—the altar in the Temple of Apollo (*CIL* 10.800). Other civic improvements were also undertaken as a result of colonist infusion (e.g., Pompeii's Forum Baths and Covered Theater, as well as improvements made at the Stabian Baths). This was true for other civic centers as well. For instance, the same Quinctius Valgus who helped pay for Pompeii's amphitheater was also a public benefactor for three other urban centers at this time (Aeclanum, Cassino, and Frigento; *CIL* 10.5282, 9.1140; *ILLRP* 598). (And, by the way, he is also mentioned by Cicero as having prospered massively because of his lack of moral scruples; *De lege agraria* 3.8.) It was clear to all that new money flooding into Pompeii was linked to a pro-Roman agenda.

We have seen something similar in the case of Nonius Balbus—the elite friend of Augustus who infused tremendous amounts of money into Herculaneum to accentuate its Roman identity (chapter 6). The same was also true of a man named Marcus Holconius Rufus in Pompeii, who lived about the same time as Nonius Balbus in Herculaneum. He infused so much money into Pompeii (renovating the large theater and other initiatives) that the town councilors erected a four-pillar archway to him and his family at the busiest intersection in Pompeii and, within Pompeii's large theater, dedicated a special space reserved for him during his lifetime. Centrally placed and five rows back (where the seating on white marble slabs meets the ordinary seating of the plebs), Holconius's bronze seat inscription still records his social prominence to this day (see figure 11.3), as does the inscription on his statue base. Both inscriptions highlight a number of his roles within Pompeii, each saving for last his identity as "priest of Augustus and patron of the [Roman] colony" (*CIL* 10.837, 10.838).

Figure 11.3. Two photos from Pompeii's Large Theater (8.7.20); left: the space for Holconius Rufus's seat (five rows back from the front), marked out by an inscription in his honor; right: a photo of seating in the Large Theater, with the central place of Holconius Rufus's seat in the white marble evident toward the center left

These civic improvements were splendid, and the money for them came with strings attached to the legitimacy of Roman rule.

Evidence of a similar kind comes from a group of men known as the *Augustales*. The *Augustales* (singular *Augustalis*) were deemed to be "priests" who helped to foster devotion to the emperor cult in their local region. A good many of them (we will never know the percentage, but probably a majority of them) had been born in slavery but earned their freedom and subsequently became men of significant wealth. These men were prohibited from serving in public office by the fact that they had originally been slaves. (Former slaves were not allowed to hold a civic position.) In order to harvest their resources for public initiatives, Tiberius (emperor from 14 to 37) created an order of the *Augustales*. Regardless of whether they had been born in slavery or not, the *Augustales* were men whose status was recognized by the emperor. Being promoted to the ranks of the *Augustales*, these men were then expected to use their wealth for purposes of public beneficence. For instance, an *Augustalis* from Herculaneum named Lucius Mammius Maximus donated six statues

of imperial family members to that Vesuvian town (*CIL* 10.1413, 10.1415, 10.1417, 10.1418, 10.1419, 10.1422). Once again, the infusion of economic resources into the civic infrastructure was configured with a significant pro-Roman spin.

It is worth lingering with the *Augustales* for a moment longer, to notice the artwork in what seems to have been the clubhouse of the *Augustales* in Herculaneum (located at 6.21). Two prominent wall paintings survive that depict two moments in the adventurous life of Hercules, the semi-divine son of the deity Jupiter (or Zeus, who fathered Hercules through the mortal woman Alcmene). One fresco in the clubhouse depicts Hercules with a competitor whom he will go on to defeat in order to marry Deianeira, who became his second wife (see figure 11.4). The other fresco shows Hercules being welcomed into heaven at the end of his life, promoted to the status of a full deity (see figure 11.5). For those *Augustales* who were former slaves, these two frescos must have represented their favorite parts of the Hercules story. Formerly slaves but now wealthy and prominent members of society and priests of the divine Augustus, these

133

Figure 11.4. Hercules (left) and Achelous, whom Hercules will defeat in order to marry Deianeira (far right) (from Herculaneum's College of the *Augustales*, 6.21, in situ)

Figure 11.5. The fresco of Hercules being welcomed to heaven by Minerva (left), Juno (middle), and Jupiter (in the form of a rainbow) (from Herculaneum's College of the *Augustales*, 6.21, in situ)

Augustales must have sought out prominent women to be their wives (just as Hercules got the woman he wanted through diligent effort); moreover, they would have resonated with the pattern of promotion and "upward mobility" that Hercules's ascension into the heavens represents. For these *Augustales*, the story of Hercules was a mythic template of their own success story.

We have already seen that civic benefactors were not always men. Sometimes circumstances transpired that enabled women to become enormously wealthy. As we have seen (in chapter 6), Eumachia was one of these women, donating a huge public building to Pompeii's forum in honor of (1) the Roman values of piety and concord and (2) the Roman imperial family of Augustus. Here we should add that Eumachia's sponsorship of Roman imperial reign was on display by way of two statues placed at the very front of her impressive building, facing the forum. These were statues of Romulus and Aeneas, two men important in the mythology of the founding of Rome's eternal reign, blessed by the deities. (See further on Aeneas below.) A plaque fixed below the statue of Rome's founding father notes that Romulus was "received among the deities" upon his death (see figure 11.6). (The plaque honoring Aeneas has not survived well.) Rome and money went hand in hand in the civic initiatives undertaken by this prominent woman in Pompeian society.

Money and Temples of Political Significance

At about the same time that the woman named Mamia was contributing funds for a new temple for "the *genius* of the region" in Pompeii (i.e., early in the first century; see chapter 7),

Figure 11.6. The Romulus inscription at the front of Eumachia's building (7.9.1), declaring him to be "among the deities" (*in deoru[m]*)

a Pompeian magistrate named Marcus Tullius used "his own land" and "at his own expense" (compare Mamia in both of these aspects) to erect a temple just north of Pompeii's forum, dedicated to Augustan Fortuna—or the deity Fortuna in her role as the overseer of the Augustan era (*CIL* 10.820; see figure 11.7). And just as Mamia was honored with a tomb sponsored by the town council (also noted in chapter 7), so too was Marcus Tullius.

Late in the life of Pompeii, funds were given to build a temple in the town's forum for the imperial cult (7.9.3, which may formerly have been Mamia's temple to the *genius* of the region). Alongside it (at 7.9.2), another temple was renovated for the reverential worship of the recently deified Vespasian (who died just

months prior to the eruption of Vesuvius in 79). Donating and renovating temples was, of course, expensive business, but those expenses were seen as worthwhile in cases that supported the Roman imperial order.

In the late 60s or early 70s of the first century, the Temple of Isis was also renovated, and here again the fingerprints of influence are all over the rebuilt temple. Above the entrance to the temple stood a commemorative plaque recounting the identity of the benefactor who dedicated the funds for the rebuilding effort (see figure 11.8). It reads as follows:

> Numerius Popidius Celsinus, son of Numerius, at his own expense restored from its foundations the Temple of Isis, which had collapsed in the earthquake. Because of his generosity, the councilors enrolled him into their number without fee, although he was six years old.

This inscription advertises a situation in which a six-year-old boy from the Popidius family donated the money for building this temple; as a consequence, he was made a member of the civic ruling council. What really happened was almost certainly this:

- Celsinus's father, Numerius Popidius Ampliatus (whose name we know from other Pompeian inscriptions), had once been a slave, but he subsequently became enormously wealthy as a freedman.

- Ampliatus himself could never become a civic councilor because of his earlier years in slavery. His son Celsinus, however, had been born free and was therefore eligible to become a civic councilor, if money paved the way for his advancement.

135

Figure 11.7. The Temple of Augustan Fortuna, paid for by Marcus Tullius on his own land (7.4.1)

- Ampliatus donated the money to erect the Temple of Isis in return for granting councilor status to his son Celsinus, even though Celsinus was only six years old.
- Probably Ampliatus instructed Celsinus regarding how he should vote in the council meetings.

This example illustrates a number of things. First, as in the case of the father (Ampliatus), the taint of slavery restrained even the most successful freedmen by placing a ceiling on the heights to which they might otherwise have risen after gaining their freedom. Second, as in the case of the son (Celsinus), those same restraints could be bypassed generationally, with the freeborn son able to rise to civic promi-

nence even at six years of age. Third (and most relevant to this chapter's topic of interest), the position of civic prominence could be purchased by those with wealth. In this case, when a huge donation was orchestrated in the name of Celsinus, the civic councilors awarded him a position of influence (that is, being numbered among the councilors) and bolstered his public prestige (and that of his family) by agreeing to recognize the six-year-old as a person of "generosity."

Money and Games of Political Significance

Another common form of economic infusion in the civic life of Pompeii was sponsorship of

Figure 11.8. The commemorative inscription highlighting the generosity of Numerius Popidius Celsinus, in whose name funds were donated for the rebuilding of the Temple of Isis

gladiatorial competitions in the amphitheater. These sponsored competitions were known as *munera*, or "gifts" to the local people, paid for by leading officials. Archaeologists have found over seventy notices on Pompeian walls announcing gladiatorial contests. One of the most prominent providers of these "gifts" was the civic official named Gnaeus Alleius Nigidius Maius, self-proclaimed as "leader of the [Roman] colony" (*CIL* 4.1177). So prolific were the games he sponsored that Nigidius Maius was referred to as the "chief of games" (*CIL* 4.7990). But his lavish games were not simply for the sake of entertainment. They came with a political agenda that coincided with his identity as a "priest of Caesar Augustus" (= the emperor Vespasian). On one occasion, for instance, the games he sponsored were explicitly said to be "for the well-being of Caesar Augustus and his children," with the games coinciding with the "dedication of the altar" for the imperial cult (*CIL* 4.1180).

(Interestingly, Eumachia's huge tomb outside Pompeii's Nucerian Gate housed the funerary urn containing the cremated remains of Nigidius Maius's adoptive mother, Pomponia Decharis. Here we see a point of inter-section in the lives of two prominent public figures, Eumachia and Maius—both individuals having been public benefactors and advocates of the Roman imperial order.)

Gladiatorial games in general helped to reinforce the narrative of the Roman program. The wild-beast hunts of a gladiatorial event usually paraded a variety of exotic animals whose natural habitats were spread far and wide throughout the world that Rome controlled. Their presence in a local amphitheater extravaganza highlighted Rome's magnificence and reinforced the narratives of its grandeur. Although the gladiators were usually "scoundrels" to society (i.e., robbers, murderers, villains, escaped slaves, and foreign prisoners of war), they nonetheless embodied some of the characteristics that Rome cherished about itself: bravery, endurance, and might. Amphitheaters were places that reinforced the structures of Roman power, and gladiatorial competitions boosted the narrative of Roman legitimacy. It is little wonder that adding an amphitheater to Pompeii's infrastructure was one of the first things that Quinctius Valgus and Marcus Porcius did when turning the town into a center of pro-Roman sentiment.

Figure 11.9. Left: a gladiatorial announcement on a Pompeian tomb (see "GLAD" clearly written toward the top left; the "XX" near the center announces that there will be twenty gladiators fighting; the "NOV" on the bottom line, directly under the "D" of "GLAD," probably announces the date in November); right: a gladiatorial announcement on an external wall, advertising games sponsored by Alleius Nigidius Maius (with the word "Nigidi[us]" still evident below the large "C")

Challenging the Status Quo

It is not much of an exaggeration to say that all roads led to Rome, at least when those roads were financial. Money was best spent when it brought benefit to (1) the benefactor in terms of increased levels of status, (2) the local urban center in terms of enhanced levels of productivity, and (3) the Roman order in terms of augmented levels of loyalty to Rome's political ambitions.

But there were voices critical of the way that money enhanced influence. A few residents within the Vesuvian towns seem to have tired of the constant drip of pro-Roman coaxing that civic benefactors seem regularly to have peddled along with their benefactions. Two data of that kind help to make the point: graffiti and artwork. Two graffiti were already discussed in chapter 6—the graffito "I sing of launderers and an owl, not arms and a man" (*CIL* 4.9131), and the other graffito regarding Rome taking its pleasure from its citizens, who utter what Rome wants to hear, even while being abused (*CIL* 4.1261). Both of these were probably politically charged

articulations that ran against the grain of pro-Roman propaganda.

Something similar is evident in a curious piece of art that playfully illustrates an incident in the life of Aeneas. The moment of Aeneas's departure from Troy was depicted in various artistic media in the Vesuvian towns (frescos and figurines). They show Aeneas carrying his father, Anchises, on his left shoulder (who himself carries the *penates*, or deities of the household, in a box) and holding the hand of his son Ascanius, who obediently trundles along beside him. But one Pompeian residence (sometimes wrongly identified as a residence in nearby Stabia) depicted the same moment in very unflattering terms (see figure 11.10). In a fresco, the great hero Aeneas is depicted as an ape with a canine head and tail, like his father and his son. And beyond the canine tails and heads, Aeneas and the other males of his family are displayed with extremely elongated phalluses—an un-Roman characterization, worthy only of uncouth barbarians (since the Roman ideal was for the Roman phallus to be "diplomatically elegant," we might say, or "streamlined"). An island in the Bay of Naples was known as the

Figure 11.10. Left: Aeneas flees Troy carrying his father, Anchises, on his shoulder while leading his son Ascanius by the hand (a poorly preserved terra-cotta from 7.2.16); right: a Pompeian fresco depicting the same scene in parody, with animal features and bestial phalluses (MANN 9089, from 6.17, although the precise location is unknown)

"isle of apes," and a local tradition claimed that Aeneas had once used the island as a base, so perhaps these factors fed the imagination of the person who commissioned this bizarre fresco. That should not detract, however, from the fact that these degrading images of a great Roman hero were entertained in the first place and that someone thought such a parody was even worthy of portraiture (especially because an adjoining fresco depicted the hero Romulus in similar ways, and no tradition had him visiting the "isle of apes").

These two parodies of the famous story of Aeneas exhibit a low-grade form of resistance to the narrative that was supported by huge amounts of pro-Roman money that flowed into the Vesuvian towns. We can easily imagine that people like Nonius Balbus, Eumachia, and Nigidius Maius, together with the *Augustales* and a sizeable portion of the civic elite, would not have been amused had they come across the parodies of Virgil's *Aeneid* in the graffito or the fresco. Following in the wake of Quinctius Valgus and Marcus Porcius, these influential people (along with others beside them) had infused the Vesuvian towns with what today would have amounted to millions of dollars' worth of civic improvements. To them, the graffito and fresco would have embodied juvenile and unenlightened sentiments that, when taken to their logical conclusion, might dangerously undermine the progress of the Roman imperial order. As sponsors of that progress, they might have taken some personal offense as well. For them, the Roman program was not to be affronted, and neither were those who supported its propaganda within urban contexts of the first-century world.

In Praise of Christian Benefactors

Unsurprisingly, money had influence within early Jesus-groups as well—although to a much smaller scale and without necessarily being attached to support for the Roman imperial order. For instance, here is what Paul says at the end of 1 Corinthians regarding an important Corinthian household of Jesus-devotees who had used their resources in a way worthy of respect.

> Now, brothers and sisters, you know that members of the household of Stephanas were the first converts in Achaia, and they have devoted themselves to the service of the saints; I urge you to put yourselves at the service of such people, and of everyone who works and toils with them. . . . Give recognition to such persons. (16:15–16, 18)

Paul probably lauded the household of Stephanus because it was reliable in its loyalty to Paul's program at a time when Corinthian Jesus-followers were beginning to fragment in their support of him (as his subsequent letter to them clearly illustrates; see 2 Corinthians). Paul's charge to "give recognition to such persons" as Stephanas was characteristic of the customs of the first-century world.

Something similar probably lies behind Paul's praise of Philemon's "faithfulness . . . for the sake of all of Jesus's followers":

> When I remember you in my prayers, I always thank my God because I hear of your love and faithfulness which you have toward the Lord Jesus and for the sake of all of Jesus's followers. I pray that the fellowship of your faith may become effective in the realization of every good work that is active among you all, to the glory of Christ. (Philemon 4–6, my translation)

Here, what Paul says of Philemon's reputation for supporting other Jesus-followers fits the mold of first-century benefaction (for example, benefaction within "associations," groups that gathered for congenial and/or supportive purposes). Whether he is talking about the household of Stephanas or Philemon, Paul's comments are miniature versions of the kind of honor-for-benefaction cycle that we see prominently and repeatedly in Roman urban centers like the Vesuvian towns. At times, then, the discourse of early Christian texts flowed very much "with the grain" of how things worked in the Roman world (and beyond). Benefactors within Jesus-groups were to be appreciated for their beneficence. (As we saw in chapter 10, however, Paul wanted to ensure that those efforts were seen to be only one of many initiatives that built up the body of Christ, with no one form of "gifting" taking precedence over another.)

Challenging the Status Quo in Early Christian Texts

At times, however, the discourse of early Christian texts ran "against the grain" with regard to those urban elite who were the primary sponsors of Roman imperial propaganda in indigenous settings. For instance, Luke's Gospel remembers Jesus as saying:

> When you give a luncheon or a dinner, do not invite your friends or your brothers or your relatives or rich neighbors, in case they may invite you in return, and you would be repaid. But when you give a banquet, invite the poor, the crippled, the lame, and the blind. And you will be blessed, because they cannot repay you, for you will be repaid at the resurrection of the righteous. (Luke 14:12–14)

Here, Jesus is remembered as turning upside down the system of honor-for-benefaction that undergirded ancient societies. The people who deserve generous initiatives are not the people who can return the favor or enhance the benefactor's status; instead, they are the outcasts of society who cannot return the favor. People of that kind were rarely targeted by benefactors as the primary recipients of generous initiatives. In this text, those who extend generosity to the outcasts are promised a form of repayment for their efforts, but only "at the resurrection of the righteous." In the meantime, Jesus-followers were to "expect nothing in return" when they extended generosity toward others; instead, their "reward will be great" in the afterlife (Luke 6:35). Ultimately, then, the forms of benefaction that this text highlights reflect not the merits of the Roman imperial order but the kingdom of the deity who blesses the righteous. In this way, Jesus-followers are being taught to recognize an elongated timeline in the cycle of initiative and reward, with "the resurrection of the righteous" held out as the foremost prize of honor.

A similar challenge to the system of honor-for-benefaction is reiterated in a more pronounced fashion later in the Lukan narrative, when Jesus is remembered to have said:

> The kings of the gentiles lord it over them;
> and those in authority over them are called benefactors. But it should not be so with you; rather the greatest among you must become like the youngest, and the leader like one who serves. (Luke 22:25–26; see also Mark 10:41–45)

This text does not perpetuate the macro-narratives promoted by powerful benefactors but, instead, focuses on the micro-narratives of the socially insignificant people, "the young-est" or "one who serves." Just as the graffitist wrote "not" in relation to "arms and a man," so too Jesus says "not" to the narratives that prop up "the kings of the gentiles . . . and those in authority."

One New Testament text attributes much the same sentiment to James, one of Jesus's brothers. James was one of the apostolic figures who stipulated that Jesus-devotees should always "remember the poor" (as Paul records in Galatians 2:10; see Looking Further: A Conclusion). Evidently James believed that Jesus-followers were inevitably to be involved in alleviating the desperate poverty that affected so many in the ancient world. The letter that bears his name makes the point this way:

> My brothers and sisters, do you with your acts of favoritism really exhibit trust in our glorious Lord Jesus Christ? For if a person with gold rings and in fine clothes comes into your assembly, and if a poor person in dirty clothes also comes in, and if you take notice of the one wearing the fine clothes and say, "Have a seat here, please," while to the one who is poor you say, "Stand there," or, "Sit at my feet," have you not made distinctions among yourselves, and become judges with evil thoughts? Listen, my beloved brothers and sisters. Has not God chosen the poor in the world to be rich in faith and to be heirs of the kingdom that he has promised to those who love him? But you have dishonored the poor. (James 2:1–6)

For James, the stories of the poor are ideally suited to carry the message of the divine "kingdom." This is quite distinctive. In Roman times, it was the elite whose stories were prominently embedded within the ideology of the Roman imperial program. The early Jesus-movement found a way to embed

141

the stories of the poor prominently within the message of "our glorious Lord Jesus Christ." Perhaps this is one reason why Paul could say that this "good news . . . is not of human origin" (Galatians 1:11), since any attempt to formulate good news from human origins usually places the powerful front and center, as we often see in the Vesuvian towns. Perhaps, too, this is one reason why Paul sought to proclaim this good news "free of charge" (1 Corinthians 9:18). It was his way of ensuring that the message he preached was not inevitably entangled with the self-interests of the powerful.

Literacies and Status   12

> Then Peter, filled with the Holy Spirit, said to them: "Rulers and elders of the people. . . . Salvation is found in no one else [but Jesus], for there is no other name given under heaven by which we must be saved." When they saw the courage of Peter and John and realized that *they were unschooled, ordinary men,* they were astonished and they took note that these men had been with Jesus.
>
> Acts 4:8, 12–13

Schooling the Elite

Unschooled and ordinary men, like the apostles Peter and John, were everywhere in the ancient world. Generally speaking, education in things like rhetoric and philosophy was the privilege of well-placed males in the Roman population (as depicted in figure 12.1; on the education of women, see below). To become influential later in life, a young Roman male was expected to apply himself to the acquisition of rhetorical skills—skills of presentation in order to persuade others and play an active role in public life. For acquiring these skills, a boy needed to learn from either a tutor or a teacher. A householder might purchase a tutor as a slave for training members of the household. A teacher would operate a school, with students being sent to him for daily instruction. The expectation was that boys would grow up to be leaders in the civic arena, winning the approval of others through various mechanisms, including rhetorical ability and an educated mind. Meanwhile, they were also to know the literary classics—Homer's *Odyssey* and *Iliad*, for instance, and especially the recently published epic by Virgil, the *Aeneid*, which was equivalent to a first-century "bestseller." Effective rhetorical skill and an intricate knowledge of classical literature were a powerful combination that helped to ensure a young man's ascendancy in the civic arena, modeling what the elite generally saw as the ideal citizen. These skills also enhanced what the Romans called *otium*—the pleasant balancing of refreshment, recreation, and learning. *Otium* was a luxury that only the elite could enjoy, since it required one to be free

Figure 12.1. Drawings of two Vesuvian frescos depicting elite men studying scrolls (see credits)

from the everyday demands that pressed down on the majority of the population.

This setting of elite opulence and learning is on display in one of the most tremendous discoveries among the Vesuvian realia:

Herculaneum's luxurious Villa of the Papyri, with its extensive library. Within that magnificent seaside residence, archaeologists have found approximately eighteen hundred papyrus scrolls containing philosophical treatises

Figure 12.2. Left: scrolls of papyrus from the impressive collection of philosophical treatises in the library of Herculaneum's Villa of the Papyri; right: a Greek papyrus scroll unrolled, from the same collection

in Greek and Latin. Most of these scrolls are highly charred and, at present, remain largely unreadable (see figure 12.2). But from close investigations it seems that the library contained many of the works of Philodemus—an Epicurean philosopher, poet, and rhetorician of some significance in the first century BCE. This villa, then, exemplifies the intersection of wealth and education that were prized by the elite of the Roman world.

Permutations of Literacy

Education did not go on simply in the houses of the opulent, however, and literacy was not exclusive to those at the upper echelons of the socio-economic scale. There were many permutations within the spectrum of education—with tutors, teachers, and their students having a variety of profiles in terms of their educational abilities. We see some of this rich variety in the Vesuvian towns themselves. A good

number of people in those towns were literate in some fashion, although there were often wide divergences in their literacy competencies, depending on their education and status.

Several frescos in the "country club" owned by Julia Felix (covering the whole block of 2.4) depict snapshots of moments in the everyday lives of ordinary Pompeii residents (rather than the mythological scenes normally depicted in Pompeian art). Two of those frescos have implications for our understanding of ancient literacy (both depicted in figure 12.3). In one fresco, several youths are hard at work in their studies, although (in a common interpretation) one of them has not met the standards expected of him by his tutor, so he is being held and whipped for his lack of diligence. (We hear of this practice in literary sources too—not least from the Roman poet Horace, who referred to his teacher as "the flogger"; *Epistles* 2.1.70.) Another fresco depicts several Pompeian residents reading a lengthy official pronouncement that had

Figure 12.3. Two drawings of frescos in the country club of Julia Felix (2.4); left: this is traditionally interpreted as depicting a school-boy being whipped by his tutor while held by two others students, as three other students continue their learning (this interpretation has been disputed, since the person being whipped could be an unschooled slave being punished for some reason; MANN 9066); right: several Pompeian residents read an official pronouncement displayed for public consideration (MANN 9068) (see credits).

been laid out for public display in the main forum.

A certain level of literacy was beneficial if one was to function effectively in business. A corpus of legal documents belonging to a leading Pompeian auctioneer and banker, Lucius Caecilius Jucundus, recorded the business dealings of many ordinary residents—especially the sale of properties among the Pompeians. Most of these wax tablets are signed by various witnesses who added their own marks of identification to the contracts, evidently in sequence according to their status on the social hierarchy (precisely the sort of thing we saw in chapter 2 regarding status hierarchies). And a certain level of literacy is also assumed in the floor mosaics at entryways to houses, where greetings of various kinds are on display—for example, "beware of the dog" (*cave canem*, at 6.8.5) and "welcome" (*have*, at 6.12.2).

Women, Literacy, and Household Management

While we would normally expect educational opportunities to be made available to boys and men, several pieces of evidence demonstrate that women also benefited from educational opportunities, at least on occasion. One collection of documents mentions a woman, Calatoria, who had a tutor by the name Telesphorus, evidently one of her household slaves. Calatoria was the matriarch of a fairly impressive household in Herculaneum (although there is some evidence that its grandest days were in the past, years before the eruption). One of Telesphorus's duties was to give Calatoria educational training of some kind. Some slaves were educated precisely for this purpose—as a kind of live-in teacher. So here

we see a household slave tutoring the matriarch of the household. (We already saw a literate slave in chapter 1, where Methe expressed her love for Chrestus in a graffito.)

Several frescos from Pompeii also demonstrate that some women had a certain level of literacy, which augmented their function as the matriarch of their household. Two frescos capture this aspect of female literacy especially well. Both depict women with a notebook tablet in one hand and a writing stylus in the other, with the stylus raised to the lips in a pose of contemplation. The notebook tablet would have contained a matriarch's list of things to be done within the household—the "to-do list" necessary to run a household efficiently. In one fresco (see figure 12.4, right side), a woman contemplates what she has written (or is soon to write) in her notebook tablet; since it is a large notebook, it seems she is the matron of a significant household. (And on the wall next to her fresco was another one depicting a man holding a scroll [MANN 9085]—perhaps her husband or son.) In another fresco (see figure 12.4, left side), a very young woman (perhaps in her early teens and newly married) contemplates the needs of the household with her (small) notebook tablet open, while another woman behind her looks on; perhaps the onlooker is the matriarch's slave seeing her duties for the day. (For a third example of this motif, see figure 16.8.)

There is no pretense here that these women have expertise in the great literature of the classical world. The literacy level of these women does not need to rise above the level of making notes and lists about what needs to be done that day for the efficient operation of the households in which they are matriarchs. In this way, the frescos serve to enhance their reputations as capable overseers of their

Figure 12.4. Left: A woman contemplates what to include on her list of household duties, while another (her slave?) looks on (MANN 9074, sometimes wrongly said to depict the writing of a love letter); right: a woman contemplates her notebook (MANN 9084, sometimes wrongly said to be the Greek poetess Sappho).

households, but they do not necessarily suggest levels of literacy beyond a household functionality. These women are not enjoying the classics of Greco-Roman literature contained in scrolls, for instance. Instead, they are depicted as efficient managers of their households.

One Vesuvian fresco (see figure 12.5) clearly links social upward mobility to these various forms of literacy (often allocated along lines of male and female functionality; see also figures 16.8 and 16.9). The five components of the fresco are as follows (from left to right):

- A woman's notebook tablet, necessary for the efficient running of the household
- Loose coins needed for the everyday running of the household

Figure 12.5. A drawing of a fresco linking literacy with status and upward mobility (see credits)

147

This fresco captures the link between the upward prospects of the household and literacy (the literacy both of household efficiency and of educated learning). It is how a thriving household of middling socio-economic status sought to present itself.

Occasionally, however, a Vesuvian fresco suggests higher levels of literacy for certain women. One fresco shows a woman whose level of literacy is quite high (see figure 12.6). She holds a scroll, rather than a notebook tablet. Living in a setting of obvious opulence, she is an elite woman whose station in life affords her the time and luxury to immerse herself in the enjoyments of high literature. Being among the lucky few at the upper levels of the socio-economic strata, this high-status woman has the opportunity to develop her mind to match the level of her first-class surroundings. Here, the luxuries of *otium* have spread even to the female members of this elite household, with the obvious enhancements in status going hand in hand with higher forms of literacy.

The Literacy of Graffiti

Since literacy came in a variety of forms, it is not surprising that many simple townspeople expressed themselves in relatively basic terms on Vesuvian walls. Of the more than eleven thousand artifacts written on the walls of the Vesuvian towns, the vast majority are simple graffiti. The external walls of houses, commercial properties, and public spaces seem to have been thought of as shared space to be used by the populace in general, fostering discourse of all kinds within the public arena. Included in that discourse were dipinti—notices painted in red over white on external walls, announcing forthcoming gladiatorial games or support for political candidates (as in chapter

Figure 12.6. A drawing of a Vesuvian fresco depicting an elite woman reading from a scroll (see credits)

- A business contract, demonstrating the entrepreneurial ambitions within the household (usually represented by the householder, the male patriarch of the family)

- A bin containing the household scrolls, showing the learning that went on within the household (usually referencing the householder and his legitimate male offspring)

- A sizeable sack containing (what must certainly be) the household's nest-egg of valuable coins

10). These were painted by sign writers who sometimes put themselves in the picture, as in this case: "Aemilius Celer wrote this on his own by the light of the moon" (*CIL* 4.3884). Or this: "Unico writes, without the rest of the team" (*CIL* 4.222). Or this: "Onesimus was the whitewasher" (*CIL* 4.222). One painter excoriated his partner: "Lantern carrier, hold the ladder" (*CIL* 4.7621).

Most of Pompeii's graffiti were not so professionally produced. These were either etched into plaster with a hard object or written with simple charcoal. These graffiti (some of which we canvassed in chapter 1 and elsewhere in this book) were not restricted to external walls but were sometimes written on internal walls as well, in properties covering the whole of the socio-economic spectrum. These inscriptions often captured key moments of life: "January 23rd, Ursa gave birth on a Thursday" (*CIL* 4.8820). Some recorded mundane moments: "It took 640 paces to walk back and forth between here and there ten times" (*CIL* 4.1714); or "On April 19 I made bread" (*CIL* 4.8792). Devoid of any puritanical sentiment, their inscribers often stated things bluntly: "I screwed many girls here" (*CIL* 4.2175); "If anyone wants a screw, he should look for Attice—she costs four sesterces" (*CIL* 4.1751). Slightly less explicit is a graffito evidently inscribed by someone relatively well placed within the empire: "Apollinaris, the doctor of emperor Titus, defecated well here" (*CIL* 4.10619). Since Titus had been emperor for only a few months before Vesuvius erupted, this graffito must have been one of the last inscribed in the Vesuvian towns (in this case, in Herculaneum's House of the Gem).

Sometimes inscriptions simply stated that their inscriber "was here" or advertised premises for rent or noted that the inscriber made "a vow to the household deities" in that place or offered "good wishes and good health" to members of the imperial family. Sometimes they allowed students to practice writing the alphabet; other times they contained complex palindromes in alluring word-squares.

Sometimes they teased. "Epaphra, you are bald!" (*CIL* 4.1816). On the wall of a residential latrine we read the chiding of a slave named Martha: "This is Martha's dining room; she defecates in [her] dining room" (*CIL* 4.5244, in 9.8.6). Sometimes they are touching. "Pyrrhus to his colleague Chius: I am in sorrow because I hear that you have died; and so, farewell" (*CIL* 4.1852, from Pompeii's basilica). Sometimes they offer words of wisdom: "A small problem gets larger if you ignore it" (*CIL* 4.1811). A notable number of graffiti even cite sentences from authors of classical literature, such as Homer, Ovid, Seneca, Lucretius, and most of all, Virgil (forty-eight occurrences, including three dozen from the *Aeneid*, as noted in chapter 6). Many of these might have been written by young students learning to write, their teachers having assigned them exercises from literary classics.

This small sample of graffiti offers insight into the lives of ordinary people on the streets of the Vesuvian towns. But these graffiti and other artifacts also reveal something of the contours of ancient literacy. Gone are the days when it was commonly said that only the top 5 percent of the Roman population were literate. Pompeii was awash with low-grade forms of literacy that included a breadth of genres targeted for readerships across a broad spectrum of the populace. This does not mean, of course, that everyone was literate. Far from it. For many people, most inscriptions and graffiti on Pompeian walls must have been little more than lines and curves joined together

Figure 12.7. A fresco depicting a young man holding a scroll, with the word "Plato" written on it; a similar fresco nearby depicted the same youth or one that looked much like him holding a scroll of Homer (MANN 120620a and 120620b; from 5.2.h).

sentation of things, Jesus had at least an elementary reading ability—hardly surprising for someone raised in a Judean (i.e., Jewish) home who, consequently, was probably very acquainted with reading the scriptures of the Judean people.

But it is also the case that Jesus's level of literacy was probably not like that of the Judean leaders, who had benefited from a much more extensive educational training than a common carpenter. Much of the tension between Jesus and the Judean leaders of his day probably derived from this conflict in authority styles between the "established" interpreters of scripture (who had enjoyed a notable level of reputable education) and the "backwater hick" from Nazareth (who could list no conventional training as the basis for his authority). That tension between the perceived statuses of different interpreters of the divine will animates Mark 6:3, for instance. In that passage, even members of Jesus's own hometown react negatively to his astounding teaching in the synagogue: "Is not this the carpenter, the son of Mary and brother of James and Joses and Judas and Simon, and are not his sisters here with us?" The reader is told that the people of his hometown "took offense at him" (Mark 6:3; compare Matthew 13:55). He was a simple artisan. He had grown up among them. They knew his simple family. What status could his teachings have? Who did he think he was?

What about the apostles Peter and John? As depicted in Acts 4 (cited at the start of this chapter), they were evidently unschooled and ordinary men—hardly surprising since they had been Galilean fishermen before they began to follow Jesus. As unschooled, ordinary men, they would have been in good company alongside the majority in the Roman age who were

that meant something to others within the town. We know, for instance, that someone by the name Mammius wrote a legal testimony "at the request of Marcus Calatorius Marullus, in his presence, because he says he does not know how to write" (VAR Tab. 24; see also *AE* [2002], 342). But neither is it the case that literacy pertained only to the urban elite and/or their retainers. The Vesuvian remains problematize any attempt to distinguish between "literate" and "non-literate" in relation to general sectors within the populace; what is on display instead is a spectrum of literate competencies or "literacies."

Literacy, Jesus, and His Followers

What might be said about Jesus himself with regard to literacy? Jesus was remembered as having read scripture in his hometown synagogue (Luke 4:16–17), so in Luke's prelow in literary status. As men who cherished their Judean identity and heritage, Peter and John may have benefited from a dose of training in reading the Judean scriptures (much like Jesus). It is unlikely, however, that they would have needed to be proficient in anything more than a basic form of literacy. (Their literary skill might have been restricted to reading rather than writing.) It is precisely because the first disciples of Jesus were "unschooled" that the people who listened to Peter and John in the Acts 4 account are said to be "astonished" when those disciples speak so eloquently, even addressing the "rulers and elders of the people" with "courage." The author of Acts supplied the reason for their courage. It was not simply that "these men had been with Jesus"; it was because they were now "filled with the Holy Spirit" (4:8, 12–13).

The apostle Paul seems to have been highly literate, and yet he also chose to dictate his letters to a scribe rather than "penning" his letters himself. One of those scribes even speaks to the audience at one point (Romans 16:22): "I, Tertius, who wrote down this letter, greet you in the Lord." At times, however, Paul picked up the stylus himself. He signaled this in Philemon 19: "I, Paul, am writing this with my own hand." It is difficult to know whether he means that he has written the whole of that short letter himself or whether (and more likely) he means that, although dictating most of the letter, he is now writing the content of that particular sentence (which contains an important financial guarantee that is best made in one's own hand). Something similar happens at the end of his letter to Jesus-devotees in Galatia: "See what large letters I make when I am writing in my own hand" (Galatians 6:11). Here, Paul picks up the stylus to introduce his final paragraphs of the letter, where he summarizes

what the letter is all about in emphatic terms ("large letters")—almost like bold or italic font. If you want to see Paul's synopsis of what Galatians is all about, the final verses of that letter (6:11–18), written large and in his own hand (in the original manuscript), are a good place to start.

In 2 Timothy, readers hear Paul instruct the younger man Timothy in this way: "When you come [to me], bring the cloak that I left with Carpus at Troas, and my scrolls, especially the parchments" (4:13). This intriguing reference raises curiosity as to what those scrolls and parchments (skins of animals used as a medium for writing) may have been. Could the scrolls have been some select passages from the Judean scriptures or passages from the Hellenistic literary "canon" of the day? Could the parchments have been copies of letters that Paul had previously sent to churches? Of course we will never know. But the passage is suggestive of Paul's own high level of literacy—something that has never really been called into question.

It is likely that at least one woman in Paul's circle also enjoyed a notable level of literacy. This was Phoebe, "a deacon of the congregation at Cenchreae [the port of Corinth] . . . [who] has been a benefactor of many people and of myself as well" (Romans 16:1–2). It seems likely that Phoebe was the person who traveled from Corinth to deliver Paul's letter to Jesus-groups in Rome. As the letter carrier, Phoebe would probably also have read the letter to the various Jesus-groups in that city. This means that she probably also helped Jesus-followers in Rome to interpret Paul's letter (we might imagine them asking her, "What does Paul mean by the righteousness of God?" and things of that sort). This would suggest that Phoebe enjoyed a notable level

151

Figure 12.8. A fresco depicting the Greek comic dramatist Menander, whom Paul quotes in 1 Corinthians 15:33 (from 1.10.4, in situ)

of literacy—one that went beyond the skill necessary for a matron to manage a household efficiently. And if she had been successful in business (as "a benefactor of many people" might suggest), her literacy would seem to have excelled beyond the skill necessary for the effective management of a business. Phoebe seems to have been a woman whose level of literacy was quite impressive within the range of literacies of her day.

Literary Oddities as Theological Contributions?

One intriguing dimension of literacy in early Christianity comes into view in the final book of the New Testament. The author of the Johannine apocalypse, the book of Revelation, wrote in a style that at times causes one's grammatical eyebrows to rise in curiosity. This happens at the very start of the text, where John sends greetings to the seven churches of Asia Minor, using these words: "Grace to you and peace from the one who is and who was and who is to come" (1:4). As any good schoolchild would have known, the Greek preposition here that is translated "from" requires the words it modifies to be placed in the genitive form, but John instead used the nominative form—the form reserved for the subject of a sentence, not the form that follows a preposition. In fact, John knew that this was "incorrect" grammar, as illustrated throughout his text—not least in the very next phrase, where the same preposition appears together with the genitive form of the words it modifies ("and from the seven spirits who are before his throne"). What's going on here? Perhaps John was making a theological point with his tortuous grammatical oddity—that "the one who is and who was and who is to come" is always the subject of things and never anything less. Or perhaps it was simply that this deity cannot be contained within rule books of our common ways of expression; that this deity is beyond our control; that this deity lies in territories that look odd to normal perceptions. Who knows? But since John clearly knew the rules of grammar (specifically, syntax), a theological explanation of some kind may have the most merit.

A similar oddity appears in Revelation 5:6. There John spoke of "the seven spirits of God that were sent out into all the world." The word "spirits" is a neuter plural noun, but the word that amplifies that neuter noun (the participle "sent out") is formed not as a neuter

152

plural, as expected, but as a masculine plural. Would John's teacher have whipped him if, as a schoolboy, he produced sentences like this? Is this just bad grammar? John knew that the Greek word "spirit" is neuter in gender, and he uses a neuter pronoun earlier in the text to refer to "spirit" (1:4). So perhaps his use of a masculine form here has some theological point to it. Perhaps his peculiar grammar was intended to signal to his readers that the sending of the (neuter) Spirit throughout the world is not some numinous, ethereal happening but is instead embodied in the lives of *people*—the masculine "sent out" doing double duty for both males and females. In this case, a grammatical peculiarity jars the audience's attention and signals John's theological conviction that the divine Spirit moves through this world in embodied form, within the lives of the devotees of that deity.

The same practice of doing theology through grammatical oddity is probably evident in one other phenomenon that appears in various places in Revelation—that is, the mismatching of the subject and the verb in sentences. In 11:15, for instance, having mentioned "our Lord and his Messiah" as two separate figures, John continues his sentence with a singular subject of the sentence's verb: "and he will reign forever and ever." Is the one who reigns the "Lord" alone or his "Messiah" or both together as a single unity, "he"? In 22:3–4 the same thing happens. John refers to "the throne of God and of the Lamb," but immediately, instead of using plural personal pronouns (e.g., "their"), he switches to a singular personal pronoun, "his"—"his servants," "his face," and "his name." (The same thing happens in 6:17, where the original text probably did not include the word "their," which seems to be an attempt by a later scribe to improve the grammar, but "his.") While John consistently placed Christ within the realm of the divine, he seems to have been aware of the danger of referring to "God" and "the Messiah/Lamb" as separate deities. Seeking to avoid a polytheistic relationality within his depiction of the divine, John broke grammatical rules by using the singular verb form whenever "God" and "the Messiah/Lamb" are the verb's subjects and by using singular pronouns when referring to them both.

Should the author of the Johannine apocalypse have spent more hours studying Greek grammar from his schoolteacher? Was his literary skill of inferior status? Or are these instances of an author intentionally breaking the rules of grammar in order to drive home important theological points?

Combat and Courts

As for us [apostles], why do we endanger ourselves every hour? I face death every day. . . . If *I fought wild beasts in Ephesus* with no more than human hopes, what have I gained?

1 Corinthians 15:30–32 NIV

Spectacles of Combat

Fighting wild beasts were regular displays in many urban centers of the Roman age. In amphitheaters like the one in Pompeii, arena fights were spectacles that urban populations seem to have eagerly anticipated and regularly consumed. Fights between groups of wild beasts, between gladiators, and between gladiators and wild beasts were exhilarating high points in the civic life of an urban center. In the coming together of all strands of society, people could enjoy viewing competition, combat, danger, and occasionally the death of other human beings. Some gladiators became superstars among the local population. Pompeii's *spectacula* (as the amphitheater was called) provided enough seating for twenty thousand people—almost twice as much as the population of the town itself. Judging by the Pompeian announcements of games

in other nearby urban centers (like Cumae, Nola, Nuceria, and Puteoli), people must have come to Pompeii from far and wide within the region to watch these spectacles of wonder. To ensure the best quality of competition within their town, the magistrates of Pompeii converted what had once been a large public portico in the "theater district" into a barracks and training ground for many gladiators (see figure 13.1).

Gladiators were usually slaves, their masters owning a gladiatorial troupe. The gladiators would have lived together in the barracks, trained together in the courtyard of the barracks, and then been forced to compete against each other (and against members of other gladiatorial troupes) in the amphitheater. Many of Pompeii's gladiators resided in the very small rooms dotted around the courtyard of the barracks. When the rooms were excavated in the eighteenth century, some

Figure 13.1. The barracks and training area for some of Pompeii's gladiators (8.7.16)

skeletons were found in some of the rooms, some skeletons having iron chains and fetters on their legs and arms—indicating that these gladiators had been restrained throughout the eruption of Vesuvius, with no one coming to release them.

Pompeians had plenty of exposure to gladiatorial combat (except for a few years after the riot of 59 CE, when such Pompeian contests were suspended by the Roman senate). Those contests were announced in advance by way of graffiti painted on the exterior walls of residences or shops. One of these graffiti reads, "The gladiatorial troupe of the aedile Aulus Suettius Certus will fight at Pompeii on May 31; there will be a hunt [of wild animals] and awnings [for shade]" (*CIL* 4.1189). Almost exactly the same notice was painted near one of the town's brothels. Evi-

dently this civic official, who also sponsored his own troupe in the competition, wanted people to know of his beneficence to the town and its people. In another gladiatorial advertisement, the prominent magistrate Gnaeus Alleius Nigidius Maius (seen in chapter 11) announced that in the games he sponsored, gladiators would "fight without interruption" (*CIL* 5.1180)—to ensure that the action moved at a fast pace, for the enjoyment of the spectators.

Frescos depicting gladiators and graffiti about them are found throughout Pompeii. One residence, the so-called House of the Gladiators (at 5.5.3), features over 140 graffiti about gladiators etched into the twenty-four columns of its peristyle courtyard. Some of these graffiti (perhaps even all of them) seem to have been inscribed by gladiators themselves,

155

who evidently lived within the residence. Their graffiti include the following:

- "Samus, the pseudo-Gallic fighter: 1 fight, 1 win. The same horseback-and-sword fighter lives here" (CIL 4.4420).
- "July 28, Florus won at Nuceria. August 15, he won at Herculaneum" (CIL 4.4299).
- "Rusticus Malius: 12 fights, 11 wins. Marcus Terentius: 3 fights, 3 wins" (CIL 4.4302).
- "Felix, belonging to Cassius: 13 fights, 13 wins. Florus, belonging to Octavius: 14 fights, 14 wins" (CIL 4.4378).
- "The heart throb of girls—Thracian fighter, Celadus, belonging to Octavius: 3 fights, 3 wins" (CIL 4.4342).
- "Celadus, Thracian fighter—girls' pride" (CIL 4.5142b).
- "Crescent the net fighter, doctor . . . of girls in the night, in the morning, and at other times" (CIL 4.4353).

Throughout this same house, an inordinately high number of frescos illustrated scenes in which predatory animals were seeking to devour their prey, including the following:

- A dog attacking a boar (two frescos of this)
- A dog attacking a deer (three frescos of this)
- Two dogs attacking a lion
- Two dogs attacking a bear
- Two dogs attacking a boar
- Two dogs attacking a panther
- Four dogs attacking a boar
- Deer in flight in fear of their attackers

This is a clear case of the artwork matching the ethos of the residence (something that we regularly see in the Vesuvian residences and buildings). These frescos must have been selected to reinforce the sense that predatory relationships are built into the structure of reality, augmenting the predatory instincts of those preparing for battle in gladiatorial contests. When gladiators were placed together to compete, they were expected to draw inspiration from these frescos. They were not to think of themselves as human beings whose relationality was to be set apart from bestial forms of the survival of the fittest; instead, they were to embody that ultimate struggle for life in the face of death. Perhaps the life-and-death contests of the gladiators were perceived by ancient audiences as the externalized performance of their own experiences of the struggle lying at the heart of human existence.

If the gladiators were to survive their ordeal through connecting with their bestial impulses, the spectacles themselves connected spectators with the same impulses. This, at least, was how Seneca (the influential Stoic philosopher and Roman statesman, who died in 65 CE) experienced the spectacles, as he noted in this report (*Moral Letters to Lucilius* 7.2):

> There is nothing more damaging to good character than attendance at some spectacle. For it is through this thrill that vices more easily creep into your soul. What do you imagine I mean? When I return home, I'm more greedy, more ambitious, more addicted to sensuousness; I am more cruel and inhumane.

If Seneca's testimony is anything to go by, rather than purifying and purging aggressive competitiveness and greedy ambition from the "soul" of Roman audiences, these gladiatorial contests often stirred up precisely those sentiments.

Metaphors of Combat in Pauline Texts

The apostle Paul incorporated combat imagery at various points in his letters. Most notably, he mentioned to the Corinthians that he had "fought wild beasts in Ephesus" (1 Corinthians 15:32, as noted at the start of this chapter). Although it is intriguing to imagine this literally having taken place in the Great Theater of Ephesus, it is more likely that Paul was simply speaking metaphorically in this case. This is for two reasons.

Figure 13.2. A fresco of a gladiatorial competition, with one gladiator down and the other poised for the kill (from the tomb of Gaius Vestorius Priscus at Pompeii's Vesuvian Gate, in situ)

First, it went against Roman law to put a citizen into an arena contest, and Paul seems to have been a Roman citizen (if Acts 22:25–29 is anything to go by; see discussion in chapter 2). Second, in a later letter Paul listed a catalogue of hardships he had undergone, but he does not mention fighting with wild beasts in that catalogue (see 2 Corinthians 11:23–28). Additionally, we might suspect that Paul (unlike a trained gladiator) would not have survived an encounter with wild beasts. So it seems that Paul experienced a serious ordeal of some kind while he was in Ephesus (from 52 to 55), which he likened to an arena spectacle in which he found fierce danger on every side of him. The author of 2 Timothy elaborates on this motif: "The Lord stood by me and gave me strength . . . so I was rescued from the lion's mouth" (4:17).

Paul used metaphors of combat in other ways too. Some people who assisted in the task of bolstering Jesus-groups were said to be "fellow soldiers" with Paul (Archippus in Philemon 2; Epaphroditus in Philippians 2:25). Jesus-followers are exhorted to protect themselves with the metaphorical "armor of God" (Romans 13:12; Ephesians 6:11 and 6:13). In 1 Thessalonians this includes putting on "the breastplate of faith and love, and for a helmet the hope of salvation" (5:8). In Ephesians this includes putting on "the belt of truth," "the breastplate of righteousness," and "the shield of faith, with which you will be able to quench all the flaming arrows of the evil one" (6:14 and 6:16). But the targeted enemies are not the ones human beings normally think of as military opponents. The author of Ephesians saw things this way: "Our struggle is not against enemies of blood and flesh, but against the rulers, against the authorities, against the cosmos

Figure 13.3. A nineteenth-century drawing of a carved stucco relief that depicts gladiators in competition with each other (top section) and a wild animal hunt (from tomb HGW17, perhaps the tomb of Aulus Umbricius Scaurus; see further at figure 10.3; see credits)

grabbers of this present darkness, against the spiritual forces of evil in the heavenly places" (6:12). Here the narrative of conflict is placed on a canvas of cosmic proportions.

Paul used a similar metaphor in 1 Corinthians 4:9. There he depicted himself as a defeated enemy of the state, paraded by the conquering general as a war trophy, a prisoner of war in a cosmic battle, being "a spectacle to the whole universe, to angels as well as to human beings" and "on display at the end of the procession, like those condemned to die in the arena" (NIV). These were graphic metaphors in the urban world of Paul's day. Paul knew what it was like to experience life as one threatened from all sides. His ministry placed him front and center in a combat zone, with forces larger than him conspiring against him.

Paul elaborates the same theme in another letter that he wrote to the Corinthians, as we see in 2 Corinthians 10. When he wrote this letter, Paul was in the midst of a tough situation with some Corinthian Jesus-followers. They thought he was not impressive enough in his stature. So he wrote the following, contrasting the way in which Jesus-devotees

should relate to one another with the way of relating that characterizes "the world"—which he depicts as a form of warfare:

> I beg you that when I come I may not have to be as bold . . . toward some people who think that we live by the standards of this world. For though we live in the world, we do not wage war as the world does. (2 Corinthians 10:2–3 NIV)

Those who "live by the standards of this world" are those who judge by the appearances of status (10:7). They are enmeshed in a quest for status capture that makes them fools, says Paul (chapters 11–12), since the "divine power" that destroys all the "strongholds" of status resides in the gospel of foolishness (10:4; compare his argument in 1 Corinthians 1–2). But since Paul felt himself forced to respond to the status challenges of some Corinthian Jesus-followers, he allowed himself to "play the fool" and to boast momentarily in status registers that should not really have mattered among devotees of Jesus. "I have made a fool of myself," says Paul in the process, "but you drove me to it" (12:11 NIV).

Figure 13.4. A mosaic (left) and a fresco (right), both highly damaged and both depicting Achilles drawing his sword to attack his adversary Agamemnon (left: from 7.7.23, MANN 10006; right: from 6.9.6, MANN 9104)

Competing at Court

Since Paul often placed the "good news" in direct opposition to the dog-eat-dog world of status capture, he sometimes found his congregations to be "waging war as the world does" in order to enhance their own prospects at the expense of others—even other Jesus-followers. Some Jesus-devotees in Corinth, for instance, had grievances against one another and deemed the solution to lie in the court system, where a judge would cast the deciding verdict. Paul had a lot to say about this (see 1 Corinthians 6:1–8). He thought that the matter should be considered internally within the community, using the resources of the community's decision-making faculties. But because a courtroom drama looked inevitable, when describing that scenario Paul highlighted the theme of "defeat," which was an ominous prospect in both combat and court

contexts: "In fact, to have lawsuits at all with one another is already a defeat for you" (6:7). In view of that impending defeat, Paul dangled a less serious outcome before them, for their consideration: "Why not rather be wronged? Why not rather be defrauded?" In fact, he suspected that their motivations themselves were not right: "But you yourselves wrong and defraud—and believers at that" (6:8). These are the motivations that Paul saw as rampant outside the community of Jesus-followers, motivations that characterize "waging war as the world does." In Paul's view, that kind of motivation is a cancer within the eschatological community, which is to be permeated by a different moral ethos altogether.

Paul's view has some overlap with the view of Musonius Rufus, a first-century Stoic philosopher (ca. 20–100) who was banished from Rome on two occasions during his lifetime for adopting views that were thought to threaten the stability of society. Some overviews of his lectures have survived, and one of them discusses "whether a philosopher will file a suit against someone for assault" (Lecture 10). He characterizes "those who are overly concerned with their own fame" as quick to take others to court for injuring them by insults (even if someone simply "glares at them" or "laughs at them" or "mocks them"). By contrast, the wise person is not disturbed by insults and, consequently, "would not resort to lawsuits or indictments since he would not think he had been insulted." Musonius Rufus continued with this reflection: "Indeed, it is petty to be vexed or put out about such things. He will calmly and quietly bear what has happened, since this is appropriate behavior for a person who wants to be magnanimous." Musonius Rufus expected the wise to be above the fray of lawsuits; Paul exhorted Corinthian Jesus-followers to rise above the fray of lawsuits. Both arrived at much the same exhortation, albeit by different routes and for different ends (personal magnanimity for Musonius Rufus, corporate health for Paul).

Lawsuits were often extremely combative, and strategies for winning a lawsuit included "going negative" through defamation of another party's character. The trick was to make one's opponent look like a villain by slander, especially in instances where the lawsuit itself was weak or had very little merit. The first-century rhetorician Quintilian, for instance, advised legal rhetoricians (that is, lawyers) that when their client's case is weak, they should resort to damaging the moral character of the other party, in order "to gain more favor than our adversary . . . [and] to incur less dislike" for the lawyer's own client (*Institutio oratoria* 4.1.44).

This perniciously combative ethos could easily transpire within court contexts and may help to explain Paul's counsel to avoid lawsuits among the small groups of Jesus-followers in

Figure 13.5. A (damaged) mosaic depicting the battle between Alexander the Great of Greece (left of photo) and King Darius of Persia (almost centered in this photo) (from the House of the Faun, 6.12.2/5, MANN 10020)

Corinth. Paul did not want the social fabric that held Jesus-followers together to split, and to do so in public, since legal cases were heard not behind closed doors but in public contexts (see figure 13.8).

The Gospel of Luke records similar concerns about the legal procedures in the civic arena. Here Jesus is remembered to have spoken this stark saying:

> Why do you not judge for yourselves what is right? When you go with your accuser before a magistrate, on the way make an effort to settle the case, or you may be dragged before the judge, and the judge hand you over to the officer, and the officer throw you in prison. I tell you, you will never get out until you have paid the very last penny. (Luke 12:57–59)

If lawsuits were potentially divisive, they were also means to (1) protect status or (2) augment status. With regard to status protection, the courts were often places where people of superior status could seek a judgment against inferiors who may have spoken against them or tarnished their reputation in some way. These moments in the enterprise of status protection may be what the author of James had in mind when asking, "Is it not the rich who oppress you? Is it not they who drag you into court?" (2:6). Perhaps criticisms of the rich as fraudulent (criticisms evident in James 5:1–5, for instance; see chapter 14) would count as slander, leaving one exposed to retribution in the courts. With regard to status augmentation, the courts were often places where people of similar status lodged civil suits against each other for a grievance of some kind. In those instances, a favorable court hearing could prove socially advantageous in one's competitive quest for security and advancement.

The Case of Publius Vesonius Phileros

The Vesuvian remains give us a notable example of the attempt to augment status through gaining a favorable judgment in the courts. One memorial in Pompeii celebrates three people. Their statues were placed high up within a tomb memorial, but the heads of those statues have all been severed from their bodies due to damage during the Vesuvian eruption (see figure 13.6). The tomb was erected by the headless man on the left, who was able to convey a lot of information by means of inscriptions attached to the front of his tomb. His name was Publius Vesonius Phileros (who was mentioned briefly in chapter 9), and he erected this memorial tomb while he was alive—as was commonly done (see chapter 19).

There are two inscriptions on the face of Phileros's tomb (see especially figure 13.7). The top inscription coincides with the time of the tomb's construction; the bottom inscription was attached to the front of the tomb at a later date. The top inscription reads:

> Publius Vesonius Phileros (freedman of a woman, himself an *Augustalis*) built this monument for himself and his family during his lifetime; for Vesonia, daughter of Publius, his patroness; and for Marcus Orfellius Faustus, freedman of Marcus, his friend.

From the names on this inscription, we can reconstruct the basic timeline of Vesonius Phileros's life. Having been born into slavery, he had gained his freedom from the Vesonian household (from which he also inherited his first two names). He continued to benefit from his association with a female member of that family, Vesonia, whom he called his patroness. The family (the Vesonii) enjoyed some political prominence in Pompeii, so it is not surprising use of the word "*Augustalis*" to describe Vesonius Phileros and (2) its odd placement within the inscription.

First, the fact that Vesonius Phileros identified himself as a member of the *Augustales* tells us something about his economic profile after he earned his freedom. As we have seen (in chapter 11), many *Augustales* were men who had been born in slavery but later earned their freedom and subsequently acquired vast amounts of wealth. Becoming an *Augustalis* granted these prosperous former slaves a public profile and social prominence (although they could never be elected to public office). In return, they were expected to use their wealth for purposes of public benefaction, much like those who were elected to public office.

The second thing to notice about the inscription on Phileros's memorial tomb is the odd placement of the word "*Augustalis*." Squeezed into the inscription between the words "Phileros" and "*patronae*," the word "*Augustalis*" seems not to have been original to the inscription; it was added later. Evidently, when Vesonius Phileros erected the tomb, he had not yet become one of the *Augustales*. He must have been admitted to their ranks afterward. In fact, it would not be surprising if the construction of this tomb was itself part of his campaign to be included among their ranks, aiding his nomination for inclusion into their prestigious membership. This tomb testifies to the upward advancement of a slave who earned his freedom, acquired significant sums of money, and sought a notable public profile by being included among the ranks of the *Augustales* of Pompeii, from where he could flex the muscles of benefaction.

If the first inscription testifies to Vesonius Phileros's considerable upward mobility, the second inscription testifies to a rough patch in

Figure 13.6. The tomb of Vesonius Phileros in the necropolis of Pompeii's Nucerian Gate (NG23OS)

that Vesonius Phileros had hitched his own star to Vesonia's in this monument. (We know of several women in Pompeii who held significant social status; Vesonia may well have been among their number.) Orfellius Faustus, Phileros's "friend," gained his freedom from the household of Marcus Orfellius, but we do not know any more about him from this first inscription.

We can reconstruct two other things about Vesonius Phileros's life story from two particular features of this first inscription: (1) the his upward mobility. It was caused by the very man whom Vesonius Phileros honored in his tomb—Orfellius Faustus, the man depicted in the statue on the right. The later of the two inscriptions, lower and newer than the original, explains a bit of the story:

> Stranger, if it is not too much trouble, delay a brief while and learn what to avoid. This man whom I had hoped was my friend, I am forsaking. A legal case was maliciously brought against me; I was accused and proceedings were instituted. Thanks to the deities and my innocence, I was freed from all distress. I ask the household deities and the deities below not to receive the man who misrepresented our affairs.

Here Vesonius Phileros recounts an attack on his status, mounted not by "the rich who oppress you" but by the very person whom he had previously called "friend." It was a very public attack, carried out in the context of a legal challenge in public court.

Vesonius Phileros survived the attack on his status, with the judgment of the court falling in his favor. Since ancient lawsuits were usually decided on the basis of the testimony of witnesses favoring or denigrating the accused, Vesonius Phileros must have been more successful than Orfellius Faustus in mustering support from high-status people.

The enmity that transpired between these two men is evident also in the tomb area hidden beneath the visible statues and inscriptions. There, the headstone representing Faustus, which Phileros had prepared to sit alongside his own headstone, had been beheaded—no doubt, at Phileros's instruction or initiative. Moreover, a cremation urn had been sunk into the ground in preparation to hold Faustus's ashes. This urn was covered over with mor-

Figure 13.7. The two inscriptions on the tomb of Vesonius Phileros, the earlier inscription at the top and the later inscription at the bottom

tar (presumably without Faustus's ashes being added to it). Moreover, the name "Phileros" was written into the mortar, signaling who had carried out the sealing of the urn. Phileros seems to have taken his anger against Faustus with him to the grave.

What we are seeing with this tomb, then, are stages of status increase throughout the impressive career of Vesonius Phileros—stages that were on display for any member of the public who might be interested. Part of that upwardly mobile status included competitive combat played out even between friends, or former friends. Notice that Vesonius Phileros did not do what most of us would probably be inclined to do in a similar situation—that is, simply remove our ex-friend from our memorial tombs and rewrite the original inscription. Instead of removing Faustus's statue and replacing the original inscription, Phileros left Faustus (now his enemy) displayed as a statue within his tomb and simply added a supplemental narrative regarding his own continued successes, even in times of ordeal and adversity. That powerful narrative enabled him

Figure 13.8. Pompeii's basilica (at 8.1.1) would have served primarily as a courthouse where magistrates, seated in the covered tribunal depicted here, heard the cases of local residents in the open (such as the case against Vesonius Phileros).

to present himself as one wrongly accused, whose innocence had been testified to by the deities (by means of men of some status who must have supported him in the court of Pompeii). And, of course, all of this is embedded in his monument that he constructed while he was living in order to ensure how he would be remembered after his death. The person reading the inscription is, in a sense, already on his side, knowing that, as an *Augustalis*, Phileros sought to benefit the people. Meanwhile, shame falls on Orfellius Faustus, who tried to steal those benefactions for his own personal benefit. This is the unstated implication of Phileros's warning to those passing by.

Of course, Orfellius Faustus might have had his own narrative, contending that the courts were biased in Phileros's favor. Faustus could have backed up his charge on the basis that already Phileros had more social prestige than he (Faustus) had, so the judge was blinded to the specific merits of Faustus's case. This kind of charge would fall in line with some of the evidence of the ancient world—both biblical (see the section "Court Judgments" below) and non-biblical pronouncements. For instance, Pliny the Younger held the view that judges hearing legal cases should ensure that "the distinctions of rank and dignity" are maintained in their legal judgments; it is, he said, "the most unequal thing imaginable" for judges "to level and confound [i.e., confuse] the different orders of humanity" since treating everyone equally before the law "is

Figure 13.9. A fresco of two warships in battle (from the House of the Vettii, in situ)

far from producing equality among them" (*Epistulae* 9.5). Evidently this elite Roman senator held the view that legal systems should rightly be skewed in favor of the elite, rather than allowing the social orders to intermingle in their privileges. Of course, favoring those of higher status could be done only at the expense of those less securely positioned.

Court Judgments

These assessments of the Roman legal system may be part of what Paul meant when he spoke of the absurdity of Jesus-followers taking each other to "court before the unrighteous" (1 Corinthians 6:1; the same Greek word for "unrighteous," *adikoi*, appears also in 6:9 although in 6:9 it is usually translated "wrongdoer"; the word connotes fraudulent use of money in 2 Corinthians 7:2). Did Paul hold the view that the judgments of the courts are skewed toward injustice? If so, he would have been drawing on a motif that ran deeply with Judeo-Christian traditions. For instance, the prophet Micah had once spoken against the elite, saying:

They all lie in wait for blood, and they hunt each other with nets. Their hands are skilled to do evil; the official and the judge ask for a bribe, and the powerful dictate what they desire; thus they pervert justice. (7:2–3)

As we have already seen, the letter written in the name of James the brother of Jesus says something similar about the courts of the Roman world being dominated by the interests of the elite (2:6). And in the Gospel of Luke, Jesus is remembered as telling a parable that develops along comparable lines.

In a certain city there was a judge who neither feared God nor had respect for people. In that city there was a widow who kept coming to him and saying, "Grant me justice against my opponent." For a while he refused; but later he said to himself, "Though I have no fear of God and no respect for anyone, yet because this widow keeps bothering me, I will grant her justice, so that she may not wear me out by continually coming." (18:2–5)

Judges who pronounce judgment on the basis of what is most beneficial for them and for those who bribe them (as in Micah and the letter of James), or on the basis of what is

165

most convenient for their own circumstances (Luke)—could these be part of the context informing Paul's instruction to avoid going to "court before the unrighteous"?

We will never know the story behind Phileros's positive verdict from a local judge—a verdict that he wanted to attribute to the deities and their recognition of his innocence. Not everyone's experiences of the courts were as positive. Some would have claimed that "justice" had not prevailed because, in the words of Micah, "the powerful dictate what they desire" and "pervert justice." Similarly, in a parody of the Roman legal system, the Roman satirist Juvenal had one of the characters in his narrative speak the following words: "A man's word is believed in exact proportion to the amount of cash he keeps in his strongbox" (*Satire* Book 3, 1.141–42).

Assessing an Ethic of Detachment

We have seen that being engaged with others in a contest for social prominence often brought people into social combat with others. There was another option, however, that some Vesuvian residents preferred to pursue—that is, a life of detachment that distanced a person from the difficulties that others experience. For instance, in one magnificent house prestigiously placed to overlook the sea (7.16.22, the House of Fabius Rufus), someone scratched a graffito on a wall that said: "Pleasant it is over the sea" (CErc [1973], 102n28). This looks like a simple enough observation written by someone resident in the equivalent of a seaside mansion. But the graffito is a quotation from a famous poem by Lucretius, where the phrase does more than state pleasantries about the sea. (All quotations in the remainder of this paragraph are from Lucretius, *On the Nature*

of Things 2.1–10.) Advocating Epicurean philosophy, Lucretius's poem from the first century BCE suggests that things are pleasant for the Epicurean when he gazes "from shore onto the trials of others" along their way on the metaphorical seas of life, watching them as they struggle to survive the dangerous storms that come to them. While there is no pleasure in seeing their misfortune itself, the Epicurean nonetheless gains pleasure from the fact that he himself remains at a distance. Unlike other people, the Epicurean does not allow himself to be engulfed in emotional distress or affected by tragedies all around him. He feels the same pleasant satisfaction when he watches "armies battling on a plain," since he has "no part in their peril" one way or another. The Epicurean imagined the deities to be distant and uninterested in mortal human beings (as noted in chapter 5); Lucretius imagined that a similar lack of concern should characterize the Epicurean's demeanor toward others. In this regard, Lucretius stated that the most pleasant thing is to watch others make mistakes in life, "vainly searching for the true path of life." Content to let events unfold as they will, the Epicurean simply "occup[ies] a lofty sanctuary of the mind, well fortified with the teachings of the wise." The attainment of personal tranquility requires disengagement in life—especially disengagement from the hardships and misfortunes of other people's lives. The Epicurean exaltation of personal "freedom" and happiness easily translated into a posture of detachment.

From start to finish, the texts of the New Testament decry detachment of this kind, despite its claim to be fortified by "lofty" and "wise" rationality. Two of Jesus's parables (and many more of his sayings beyond that) make the point forcefully, drawing on resources deeply embedded within Judean ethics. The first is the parable of the rich man and Lazarus (Luke 16:19–31). This story contrasts the situation of two men: (1) a wealthy man who "was dressed in purple and fine linen" and "feasted sumptuously every day" (16:19), and (2) a poor man who was "covered with sores" that dogs would lick and who "longed to satisfy his hunger with what fell from the rich man's table" (16:20–21). Day after day, the man embedded in the world of opulence modeled an ethic of detachment in relation to the impoverished man. The parable says nothing about the rich man having a long list of ethical deficiencies; it simply implies (since Lazarus continues in his state of abject need) that the rich man lived his life on the basis of non-involvement toward "the trials of others." Like someone in Pompeii's opulent House of Fabius Rufus, this rich man might have gone from sumptuous feast to sumptuous feast, reciting the words, "Pleasant it is over the sea." The sting is found as the parable extends the narrative of the lives of these two men into the realm of the afterlife, where their situation is dramatically reversed: Lazarus is blessed while the rich man suffers in perpetual agony (16:22–31).

The second example is the parable of the Good Samaritan (Luke 10:30–37). This story recounts different reactions three people have when they encounter a person in need—specifically, a man who had been robbed, stripped, beaten, and left for dead along a roadside. Two socially prominent people come upon him, one after another, but they simply pass him by in a state of detachment. The third person (himself a social outsider) extends assistance to the man in tragic need. Luke remembered Jesus as ending the parable with the words, "Go and do the same" (10:37).

These two parables disparage an ethic of detached non-involvement. And within the canon of early Christian writings, they are not outliers; instead, they lie at the heart of the social ethic of the early Jesus-movement. Following the lead of the one they called "Lord," the apostolic voices within that movement denounced an ethic of "pleasant" disinterestedness; instead, they consistently advocated a rigorously non-detached social ethic, lauding instead the posture of self-giving in the service of others. In a world marked by aggressive combat and its tragic consequences, the apostolic voices articulated a vision that ran along different lines altogether. For them, Jesus-groups were to be characterized by an ethos of non-combative relationality, enabling Jesus-followers to be refreshed by a supportive mutuality, as a foretaste of a blessedness that awaited them in the "kingdom" of their deity. They were excited by this vision. It was part of their conviction that (in the words of Mark 1:15) "the kingdom of God has come near."

In this kingdom, even the word "enemy" was not immune from being reconceptualized. Jesus was remembered as commanding his followers, "Love your enemies" (Matthew 5:44; Luke 6:27, 35). Paul interpreted this command not in terms of an emotional posture but in terms of an ethical one: "If your enemies are hungry, feed them; if they are thirsty, give them something to drink" (Romans 12:20). If there was excitement in the vision proclaimed by early Christian apostles, there was also challenge. Even the combative character of life was reconstructed in their vision of a kingdom that invoked fresh ways of seeing the world and novel forms of relationality.

14 Business and Success

About that time, a significant disturbance broke out concerning the Way [that is, the early Jesus-movement]. A silversmith named Demetrius made silver shrines of Artemis [the deity of Ephesus] and brought significant wealth to the artisans. He assembled them together, along with artisans of similar trades, and said the following.

"Colleagues, you know that we get our wealth from this business. You also see and hear that not only in Ephesus but in almost the whole of Asia this Paul has persuaded and drawn away a considerable number of people by saying that deities made with hands are not deities. And there is danger not only that *this trade of ours may come into disrepute* but also that the temple of the great goddess Artemis will be scorned, and she will be deprived of her majesty that brought all Asia and the world to worship her."

When the artisans heard this, they were enraged and shouted, "Great is Artemis of the Ephesians!" The city was filled with confusion.

Acts 19:23–29 NRSV alt.

The Deities and Business

The silversmiths of Ephesus shouted "Great is Artemis of the Ephesians." The "significant wealth" they derived from their "trade" resulted from devotion to the primary deity of their city, Artemis. We do not have much evidence of silversmiths in Pompeii, but metal workers clearly resided there, especially workers in bronze and iron (for instance, the workshops at 1.6.1, 1.6.3, 1.10.7, 1.13.6, 6.3.12/13, 7.4.60/61, 7.7.6, 8.7.5, 8.7.7/8). And, of course, some of the metalwork crafted in those shops was related to the worship of deities. For instance, archaeologists found that bronze figures of Bacchus were being produced in the Pompeian metal shop at 7.4.60/61. If the workers there were ever told that "deities made with human hands are not deities," they too might have connected the obvious dots between that message and their own economic welfare. (For further discourse about idolatry see also Plutarch's *Isis and Osiris* 379D). Perhaps Plutarch had noted that the devotional expectations of ordinary people were being stoked by craftworkers who enhanced their own incomes by promoting a fascination with deity figurines.

Of course, metal-worker entrepreneurs were no different from any ordinary individual who wanted to bolster his or her coffers. Inscriptions and mosaics at the entryway of Pompeian residences frequently expressed the entrepreneurial interests of the householder. The words "Hail profit" (*salve lucrum*) greeted visitors at one residence in Pompeii (*CIL* 10.874 at 7.1.46); "Profit is joy" (*lucrum gaudium*) at another (*CIL* 10.875 at 6.14.39); "Make profit" (*lucru[m] acipe*) at another (*CIL* 10.876, whose find-spot is now uncertain). For many Pompeians, success was enhanced through devotion to the deity Mercury, the deity of commerce. If he brought success to their businesses, they could find joy through their profits.

Figure 14.1. This silver cup was found, together with a similar one, alongside the body of a Pompeii resident who was fleeing the eruption; both cups were adorned with imagery pertaining to the worship of Isis (MANN 6045).

in early Christian texts, see especially 1 Thessalonians 1:9; 1 Corinthians 8:4–6; 10:14; 2 Corinthians 6:16; Romans 1:23; Acts 14:15; 15:20, 29; 17:24, 29; 19:26; 1 John 5:21; Jude 10–11; Revelation 9:20.)

The connection that Demetrius highlighted in Acts 19 (between the worship of deities and the economic interests of businesses) was gently disparaged by the late first- and early second-century essayist Plutarch. He ridiculed those who "give credence to workers in metal, stone, or wax, who make their images of gods in the likeness of human beings, and they have such images fashioned, and dress them up, and worship them" (*Superstition* 167D–E;

Different Attitudes within Christian Texts

Some apostolic figures within early Christianity were not opposed to people making profits. It was noted in chapter 11, for instance, that Paul praised people like Stephanus and Philemon—entrepreneurs who had used their profits in ways that met with the apostle's approval. The author of Acts depicts Lydia, a female Jesus-follower, as "a dealer in purple cloth" (Acts 16:14), whose house was available for Paul's use as he spread the gospel in Philippi. Paul himself was a tradesman, and it is possible that he may even have been in business with Philemon at some point (as some have thought on the basis of what Paul wrote in Philemon 17–19). Nonetheless, notice what

Figure 14.2. A shrine in the House of the Cryptoporticus (1.6.2) with Mercury (the deity of commerce, here holding a caduceus) in the inner fresco and a small platform for household offerings in front of him, while snakes depict the benign spirits of the house; one of the snakes climbs the painted altar while the other approaches the shrine's platform.

Paul did when calculating his profit-and-loss margins on the spreadsheet of his accumulated status:

> Whatever I considered to be assets, I have calculated these things to be losses because of Christ. Even more, I calculate *all* things to be losses because of the better value of the knowledge of Christ Jesus my Lord. Because of him, I count all things as losses, and consider them to be excrement, so that I might gain Christ. (Philippians 3:7–8, my translation)

All the items on his status account sheet that could conceivably count as "profit" Paul simply moved to the "loss" column, in order to gain the only true profit, "Christ Jesus my Lord," the only "commodity" he considered

worth "possessing." He made use of the economic metaphor earlier in the letter when he stated simply, "To live is Christ, to die is gain" (1:21 NIV alt.).

Within early Christian discourse, voices harsher than Paul's can be heard regarding "the bottom line." In chapter 11, we noted that the author of the letter of James critiqued the favoritism that privileges the rich at the expense of the poor ("you have dishonored the poor"; see James 2:1–6). The same letter offers extensive critique of the rich themselves:

> Come now, you rich people, weep and wail for the miseries that are coming to you. Your riches have rotted, and your clothes are moth-eaten. Your gold and silver have rusted, and

Figure 14.3. A fresco on the external wall of a pub in Herculaneum (6.14), advertising the cost of four types of wine (*ad cucumas*, "to the vessels," with the prices listed below), and above that a portrait of Sancus, the deity of trustworthiness (perhaps suggesting to passersby that the wine was not watered down and the prices were fair)

their rust will be evidence against you, and it will eat your flesh like fire. You have laid up treasure for the last days. Listen! The wages of the laborers who mowed your fields, which you kept back by fraud, cry out, and the cries of the harvesters have reached the ears of the Lord of hosts. You have lived on the earth in luxury and in pleasure; you have fattened your hearts in a day of slaughter. (5:1–5)

This tirade against the rich who live "in luxury and in pleasure" while oppressing their laborers and defrauding their harvesters is

not a world away from the advice of James's famous brother, Jesus of Nazareth, whom the letter of James later proclaimed to be the heavenly "Lord" (1:1; 2:1). Jesus was remembered to have told a parable in which a wealthy entrepreneur boasts about "reap[ing] where [he] did not sow and gather[ing] where [he] did not scatter"—as if there are no moral boundaries to the stretch of his business investments (Matthew 25:26). In keeping with that denunciation, Jesus was also remembered for overturning the tables of what he deemed to be opportunistic money changers ("robbers") in the temple of Jerusalem (21:12–13), and for saying:

> Do not store up for yourselves treasures on earth, where moth and rust consume and where thieves break in and steal; but store up for yourselves treasures in heaven, where neither moth nor rust consumes and where thieves do not break in and steal. For where your treasure is, there your heart will be also. (6:19–21; for other images of household security in Jesus's teachings, see 12:29 [also Luke 11:21–22]; 13:52; 24:43 [also Luke 12:39])

Figure 14.4. An ironclad strongbox from Pompeii, which would have been proudly displayed toward the front of a residence while containing money and precious items of the household

171

This contrast between storing up treasures that matter and storing up treasures that ultimately are worthless seems to have been a hallmark of Jesus's discourse. Jesus made much the same point in a story introduced by the words, "Take care! Be on your guard against all kinds of greed; for one's life does not consist in the abundance of possessions" (Luke 12:15). The story itself is as follows:

> The land of a rich man produced abundantly. And he thought to himself, "What should I do, for I have no place to store my crops? . . . I will do this: I will pull down my barns and build larger ones, and there I will store all my grain and my goods. And I will say to my soul, 'Soul, you have ample goods laid up for many years; relax, eat, drink, be merry.'" But God said to him, "You fool! This very night your life is being demanded of you. And the things you have prepared, whose will they be?" (12:16–20)

The moral of the story is then emphasized by Jesus (12:21): "So it is with those who store up treasures for themselves but are not rich toward God."

Jesus and James are remembered as sharing a common voice in this regard. Both placed stories of entrepreneurial success into a larger narrative that caused the hearer to question the very notion of what constituted "success." This is because those narratives showcase a deity whose value system challenges the most fundamental expectations about status. The "fool" in Jesus's story is much like the portrait of "those who want to be rich" in 1 Timothy 6:9, since they "fall into temptation and are trapped by many senseless and harmful desires that plunge people into ruin and destruction." The potential link connecting entrepreneurial success and spiritual failure runs throughout

many texts written by Jesus-followers. In that regard, they were articulating a sentiment that was often voiced by their lord, whom they remembered as saying radical things, such as, "Sell your possessions and give to the poor" (Luke 12:33), or more extensively, "Sell all that you own and distribute the money to the poor, and you will have treasure in heaven" (18:22; see also 19:8–9). Or even more boldly still, "No one can serve two masters; for a slave

Figure 14.5. Painted outside a workshop (9.7.7), this fresco depicts the deity of commerce in the upper register (Mercury, with his money bag, caduceus, and winged shoes) and a shop worker and customer in the lower register.

will either hate the one and love the other, or be devoted to the one and despise the other. You cannot serve God and wealth" (Matthew 6:24). Early Christian discourse makes the point repeatedly that "the lure of wealth" is so overwhelming that it can easily uproot devotion to the deity proclaimed by Jesus-followers (13:22; Mark 4:19).

Economic Critique in the Book of Revelation

In the last book of the New Testament, the Revelation of John, things come to a head in this regard. In a sense, John seems to combine the either-or articulated by Jesus (for instance, in Matthew 6:24) with the disdain for the rich articulated by Jesus's brother James (in James 5:1–5). Consequently, whereas Demetrius the silversmith of Ephesus wanted to run Christian exclusivists out of his city (according to Acts 19, recounted at the start of this chapter), John himself also wanted Christians "out," since his exclusivist commitments included a sharp economic critique. This is what he meant when he wrote, "Come out of her, my people, so that you do not take part in her sins" (Revelation 18:4). Paul had said something similar and used some passages from the Judean scriptures to make the point ("come out from them and be separate from them," citing Isaiah 52:11 in 2 Corinthians 6:15). But for Paul the call to "come out" was primarily directed against specific practices of idolatry; for John, idolatry needed to be seen as permeating the whole of Roman society, including its economic structures.

For this reason, John the Seer saw things in dramatically stark terms. He connected dots between phenomena in his world very perceptively. The interconnectivity of all aspects of the ancient world was like an ever-reinforcing spiral: politics merged with military power, which merged with business, which merged with devotion to the deities, which merged again with politics. This ubiquitous interconnectivity of phenomena meant that no matter where an analysis of the health of the ancient world might start, John was able to connect each individual component to the reign of Satan, the devilish and cunning spiritual opponent of John's deity. This is because, in John's view, Satan had managed to kidnap the whole of human society and conscript it for his own purposes. In John's estimate, although his contemporaries may not have known it, they were merely puppets in the play stage-managed by the satanic being, and they were all the worse for it.

According to John's presentation of things, there are two places where the influence of Satan is not to be found: in the heavenly throne room, where John's deity reigns as sovereign (as depicted in Revelation 4–5; see also 12:7–9, 13), and in the restored eschatological creation (as depicted in Revelation 21–22). Apart from those two places, the influence of the beguiling Satan is everywhere, permeating every aspect of human society, including politics, military, economics, and devotion to the deities. It is little wonder, then, that John identified Satan as "the deceiver of the whole world" (12:9). Although this can mean simply that Satan has deceived "the inhabitants of the earth" (13:14), it probably has a broader register, suggesting that Satan has set in place a system of tragic deception that has invaded, infiltrated, and afflicted every component of human society.

This is most clearly depicted in the symbolic narrative that weaves its way through Revelation 12–18. In Revelation 12, Satan is depicted as "a great red dragon" (12:3) who tries

Figure 14.6. A fresco depicting the Greek myth about a serpent-dragon who killed the baby Opheltes by strangulation; here the baby's mother looks on in horror (right) while soldiers attempt to kill the serpent, to no avail (from 6.17.9/10, MANN 8987).

to usurp the sovereignty of the true deity in the heavenly world by seeking to devour the special male child of a special woman. In the imagery of this apocalyptic text, the woman probably symbolizes both Israel and Mary the mother of Jesus simultaneously, while the male child symbolizes Jesus Christ. As the narrative of this chapter continues, the son is unharmed by the dragon because he "was snatched away and taken to God and to his throne" (12:5). The dragon is thrown down to earth and is now identified as "that ancient serpent" (12:9). On earth the serpent continues his assault, now directed against the woman (perhaps symbolizing the church at this point in the narrative) and her other offspring.

The fact that we have moved from the world of entrepreneurial success to the world of mythological narrative is, for the author of Revelation, precisely the point. In John's view, the trick of Satan has been to embed individual components of society within an ideological narrative that looks impressive and beneficent but is really something quite different. Throughout the rest of Revelation 12–18, John unmasks the individual components of society and places them within a narrative of a much different sort from the regnant ideology of the day. As the dragon stands on the shores of the sea (12:18), a beast emerges from the sea (the sea symbolizing the traditional abode of evil), with the satanic dragon concentrating its power within this beast (13:1–2). In chapter 7, we traced some of the components of John's depiction of this beast's satanically empowered reign—especially in terms of Rome's military campaigns, Rome's imperial rule over the world that mattered, and the cultic worship of Roman imperial figures. Without retracing those steps, we need here to see that the economic system overseen by Rome is also portrayed by John as being engulfed within the clutches of the satanic beast.

The first clear sign of this comes in Revelation 13:16–17 (see also 14:9, 11). This passage speaks of all people being required to align themselves with the beast in order simply to buy or sell. This is symbolically depicted by means of the requirement to have a mark on one's right hand (the hand used for handshakes that seal business deals) or on one's forehead (advertising one's true identity). Economic prosperity in the world narrated by John requires compliance with the satanic program (even though the satanic character of economic systems goes unrecognizable to those complicit with those systems).

In Revelation 18 the economic critique of Satan's reign through the beast is most evident. Having likened the domination system to a great whore (17:1, 5, 15; compare 19:2: "the great whore who corrupted the earth with her fornication"), John says that "she glorified herself and lived luxuriously" (18:7). This "whorific" spirituality of luxury permeates "the merchants of the earth," who "have grown rich from the power of her luxury" (18:3) and "gained wealth from her" (18:15). Similarly, "all who had ships at sea grew rich by her wealth" (18:19). If the merchants "were the magnates of the earth," it is only because "all nations were deceived" by the sorcery of the harlot (18:23).

The merchants of Ephesus saw their profits linked to Artemis (as we saw at the start

Figure 14.7. A Pompeian fresco of business being conducted on the streets of the town (perhaps in its forum; from the country club of Julia Felix, 2.4, MANN 9063 [sometimes listed as 9062])

Figure 14.8. The frescoed shrine overlooking the countertop of a fast-food and wine bar (at 1.8.8), with Mercury on the far left (holding a money bag in his right hand and his caduceus in his left) to help ensure the success of the business (Bacchus is on the far right, dripping wine down to his panther; the *genius* of the householder is in the middle of the fresco, with two *lares* on either side of him); one of the eleven countertop vats at this food and wine bar contained 1,385 bronze coins when it was discovered by archaeologists.

of this chapter). The merchants of Pompeii often imagined their profits to result from Mercury's beneficial enhancement of their profits. John wanted his readers to see another spiritual reality operating within the economic structures of his world—a satanic spirituality. In Revelation 18:12–13 John unmasked the spiritual ethos of the satanic system in concrete terms by including a list of its economic priorities:

> gold, silver, jewels and pearls, fine linen, purple, silk and scarlet, all kinds of scented wood, all articles of ivory, all articles of costly wood, bronze, iron, and marble, cinnamon, spice, incense, myrrh, frankincense, wine, olive oil, choice flour and wheat, cattle

and sheep, horses and chariots, slaves—that is, human lives.

This list overviews the basic economic drivers of the Roman age. And it seems to move from the more costly and precious entries (gold, silver, jewels) to the more ordinary and mundane (cattle, sheep, horses, chariots). Notice, however, that the last entry in this list of commodities is "slaves," with John making the point that these are "human lives." Here the economic structures of John's world are ultimately exposed as satanic in character—as illustrated by their valuing of human lives simply as commodities useful for perpetuating the economic well-being of those at the helm of the system. This damning critique is an extremely rare moment in ancient discourse about slavery—even within Christian discourse. John peered into the economic structures of his day, driven as they were by slavery, and saw Satan in the driver's seat of it all. In John's view, human lives created by the sovereign Lord of creation had been conscripted by the system orchestrated and overseen by the great deceiver.

John was confident that the true deity would ultimately triumph over the system undergirded by satanic deception. He foresaw a time when "the great city clothed in fine linen, in purple and scarlet, adorned with gold, with jewels, and with pearls" (Revelation 18:16) will be laid to waste (Revelation 18–19), causing the "weeping and mourning" of merchants (18:15) and "all whose trade is on the sea" (18:17–19). Together with the destruction of the satanic system will come the destruction of satanic commerce, with the complete disappearance of "an artisan of any trade" (18:22).

Against this backdrop, it is easy to see that John's call "Come out of her, my people" has an economic dimension to it. This helps to explain why he was so critical of some of his peers in Revelation 2–3, where the seven churches were addressed specifically (through their "angel," or *genius*, as we saw in chapter 7). For instance, some Jesus-followers in Pergamum and in Thyatira are said to "practice fornication" (2:14, 20–22). In the symbol system of Revelation, that charge is probably not literally about a deviant sexual practice; instead, it seems to point metaphorically in the direction of economic engagement with the satanic system. That metaphorical meaning allowed John to describe "the kings of the earth" in sexual terms as those "who

committed fornication and lived in luxury with her [the whore]" (18:9; see also the metaphorical use of "fornication" in 17:2; 18:3). Similarly, some Jesus-followers in Laodicea were saying, "I am rich, I have prospered, and I need nothing" (3:17). These Jesus-devotees were presenting themselves in ways not unlike the embodiment of the Roman ideal—rather like the propaganda of Roman peace and prosperity. But the one whom John called "one like the Son of Man" rebuked these same people with words that transform economic categories into spiritual ones:

> You do not realize that you are wretched, pitiable, poor, blind, and naked. Therefore I counsel you to buy from me gold refined by fire so that you may be rich; and white robes to clothe you and to keep the shame of your nakedness from being seen; and salve to anoint your eyes so that you may see. (3:17–18)

Evidently, some Jesus-devotees had not done much to divorce themselves from the economic structures of the Roman world. That simply irked John the Seer, who thought they needed to be removed from it all. Other apostolic figures were less bothered. Paul, for instance, simply assumed that Jesus-followers would operate within the economic sphere, even if their devotion to Jesus Christ was to make a difference in how they operated within it and what they did with the resources they accumulated. Paul repeatedly urged Jesus-followers to get to work and earn money in order to financially support the Jesus-movement among their contemporaries (for example, 1 Thessalonians 4:11 [see also 2:9]; 2 Thessalonians 3:6–10). But John the Seer saw things in a different light, making connections in ways that others did not.

177

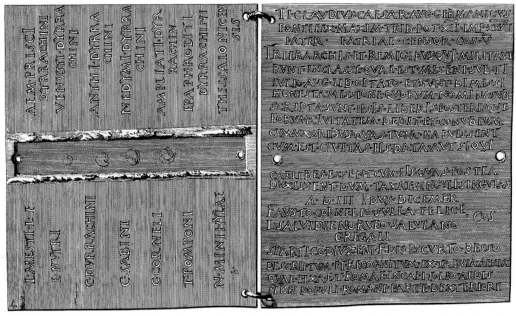

Figure 14.9. A drawing of a wax tablet from the House of Jucundus (5.1.26), with the terms of a business transaction listed on the right and the witnesses to the agreement listed on the left (the two parts linked together with modern rings; see credits)

Associations and Deity Devotion

John's denunciation of artisans and merchants probably had something to do with the fact that occupational associations of his day usually had cultic dimensions to them. In order to have success at even the most basic level, artisans and merchants would have needed to join a guild for their professions, usually known as an association (*collegium*), based within the urban center where they resided. These associations inevitably had a devotional component in which the worship of one or more deities was prioritized as part of the group's corporate gatherings. Thus in order to be successful in business, entrepreneurs had to involve themselves in dinners and celebrations in which deities of various sorts would have been worshiped. This, for John, was part of the deceit of Satan, whose system had engulfed the world and whose

tentacles had worked their way into every manifestation of civilization.

Associations were widespread by the end of the first century, but the level of their concentration seems to have varied significantly from one urban center to another. In fact, Pompeii's material record contains no definitive instances of groups referring to themselves as associations. A number of occupational groups had formed in Pompeii by the time of its destruction. From graffiti and inscriptions, we know of the existence of about two dozen occupational groups, including goldsmiths, carpenters, innkeepers, cart drivers, felt makers, cooks, laundry workers (fullers), dyers, mule drivers, shippers, fishermen, bakers, fruit sellers, garlic sellers, porters, cloth dealers, percussion musicians, shoemakers, barbers, perfume makers and dealers, and grape pickers. These occupational groups may not have

Figure 14.10. A fresco of a street procession of carpenters carrying a platform whose canopy covers several figurines illustrating carpenters' work; at the front of the platform are figurines of two people from Greek mythology—the inventor Daedalus (the patron of the carpenters) and his son Icarus, lying dead at his feet after flying too close to the sun (from the external wall between 6.7.8 and 6.7.9, MANN 8991).

been associations per se. Strictly speaking, associations (or *collegia*) were legal entities, and there is little indication that these occupational groups in Pompeii had any legal status. For that, they would have needed their own internally elected magistrates, their own bylaws, their own membership requirements, and their own common treasury. There is very little evidence to suggest that occupational groups in Pompeii had organized themselves into legally recognized associations of this kind, with local magistrates giving them the right to assemble. But whether we recognized them as occupational groups or as guild associations, it was common for groups of people working in the same line of work to meet together for meals and, often, to commit themselves to support one another in various ways, with their corporate gatherings often including a devotional dimension.

The laundry workers (or fullers) of Pompeii offer a good example of this. They seem to have been sponsored by Eumachia, the wealthy woman whom we have already mentioned on various occasions (see chapters 6 and 11). The statue of Eumachia in what is now called "the Eumachia building" was dedicated to her specifically by the fullers of Pompeii, which suggests that she had acted as their patron. In view of Eumachia's strong and explicit promotion of the Roman imperial order (as noted in chapter 6), we must assume that imperial devotion was an essential component of the gatherings whenever the fullers of Pompeii met together as an occupational group. It was precisely that combination of politico-religious and economic influence on the devotional alignments of these groups that caused John to see the whole situation as inherently diabolical.

Crafting Penultimate Solutions

Unlike other apostolic voices, John's voice called Jesus-followers to pull out of civic and occupational entanglements, since virtually all of them could in some shape or fashion be traced back to a system controlled by Satan. But what were Jesus-followers to do? Did John expect them to move out of the cities? But cities were intricately connected to rural environments, so even moving out would not keep them from exposure to contaminants. If they remained in urban centers, were they meant to eke out a living running small businesses that somehow managed to survive without any links to occupational groups or associations? Were they to operate insignificant businesses out of paltry workshops, uninfected by Satan's economic structures? Who could do that? Perhaps a barber with a pair of scissors? Perhaps an independent carpenter with a hammer, some nails, and a store of wood? Or an independent carriage-driver? A chicken keeper? A cushion seller? A "rag-and-bone man" (who collected people's unused items and sold them to others)?

All these relatively "lowly" occupations are evidenced by graffiti at Pompeii. But so too are other professions that would inevitably have inserted Jesus-followers further into the system, with the "satanic contaminants" more obviously affecting them. Would a baker who adopted Jesus-devotion in Pergamum or Thyatira or Laodicea have been expected to drop his membership with the bakers' association and suffer the economic consequences? Would this have impeded the spread of the "good news" by cutting off relationships with others who were not Jesus-followers?

These questions go unanswered. John knew the problem well, highlighting connections between cultural phenomena in a fashion unprecedented among apostolic figures. He knew that the ultimate solution rested in the hands of his deity (e.g., the new heaven and the new earth), but in the meantime, he seems to have left his first-century audiences to figure out their own penultimate solutions.

PART FOUR

Protocols of Household Effectiveness

Household and Slaves

15

There is neither slave nor free . . . for all of you are one in Christ Jesus. . . .
Through love, become enslaved to one another.

Galatians 3:28; 5:13, my translation

Slavery in Pompeii and Beyond

Slaves were incorporated into every part of the Roman world. Each facet of that world had been built on the sweat (and often the blood) of the servile workforce. No part of that world could have functioned without slaves. They served an endless range of functions. Wherever you looked, slaves were there. They were like the electricity that the whole system relied on. If a magic wand could have removed all the slaves from ancient culture, everything would have come crashing down immediately, with anarchy rising in the aftermath.

As we saw in chapter 14, John the Seer captured something of this when he listed slaves as part of the commodities that ensured the perpetuation of the system (Revelation 18:12–13, with slaves being at the bottom of the list). The only places where slaves might not be found were the very small workshops in which poor artisans worked for themselves—perhaps

having been recently freed and being unable to do much more than simply get by. With the possible exception of those small residential hovels, slaves would have been everywhere—in the civic administration buildings (as scribes, accountants, etc.), in public baths (e.g., as fire stokers), at temples (as assistants to priests), in workshops (as workforce commodities), and in the households of the majority of Vesuvian residences. Although this chapter will discuss slaves within the ancient household, it is already obvious that this is only one slice of the much larger pie. But it is in the household that we see the functions, identities, and relationalities of slaves particularly clearly.

Artifacts and graffiti attest to some of the tasks carried out by slaves within the households they served: cleaning premises, preparing and presenting food and wine to the householder and his family, and washing the feet of the householder's guests. One inscription from the House of the Moralist captures one

Figure 15.1. A fresco of diners who have gathered for a dinner party, as a young slave waits to assist them as instructed (from 5.2.4, MANN 120031; the words written above the diners read, "Make yourselves comfortable, I'm going to sing" on the left and, on the right, "That's right! To your health!")

of these rather basic tasks: "Let water wash your feet clean and a slave wipe them dry" (*CIL* 4.7698a).

There was, however, a much uglier side to the master-slave relationship. This went beyond the iron stocks that some masters used to chain their slaves—as was the case for one unfortunate slave in the Villa of the Mosaic Columns (HGE12), who died in the eruption with shackles around his legs, and fastened to the ground, leaving him unable to attempt an escape from the volcanic chaos all around him. The uglier side of the master-slave relationship often included sexual relations. "Take advantage of the cook, whenever you like, as it suits you" (*CIL* 4.1863). Perhaps no other graffito from the Vesuvian towns captures the essence of the relation of householder and slave as well as this one. It suggests that the cook of the household was subject to the householder's advances whenever the householder had sexual desires. Simply put, the household sustained relationships between householder and slaves that were often abusive by today's standards. The householder had the dominant (domineering) power, and the slave was usually little more than his property, his chattel, his possession. If the householder was tired, he went to his bed; if he was hungry, he ate food that his resources had purchased; if he had sexual desires, he had sex with a slave (or two) whom he had bought. It was as simple as that. The slave might be female or male, according to the householder's preference and regardless of the slave's own well-being. (Compare the case of the male slave Icarus, who was teased by a friend for having to penetrate his master Ampliatus sexually [CIL 4.2375, near 7.12.15].) A slave was ultimately the possession of his/her master, and a possession does not determine its own use or function.

It is not surprising, then, to hear this advice from the Roman poet Horace (65–8 BCE): "If your groin is swelling and a housemaid or a slave boy is at hand, arousing constant desire, do you prefer to burst with tension? Not me: I enjoy love that is available and easy" (Satires 1.2.116–19). Along the same lines, the Latin poet Martial (about 40–103) praised a man for being frugal with his resources, since the man chose to have sex with his slaves' wives free of charge instead of having to purchase the services of prostitutes (Epigrams 4.66). Even the "wife" of a slave was the possession of the householder. So too was the slave's peculium—the money a slave might have been able to accumulate during his/her time in servitude. Although a slave could use his/her peculium to eventually buy his/her freedom, at any point a master could take possession of the peculium to fund any purposes of his own choosing, to the loss of the slave's prospects. If a female slave were to be freed by her master, her past would continue to plague her survival strategies. A female who was a former slave had inevitably been used to offset her master's sexual desires; this set her apart from the ideal of the marriageable female, who was to be chaste prior to marriage.

Slavery and the Sex Trade

Some householders bought slaves precisely for the purpose of the sex trade. Some spaces within larger Pompeian houses have a high concentration of frescos depicting ordinary men and women having sex. It is hard to know what the purpose of those frescos might have been. It is possible that they simply adorned a room in the slave section of the house. In that case, they might have reinforced the slaves' identity as sexual possessions of the householder. But is also possible that these frescos reinforced the sex trade operation within the house itself.

This has sometimes been suggested for the House of the Vettii in Pompeii. The owners of this house (named Restitutus and Conviva, perhaps brothers, but not necessarily so) began life as slaves, but they eventually gained their freedom and went on to become extremely wealthy Augustales, their house being one of the more impressive of the Pompeian houses (6.15.1, although it is not as opulent as the houses of the "old-money elite"). They made a large portion of their wealth from their rural vineyards and their participation in the wine trade. One section of their house was adorned with

Figure 15.2. Frescos in the public space of the House of the Vettii often depict mythological scenes of love gained and love lost (such as this, as Theseus abandons Ariadne, who is comforted by a cupid, in situ); by contrast, frescos in the service area of the house (populated by household slaves) regularly featured couples having sex.

Members of the household, together with their invited guests and clients, would have entered the house through the grandest of the house's entrances (at 9.5.14). The other two entrances into the house tell a slightly different story, however. The second entrance had a phallic symbol above it (9.5.15; see figure 15.3), and next to the third entrance a graffito announced the price of "Optata," who "sells herself for two asses" (the "ass" being the smallest monetary coin in circulation, with two asses being about half the price of a glass of wine; *CIL* 4.5105, inscribed outside 9.5.16). A large erotic fresco greeted the person who entered through this third entrance, being placed centrally on the wall of the room that the entrance opened onto. Set between these two entrances is a room decorated with five frescos of couples having sex. With this combination of features, archaeologists have identified this as a "little brothel"—a larger one being situated a few streets to the west (at 7.12.18). This business operated within the household of an elite resident and his family. And in that light, rather than simply "selling herself," Optata was probably a slave who worked in these premises to bolster the coffers of her master's household.

provocative frescos. If this was an area where slaves were used in a sex-trade operation, it would seem that at least some of the great success of these prominent businessmen resulted from their use of their own slaves for purposes of prostitution. These two entrepreneurs had gone from being someone else's possessions (during the time of their own enslavement) to being owners of many other possessions—including slaves used in the sex trade.

Another house where this situation is possible, perhaps even likely, is the so-called House of the Little Brothel (at 9.5.14 through 9.5.16). Although we know very little about the owner, this grand house suggests that the householder came from a family whose wealth reservoirs tapped into "old money."

Perhaps this is the sort of thing that the Christian theologian John Chrysostom (349–407) was speaking about when listing ways that masters sexually abuse their slaves: "Many [slave-owners] have thus [sexually] compelled their domestics and their slaves. Some have drawn them into marriage against their will, and others have forced them to minister to disgraceful services, to infamous love, to acts of rapine and fraud, and violence" (*Homiliae in epistulam ad Philemonem* 1). Early in the second century the Roman orator Dio Chrysostom (40–120) wrote in a fashion similar to John Chrysostom (no relation) when he spoke of how some people "take hapless women and children, captured in war or else purchased with money, and expose them for shameful ends in dirty booths which are flaunted before the eyes in every part of the city" (*The Hunter* 7.133). There is Pompeian evidence of "booths" of this kind (see figure 15.4), where slaves were required to perform sexual services for paying customers. (A multi-room brothel at 7.12.18/19 must have relied primarily on slaves to provide the necessary services.)

We should not imagine that all master-slave relationships were necessarily severe. But the master-slave relationship was inevitably built on the foundation that the slave was the property of the householder, to be used in any way that was deemed most beneficial to the householder. Clearly there was plenty of scope for abuse. The sex trade is one of the most glaring forms of power abuse.

Slavery in the Oplontis Villas

The distinction between slave and free was one of the fundamental contrasts of the Roman world. The contrast may even be displayed in a certain form of decor incorporated into some of the Vesuvian buildings. For instance, a sizeable villa about two miles outside of Pompeii (known as Oplontis Villa A or, sometimes, the Villa of Poppaea) was owned by someone extremely rich. Some of the frescos within this villa are among the most beautiful of the Vesuvian material remains. Wonderfully conceived and executed frescos saturate the living space of the elite, with vividly colorful displays that catch the eye for their depth and detail (see figure 15.5). By contrast, however, the common spaces where slaves would have

Figure 15.3. One entryway to the "House of the Little Brothel" (9.5.15), with a phallic symbol (dark toward the top of the photo) advertising one of the businesses that the householder oversaw within his house

worked were clearly demarcated by a basic, ordinary form of decor. Almost like the black-and-white stripes of a zebra (see figure 15.6), this decor was deemed sufficient for the spaces of the villa where slaves were concentrated in number. Accordingly, the firmly entrenched social distinction between common space and elite space was translated to the walls of this opulent villa in the form of a sharp differentiation in decor.

187

Figure 15.4. A one-room "booth" accessed directly from the street, outfitted with a bed (made of stone, on which a straw mattress would have laid) for purposes of prostitution (at entryway 7.11.12); a phallic symbol exactly like the one shown in figure 15.3 was above the entryway to this booth.

a lowly bakery in Pompeii, for instance, you would probably find a slave or two working alongside the baker's son, getting the baked goods out to the town's residents. But if concrete situations did not always permit the distinction between slave and free to emerge clearly, that distinction nonetheless ran deep within the social fabric of Roman society.

If people lived with a consciousness of this deeply entrenched social differentiation, at times they also died fully aware of that differentiation. A little over three hundred yards away from Villa A in Oplontis, archaeologists have found another villa that operated as a local storage and distribution center for wine and other goods produced in the region. In this working villa, fifty-four skeletons were found in a room looking south to the sea that bordered the villa. Presumably these people were hoping for a maritime rescue from the

Of course, most ordinary residences and workshops did not have the luxury of making such a clear distinction between common space demarcated primarily for slaves and space demarcated primarily for the elite. In

Figure 15.5. Two of the many beautiful frescos that decorate elite space in Oplontis Villa A (painted on flat walls but with effects to suggest otherwise; notice the columns, ledges, niche)

Figure 15.6. The plain wall decor for the common (slave) spaces of Oplontis Villa A

dangers of the angry mountain behind them. But instead of being rescued, they died together when the first of six deadly pyroclastic flows sped down the mountain and destroyed all life.

What is interesting about the unfortunate deaths of these people is how they had assembled themselves in the room that would turn out to be their last abode. The arrangement of their skeletons suggests that these fifty-four people were exceedingly conscious of their social differences even as death was imminent. People who carried nothing of value (or nothing that survived the pyroclastic flows of the eruption, at least) had huddled together toward the rear of the room. They were separated from another group of people huddled together toward the entrance of the room. Those people carried possessions of considerable wealth—coins and jewelry indicating this group to have comprised elite men

and women. For instance, one of the women in this group (who was eight months pregnant) wore a necklace of gold and emerald, together with pearl earrings. People of such elite status would not have been resident in this working villa. This elite woman and her companions must have sought the strategic setting of Villa B when seeking a sea rescue from the eruption. But in their assemblage within their final resting place, they adopted patterns of social separation that coincided with the ideology of slave and free advertised on the frescoed walls of Villa A.

Varieties of Slavery

There were, of course, varieties of slave status. For instance, even within the ranks of the slaves of Oplontis Villa A, the household manager (who himself was probably a slave)

189

seems to have been given a bedroom that was perhaps superior to the kind of sleeping situations that most other slaves would have had (for instance, sleeping in hallways; one hallway had small stone benches perhaps for this purpose). Some kinds of servitude commanded status more than other kinds.

Moreover, some slaves had more opportunity than others to capitalize on their status. At times a slave could benefit from strategically advantageous opportunities even beyond the opportunities of a free person with low status. This was the case for a Pompeian slave named Hesychus. His name appears in the official receipts of Caecilius Jucundus, the Pompeian auctioneer and banker in whose house were found 154 documents outlining financial transactions between Pompeian residents. From five of those documents we can reconstruct that Hesychus was the servile manager of his master's household. In that role, he undertook two transactions on behalf of his master's household. But he also undertook three further transactions as an independent financial agent, including the lending of sizeable amounts of his own money (no doubt, officially part of his *peculium*) to a free(d) man. Clearly Hesychus the slave had time for his own pursuits beyond his obligations to his master's household, and he had reserves of his own (permitted by his master) to finance his own interests.

But even if Hesychus was in a more strategically advantageous position than a certain free(d) man, he was still a slave. The man to whom he lent money might well have been seen at the voting booth on election day, for instance, whereas Hesychus would probably have been flogged if he had tried to cast a vote. Regardless of the extent to which other status indicators might complicate the relational dynamics between free and slave, the binary opposition of slave and free was always in place.

Interpreting status was a never-ending process in the Roman world. Who had more, who had less, and how was that decided? In the binary "slave versus free," sometimes things were simple, sometimes things were complex. But no matter its level of complexity in any situation, this category was always one of the first ones to be employed when determining status in the Roman age.

Neither Slave nor Free?

Against this backdrop, we can imagine how a text like Galatians 3:28 (quoted at the start of this chapter) might have been heard in Jesus-groups of the first century. When the phrase "there is neither slave nor free . . . for all of you are one in Christ Jesus" was read to Jesus-groups, we might hope that slave-owners among them would have rejoiced in the possibility of new forms of relationality emerging between them and their slaves, but the reality was probably somewhat different. Householders might have tilted their heads guardedly, distrusting whether such a wild scenario could even be practicable in any meaningful way. Meanwhile, a few of the braver slaves within the group (including slaves in situations like that of Optata) might have lifted their eyes cautiously, seeing if others had registered the implications of what Paul had written. People would have taken notice of the phrase and given it some thought, one way or another. The negation of the binary opposition in Galatians 3:28 had radical potential: "Neither slave nor free" (see also 1 Corinthians 12:13 and Colossians 3:11).

But what did that mean? What did it look like in practice? Paul says nothing in Galatians to elaborate the point. He spends most of his time exploring another phrase from Galatians 3:28, "neither Jew nor gentile." With regard to ethnic identity, Paul was perfectly clear: one form of identity should not be allowed to dominate over the other. Is that also, then, the implicit point of the phrase "neither slave nor free"? If so, how could that be implemented in realistically meaningful terms in Jesus-groups of the Roman world?

There is little in his letters to suggest that Paul saw this as a radical inversion of social relationships beyond the occasions when Jesus-devotees gathered to celebrate their deity. If Galatians 3:28 served a programmatic function, it was primarily during those celebrations. According to the author of Ephesians, when Jews and gentiles gathered in association "in Christ," the "dividing wall of hostility" between them is removed, with Jesus-devotees being created as "one new humanity" whose representatives live together in peace (2:14–16 NIV). This happened in weekly celebrations of Jesus-followers. In theory, at least, those gatherings allowed for relational innovation as the Spirit of their resurrected lord relativized potential hostilities between different identities. In those meetings, the eschatological reconfiguration of the "one new humanity" was already to be evident.

But what kind of relationality was to take place between slaves and masters beyond the context of those meals? What happened during the ordinary times throughout the week when things needed to be done? Were slaves still slaves then? If slaves were part of the "new creation" in Christ, how applicable was the encouragement that "everything old has passed away; see, everything has become new"

(2 Corinthians 5:17)? To address these questions, we need to look to the letters Philemon, 1 Corinthians, and Colossians/Ephesians.

Master, Slave, and Mission

In a short letter written from prison (see Philemon 1, 9–10), Paul gave recommendations concerning the relationship between a Jesus-follower named Philemon and his slave Onesimus. In that letter, Paul insinuated that Philemon was to devise strategies for mission regarding Onesimus, strategies that followed pathways unhindered by cultural assessments of status. Because Philemon and his slave Onesimus were to be considered "brothers" in Christ (Philemon 16), their relationship needed to be reimagined along fresh lines. This was true both in terms of their relational complexities of the past (11a, 17–19) and of the possibilities for the future (11b, 20–21). Paul does not say exactly what he is thinking regarding what the future possibilities might look like, but a likely scenario is that he wanted Philemon to send Onesimus back in order to assist Paul in his ministry.

Was Philemon to release Onesimus from servitude? Paul makes no explicit suggestion along these lines. We might imagine that scenario to be preferable. Paul, however, might have preferred Onesimus to remain Philemon's slave even while away from Philemon's household. (That sort of thing was not unusual.) If that were to happen, Onesimus's living expenses would have been the responsibility of Philemon. If Philemon were to release Onesimus, however, those expenses would need to be covered by Paul or Onesimus, creating a distraction from their intended mission. Paul left the decision to Philemon, but he may have

191

preferred this Christian slave-owner not to grant freedom to his Christian slave.

Ironically, this sort of thing is possible precisely because the slogan "neither slave nor free" has moved identities of that kind to the periphery within Jesus-groups, reconfiguring cultural expectations about master-slave relationships by the infusion of fresh relational dynamics, even while the master-slave relationship itself remained intact. In other words, if Paul did not necessarily insist on Onesimus's manumission in his letter to Philemon, that was because Paul was realigning lines of relationality and status in Christ, with Philemon and Onesimus now sharing a mutual standing before their deity and sharing a common mission in Christ. The important thing, in Paul's view, was how best to advance that mission and to bring that mutual standing into responsible social embodiment within their own unique historical moment. In that regard (and regardless of what else we might want to say about this), the overturning of slave status was a rather peripheral matter in Paul's strategic thinking about the advancement of his mission.

Much the same is evident in 1 Corinthians 7, where Paul again addressed the practicalities of Christian relationality that is both innovatively new and yet contextually embedded. Before addressing the issue of slavery, Paul gave instructions urging gentiles to remain as gentiles and Jews to remain as Jews (7:17–20)—perhaps filling out the implications of what it means for there to be "neither Jew nor Greek" in Christ. Since neither of these status identifiers means anything of significance (7:19), Paul concluded this section of his discourse saying "Let each of you [i.e., Jew and gentile] remain in the condition in which you were called" (7:20). This echoes the instruction

Paul gave at the beginning of the paragraph: "Let each of you lead the life that the Lord has assigned, to which God called you. This is my rule in all the churches" (7:17).

Having established this "rule," Paul then turned to the issue of slavery in the next paragraph, where he says much the same thing: "Were you a slave when called? . . . In whatever condition you were called, brothers and sisters, there remain with God" (1 Corinthians 7:21, 24). Along the way, however, conventional forms of assessing status are shredded, so that an enslaved Jesus-follower is to be seen as "a freed person belonging to the Lord" and a free Jesus-follower is to be seen as "a slave of Christ" (7:22). Tucked away in Paul's discussion is another instruction: "You were bought [like a slave] with a price; do not become slaves of human masters" (7:23; compare 6:20 and Galatians 4:5). This instruction seems driven by a concern for mission; if you become a slave, your freedom to serve the Lord will be restricted. The same missional concern probably lay behind Paul's lackadaisical attitude toward the prospect of enslaved Jesus-followers remaining in slavery: he seemed to imagine that they were imbedded in situations that otherwise might not be reached. Because enslaved Jesus-followers were well placed to bring Jesus-devotion into such contexts, they should "not be concerned" about their servile status (1 Corinthians 7:21). Moreover, because Paul thought that "the appointed time has grown short" and "the present form of this world" is soon to pass away (7:29, 31), his top priority was to get the word out before "the impending crisis" comes upon this world (7:26). Paul imagined that getting the word out was best done if people remained in the positions they were in when they first became Jesus-devotees, regardless of the social status

Figure 15.7. A fresco of male diners getting ready to leave a dinner party, with three slaves attending them: a young child puts on the shoe of the man at the far left, who is being served a goblet of wine from another slave in the middle of the painting, while another slave assists a man who has had too much to drink at the lower right (from 5.2.4, MANN 120029).

attached to those positions. (Paul seems to recognize in 7:21, however, that if a slave could become free, certain missional advantages could come with that scenario.)

Two other Pauline texts address the issue of slavery—Colossians and Ephesians. Since Colossians is slightly fuller in its coverage of the matter, we will focus on its discourse, with much the same view being evident in Ephesians (see Ephesians 6:5–9).

According to Colossians 3:11, "there is no Gentile or Jew, circumcised or uncircumcised, barbarian, Scythian, slave or free, but Christ is all, and is in all" (NIV). This verse is similar to Galatians 3:28 in placing specific identities to the periphery in order for Christ

193

to be put at the center. But whereas Galatians 3:28 does not spell out the social implications regarding slave and free, Colossians elaborates those implications. According to Colossians, enslaved Jesus-followers continue to be slaves, and householders continue to be masters who deserve obedience from their slaves: "Slaves, obey your earthly masters [*kyriois*] in everything, not only while being watched and in order to please them, but wholeheartedly, fearing the Lord [*kyrion*]" (3:22). If someone like Optata in the House of the Little Brothel had high hopes when she heard that "there is no . . . slave or free" (3:11), she might have lowered her expectations when she heard about her need to be obedient to her master. In fact, the author of Colossians continued in ways that might have confused her:

> Whatever your task, put yourselves into it, as done for the Lord and not for your masters, since you know that from the Lord you will receive the inheritance as your reward; you serve the Lord Christ. For the wrongdoer will be paid back for whatever wrong has been done, and there is no partiality. (3:23–25)

Was Optata to carry out her sexual tasks within the household of her master, in the service of "the Lord Christ"? Was her master "the wrongdoer" who would receive divine punishment for putting her to work as a prostitute? Or would Optata herself be "the wrongdoer" if she failed to obey her master's expectations?

If there might have been some confusion regarding the implications of Colossians 3:23–25, the concerns of people like Optata might have been alleviated by the very next verse, where masters are explicitly addressed. Most ancient codes that regulated behavior within households addressed only those with inferior status in the household. The Colossian code,

however, broke out of that restriction and placed even masters within the frame of regulation. If that aspect of the author's discourse was unusual, the content of that discourse would have been refreshing for someone like Optata: "Masters [*kyrioi*], treat your slaves justly and fairly, for you know that you also have a master [*kyrion*] in heaven" (4:1). Here the Christian householder is not the sole lord of his household; he stands under the authority of a higher lord, "a master in heaven" who expects that slaves should be treated "justly and fairly." If Optata (and others like her) had heard these words, she might have been heartily encouraged, especially if her master was already a Jesus-follower. (After all, the divine master of her earthly master expected Jesus-followers to live lives of moral purity, including the avoidance of "sexual immorality" and "impurity"; Colossians 3:5 NIV.) If her master was not a Jesus-follower, she might have hoped that the message of the Jesus-followers might somehow get a toehold within her master's own household.

Gentle Masters and Harsh Masters

There must have been Roman-era households where being treated "justly and fairly" was not out of the ordinary. Luke 7:1–5 gives an example of what might have been an equitable relationship between a master and his slave. In that account, a centurion appealed to Jesus to heal his treasured slave who was at the point of death. The assumption in this story is that a healthy relationship existed between master and slave, one that was respectable by Judean standards.

Perhaps we see other glimpses of these healthier forms of relationality between master and slave in the Pompeian artifacts. For instance, a prominent man by the name of

Figure 15.8. A fresco from the wall of a small Pompeian pub depicting a barmaid (probably a slave) taking wine to two waiting customers (one saying, "Bring it here," the other saying, "No, it's mine," with the woman responding, "Whoever wants it should take it"; from 6.14.35/36, MANN 111482)

Munatius Faustus erected a tomb to honor himself and his wife, but others within his household were also buried within the tomb, including some of his slaves (perhaps some being his own biological offspring): "Helpis, who lived three years" (DADC 4); "Arsinoe, who lived three years" (DADC 6); "Psiche, who lived three years and six months" (DADC 7); and finally "Atimetus, who lived twenty-six years" (DADC 8). (We will see more of Munatius Faustus in chapter 19.) Of course, we never get to hear the voices of these slaves, so we cannot know what their own estimate of Munatius Faustus's character might have been. But if any Pompeians treated their slaves "justly and fairly," perhaps they were people like Munatius Faustus. When New Testament authors imagined that slave-owners should be people of just character in their relations toward their slaves, they might have had in mind people like Munatius Faustus (at least as I have reconstructed him).

But clearly many slave-owners were not "just and fair." At times, Pompeian data seems to offer glimpses into these unhealthier forms of relationality. For instance, in several villas on the outskirts of Pompeii (for instance, villas 31 and 34), archaeologists have found stocks and restraining gear that were used to chain slaves to the premises (presumably for punishment or to prevent them from escaping in the dark hours of the night). Perhaps a good number of slaves in these villas were treated in ways that we would consider severely damaging to their human well-being. Were Jesus-followers to have heightened sensitivities in situations of pernicious mistreatment of slaves? The only New Testament text that gives instruction about harsh masters is 1 Peter. The author's advice might again have caused confusion for someone like Optata:

> Slaves, accept the authority of your masters with all deference, not only those who are kind and gentle but also those who are harsh. For it is a credit to you if, being aware of God, you endure pain while suffering unjustly. If you endure when you are beaten for doing wrong, what credit is that? But if you endure when you do right and suffer for it, you have God's approval. For to this you have been called, because Christ also suffered for you, leaving you an example, so that you should follow in his steps. . . . When he was abused, he did not return abuse; when he suffered, he did not threaten; but he entrusted himself to the one who judges justly. (2:18–21, 23)

"Accept the authority of your masters with all deference"—even masters who are "harsh"? What would this have meant for Optata (if we imaginatively think of her now as a Jesus-follower)? Was she simply to acquiesce in her master's abusive dominance? Perhaps she would

have followed this line of thinking in response: "But didn't the same heavenly master overturn tables of the opportunistic money changers in the temple of Jerusalem? Didn't he speak truth to the powers that be? Why aren't his prophetic acts examples for me to follow in abusive situations?"

Perhaps Optata found the passage's later statements to offer assistance in that regard. "If you endure when you do right and suffer for it, you have God's approval," the author had said. Perhaps Optata (our placeholder for a Christian female sex-slave) was to oppose her assigned role as a prostitute. This would be "doing right." Perhaps Optata was to "do right" by saying no to her master, informing him that she would no longer be used for purposes of prostitution. This would replicate the model of Jesus, who had also said no (in effect) to the ruling authorities of his day. There would be suffering as a consequence, just as Jesus suffered for standing against the authorities. But there is also approval from "the one who judges justly." Perhaps Optata would have found this passage, whose initial command looked so unpromising, to offer resources for reconceptualizing her identity in Christ and to embolden her to adopt new patterns of life, in a confident spirit, despite the prospect of suffering that might await her as a consequence.

What might Optata have thought about the kind of instructions found in Titus 2:9–10? There enslaved Jesus-devotees are instructed "to be submissive to their masters and to give satisfaction in every respect"; as they "show complete and perfect fidelity," they will prove to be "an ornament to the doctrine of God our Savior." Unlike Colossians and Ephesians, this text (like 1 Peter 2) has no instructions to masters about treating slaves justly and fairly. Without that important qualifier, Optata might not have warmed to the thought that she was "to give satisfaction in every respect" to her master. Was "the hope of eternal life" (Titus 1:2) to have so little impact on her own daily life here and now? Was the concern that Christians be respectable within society expecting too much from her?

If he had been asked, the author of Revelation might have taken a different track on things. For him (as we have already seen), the whole web of relationality beyond Jesus-groups (and sometimes even within them) testified to the domination system orchestrated by Satan. Perhaps this Christian thinker might have devised a strategy about Jesus-followers and slavery that coincided with his instruction "Come out of her, my people" (Revelation 18:4). Perhaps he would have articulated his discourse in relation to his assessment that slaves were "human lives" that mattered (18:13)—even beyond the economic structures in which they were usually embedded and the social constructs in which their identities were usually assessed.

In view of the ubiquity of slavery within the Roman world, it is not surprising that authors of New Testament texts had to consider Christian identity and mission in relation to that all-pervasive practice. When thinking about those issues, New Testament authors sometimes seem to have sought accommodation with the cultural norms of their day. At other times, they leaned toward the innovative. Or as Paul said in Galatians 5:13 (as noted at the start of this chapter), "Through love, become enslaved to one another."

16 Family and Solidarity

> I have come to set a man against his father, and a daughter against her mother, and a daughter-in-law against her mother-in-law. And *one's foes will be members of one's own household.* Whoever loves father or mother more than me is not worthy of me; and whoever loves son or daughter more than me is not worthy of me.
>
> Matthew 10:35–37; see also Luke 12:52–53

The Family in Theory

The family resided at the heart of emperor Augustus's plans to rejuvenate the Roman project. If civic order was to be maintained throughout the Roman empire, the bedrock for that was the stronghold of the family and the proper management of the household. Energizing robust families in harmonious relations was the foundation on which a strong empire was to be built.

This vision of how things should be caught people's imaginations. In practice, however, things were often much different. This was evidenced even in Augustus's own family. His daughter, Julia, for instance, engaged in a variety of promiscuous and adulterous relationships, to the extent that she was ultimately arrested for treason—her activities contradicting the official promotion of family values and representing a

political "sin." She was sent into exile on the island Pandateria, off the coast of Puteoli (not far from the Vesuvian towns). There she was prevented from seeing anyone unless Augustus gave his prior approval. She remained an embarrassment to her father's political vision, embodying a character that ran contrary to his own stipulations for the health of the empire, built on the foundations of ordered and strong relationships within the family.

The family usually revolved around the *paterfamilias*, the male head of the household. The painted frescos on Vesuvian walls frequently reinforce the interests of the *paterfamilias*. For instance, prominently displayed in Pompeii's macellum (where meat and fish were sold) are two frescos that seem to have played off each other in reinforcing a message about family values (see figure 16.1).

Figure 16.1. Two corner frescos in Pompeii's macellum (7.9.7/8), depicting Penelope with Odysseus (left) and Io with Argus (right)

- One fresco depicts Penelope and her husband, Odysseus—both central characters in Homer's epic the *Odyssey*; in that narrative Penelope waits patiently and faithfully for Odysseus while he undertakes his journey.

- Another fresco depicts the woman Io being kept in isolation by Argus, the servant of Hera (later known in Roman mythology as Juno); Argus was given this task in order to keep Io away from Hera's husband, Zeus (known to the Romans as Jupiter), who wanted to have sex with Io—and, as the story unfolds, Zeus was successful in his sexual ambitions (as usual).

The two frescos, placed near each other in the corner of the macellum walls, pose questions to the married women of Pompeii: "Are you a good wife like Penelope, who diligently pro-

tected her husband's household through her unswerving faithfulness to him? Or are you like Io, who allowed herself to be preyed upon and, thereby, was a weak link in the bonds of family?"

Characterizations in the House of Lucretius Fronto

We see similar groupings of narratological themes in other frescos as well. One of the best examples comes from the House of Lucretius Fronto (5.4.a). That house has three bedrooms for family members. The householder's bedroom had two main frescos, although only one is still intact. The fresco that remains on the wall of his bedroom depicts a mythic scene of Orestes killing Neoptolemus at the altar of the Temple of Apollo. The story referenced by this fresco involves self-interest and murder. A woman named

199

Figure 16.2. Left: the fresco in the *tablinum* of the House of Marcus Lucretius Fronto (5.4.a), depicting Mars fondling Venus; right: the fresco in the householder's bedroom, depicting the murder of Neoptolemus by Orestes (both frescos in situ)

Hermione was the daughter of Menelaus, and Menelaus had arranged for Hermione to be given in marriage to Neoptolemus, rather than to Orestes (because Orestes had killed his own mother); Orestes foiled Menelaus's wishes by killing Neoptolemus and stealing Hermione away to take her as his wife. It might be a romantic story in one sense, but it is ultimately a story about power—a story about taking whatever one wants, without moral constraints. The fact that this episode was displayed in the householder's bedroom may tell us something about his attitude toward his sexual relations, as well as his general approach to life.

The story referenced in a fresco in Lucretius Fronto's bedroom overlaps with the point referenced in a fresco in his study and meeting room (*tablinum*). That fresco depicts Mars, the deity of war, reaching into Venus's clothing to fondle her breast (a motif depicted in a variety of other Vesuvian frescos as well). In each fresco, the iconic male achieves his

ambitions through initiatives unrestrained and undiluted. Whatever or whomever the male figure wanted, he simply took for himself, by determined force if necessary; other people either served his purposes or were obstacles that needed to be removed, no matter the cost. Lucretius Fronto had these "life lessons" reinforced for him in the frescos that he chose to have painted on the walls of his bedroom and *tablinum*.

It is in the other two bedrooms that we see how Lucretius Fronto's self-image pertained to other members of his household. In those bedrooms too, frescos were object lessons in how the values of the household were to be configured. One room seems to have been the bedroom for Lucretius Fronto's two children, a boy and a girl (in fact, the same boy and girl whose portraits were shown in figure 1.5). Although the girl (perhaps ten years old) is rather plainly depicted, the boy (perhaps twelve years old) is depicted in the garb of Mercury, the deity of commerce (compare

Paul's depiction of Jesus-followers as those who are "clothed in the garb of Christ" in Galatians 3:27, my translation). Clearly, Lucretius Fronto had high hopes for his son's entrepreneurial success. (Presumably he hoped his daughter would marry someone as prominently placed as possible within the town's hierarchy and would manage her husband's household effectively.)

Two mythological frescos enhance the ethos of the children's bedroom. One depicts Narcissus staring at his reflection in the water, recalling the story of the handsome young man who became so enthralled with his own reflection that he could do nothing else except stare longingly at it, eventually dying of starvation as a consequence. The other fresco depicts Pero breast-feeding her father, Cimone, recalling the story of the daughter who saved her father's life by breast-feeding him after he had been sentenced to death by starvation in prison. In the ancient world this story was celebrated as a model of heroic compassion. In fact, as the story continues, the jailer is so impressed by Pero's innovative compassion for her father that he initiates her father's release from prison.

This combination of frescos makes perfect sense as illustrations of what Lucretius Fronto intended regarding the character of his children—perhaps especially the character of his son. The Narcissus portraiture warned against allowing self-infatuation to distract you from the path to public success; the Pero and Cimone fresco reinforced the importance of strategic altruism—perhaps in particular the care for family members, including parents who might require it later in life.

Frescos in the bedroom of the household's matron similarly reflect how Lucretius Fronto intended to orchestrate the values of those within his household. The fresco of the deity Venus on one wall sends clear signals: just as

Figure 16.3. Two frescos in the children's bedroom of the House of Marcus Lucretius Fronto (5.4.a, in situ), one depicting Pero breast-feeding her father (left) and another showing Narcissus (right; see also MANN 115398)

Figure 16.4. Frescos in the matron's bedroom in the House of Marcus Lucretius Fronto (5.4.a, in situ), depicting Theseus and Ariadne (left) and Venus the deity of love (right)

Venus was the deity of love, so too Lucretius Fronto's wife was to service the householder's needs in love and lovemaking. The fresco that partnered with the Venus fresco depicts two heroes of Greek mythology—Theseus and Ariadne, just before Theseus goes into the labyrinth to kill the Minotaur. In the story, the hero Theseus could never have hoped to reemerge from the labyrinth had it not been for the ingenuity of the heroine Ariadne, who gave him a ball of string, allowing him to retrace his steps and emerge victorious from the conflict with the Minotaur. The message is clear: a wife is to be the helpmate in ensuring the success of her husband.

These frescos in the House of Marcus Lucretius Fronto are aligned with the Augustan notion of family values. They reinforce the ideal Roman family, with each member of the family joining forces to perpetuate the success of the household, as determined by the householder.

Slaves and Concubines

As we saw in chapter 15, slaves also played an obvious role in the success of the household. They were purchased for that task, or had been sired within the household for that purpose. Biological offspring of the householder were frequently raised within the household, even though those offspring were not members of the householder's family (since legitimate offspring were members of his family only if they were birthed by the householder's legitimate wife). Instead, they were commodities acquired by the household through female slaves whom the householder had impregnated. This was a relatively inexpensive way to augment a household's workforce.

As we have seen, in this male-dominated world, it was not considered out of the ordinary for a householder to have sex with his male or female slaves. Prostitutes were probably for the economically disadvantaged men to make use of; slaves were for the economically more advantaged.

Nor was it out of the ordinary for the householder to have an officially recognized concubine, one who lived within the house. We might imagine this happening only if his wife had already died. That generous interpretation might be the situation for a Pompeian land surveyor named Nicostratus Popidius, who erected a tomb that he dedicated (in an inscription) to himself, "to his concubine Popidia Ecdoche, and to his family" (Nucerian Gate, at tomb 17a/b OS). But if Popidius's wife had already died, Popidius might have chosen to marry his concubine or to take another woman as his wife (since a man needed a wife to run his household). So because the tomb inscription fails to mention the wife by name and only mentions the concubine by name, it is most likely that both a wife and a concubine lived in Popidius's household simultaneously and served different roles. (Judging by her name, the concubine Popidia Ecdoche had first been a slave within Popidius's household but was then freed by him to live as his concubine within his household.)

Another tombstone of a similar kind (see figure 16.5) reads:

> Marcus Vennius Rufus, *sevir* [a
> municipal magistrate]
> For himself and
> Marcus Vennius Demetrius, his
> father
> Vennia Rufa, his mother
> Valeria Urbana, his wife, [and]
> Fufia Chila, his concubine.

Here again we do best to imagine that, in this stage of their lives, Rufus's wife and his concubine both lived under the same roof, each one servicing Rufus in her own way—his wife

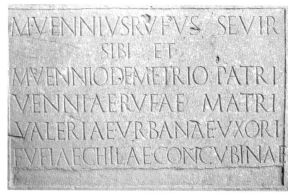

Figure 16.5. The tomb inscription of Marcus Vennius Rufus, listing himself, his father, his mother, his wife, and his concubine as beneficiaries of the tomb; the inscription is displayed in the National Archaeology Museum of Naples, but without its inventory number or provenance listed; *CIL* 4.2496 places a member of the Vennius family (Gaius Vennius) in Pompeii, so perhaps this inscription derives from there also.

overseeing his household and giving him legitimate offspring, and his concubine servicing him sexually. A Greek orator from the fourth century BCE (whose identity is disputed) had once said: "We keep mistresses for our pleasure [at parties], we keep concubines for our day-to-day bodily needs [at home], and we have wives to produce our legitimate children and to serve as faithful housekeepers" (*Against Neaera* 122, my translation). Evidently not too much had changed between the fourth century BCE and the eruption of Vesuvius.

Wives and Husbands

In the Roman age there was little expectation that a wife would object to her husband's sexual involvements beyond their "marriage bed." The wife's sexual role was to give the householder legitimate heirs, perpetuating the family line and the household's reputation. Beyond that, she was to support his efforts in anything he did and needed, conferring honor on her husband's household

Figure 16.6. A scene commonly depicted in Vesuvian art shows Medea (on right, holding a sword) with her two children and their tutor, after her husband had left her for another woman; in the Greek myth, Medea does not accept the situation but murders the other woman as well as these two children of hers in an act of revenge against her former husband; here she hides the sword that she'll soon use against her own children (from 6.9.6, MANN 8977).

by efficiently running his household affairs to suit his goals—sometimes even after her husband's death (as in the case of Naevoleia Tyche, whom we'll meet in chapter 19). A husband's sexual involvements might have been a source of frustration for his wife, but they were not necessarily seen as tragedies of relational dysfunction. In fact, Plutarch, the Roman biographer and prolific essayist, peddled the idea that a man's infidelity should actually be seen as a compliment to his wife and a sign of respect for her, since he had chosen to share "his debauchery, licentiousness, and wantonness with another woman" rather than degrading his own wife with them (*Moralia* 140B).

Proportionately few women could have taken action against the sexual involvements of their husbands. That was the prerogative, perhaps, of the admired deity Hera (later known as Juno). She did everything she could to prevent the sexual promiscuity of her husband, Zeus (later known as Jupiter), even resorting to killing some of the offspring from sexual engagements he had with other females. Most human wives did not have opportunities of that kind, however. They might have mumbled something on occasion or demonstrated dissatisfaction in some minor fashion, but there was no real expectation that anything would change as a result of such protestations. Perhaps most wives didn't even bother. Many of them probably just trudged along in loveless marriages, in accordance with their social duty in a patriarchal society (a society where well-placed men benefited from what we might call structural selfishness).

Perhaps this is why there seems to be little emotion in the fresco of the faithful Penelope and Odysseus in the macellum (see figure 16.1). She is attentive to him (as he recounts his exciting experiences to her), but it seems to be a distanced attentiveness, even if it is a faithful attentiveness. There is no joy in his presence (contrast the stylized fresco of the amorous couple in figure 1.8). There is no delight in their being together. The marriage is functional in first-century terms, since she had remained chaste during his long absence. But a twenty-first-century painter would have depicted the scene much differently, in alignment with twenty-first-century ideals about a healthy relationship between married partners. In the Roman world, it was not the wife's prerogative to expect joy and fulfillment in marriage. Her job was to be faithful to her husband, to support his interests, strategies, and goals. If love blossomed in the process, that was welcomed; if not, that was not out of the ordinary.

The dynamics of married life often depended on where the married partners were located on the socio-economic spectrum. Marriages between people higher up on the socio-economic ladder were usually arranged marriages. Their usual purpose was not to bring together two young people desperately in love. Instead, these marriages usually tied together two households and enhanced the prospects of each extended family through the bonding of male and female counterparts. Young women were typically married by the age of fifteen, although we should imagine some having been married even by the age of twelve. They were often wed to much older men who may already have lost one or two wives, usually in the dangerous process of childbirth. These marriages were established in ceremonies in which the male and the female commonly shook hands, symbolizing their agreement to enter this union of households. Marriages of this kind were expedient means of creating new households that reflected well on the households from which the two partners had come.

Of course, marriage may have fostered romance and love in some cases. We might get a glimpse of loving emotion among Pompeian spouses in rare instances. One man dedicated a tomb to his wife's memory with these words: "Lucius Caltilius Pamphilus, freedman of Lucius, member of the Collinian tribe, for his wife Servilia, in a loving spirit" (*CIL* 4.1046, at tomb HGE34). Similarly, a graffito containing a woman's amusingly ironic quip reads: "I would not sell my husband . . . for any price" (*CIL* 4.3061).

Vesuvian graffiti rarely testify to love within the boundaries of marriage. Notice, for instance, how a Pompeian man named Zosimus used a graffito to propose marriage to a woman named Victoria: "To his Victoria, greetings. Zosimus greets Victoria. I ask you to become the support of my old age. If you think I do not have money, don't love me" (*CIL* 4.1684). Here a marriage proposal virtually defines love as Victoria's support for Zosimus in his old age, based on the fact that he has money. Notice also these graffiti that seem to celebrate recently wedded partners: "Daphnicus and his Felicula were here. Long live Felicula! Long live Daphnicus! All the best to both of them" (*CIL* 4.4477); "Eulale, may you enjoy good health with your wife Vera" (*CIL* 4.1574). These graffiti are pleasantly uplifting, but they are not monuments to passionate love; only good health and long life are mentioned.

Love and the Fickleness of Men

In the grand seaside estate called Villa Arianna (south of Pompeii in Stabia), a small room displays a somewhat curious Vesuvian fresco (see figure 16.7). Its scene blends the realistic (that is, three women) with the mythic (that is, three Erotes, or cupids). In one widespread interpretation, it depicts a woman (and her female companion, on the far left) considering the purchase of a cupid of love, three of which have been brought by a female cupid peddler (on the right) for the woman to consider. (The fresco was displayed in a room depicting a number of female figures, one of whom raises her cloak to reveal a garment showing naked figures in various poses.) How is this intriguing scene to be understood? In what way might this scene of love being brought to the woman relate to the experiences of women in general?

A Pompeian graffito might be able to shed light on how the fresco is to be interpreted (*CIL*

Figure 16.7. A fresco depicting cupids being brought to a woman and her friend (from the Villa Arianna, MANN 9180)

4.5296, from 9.9.f). Scholars are divided over whether the author of the graffito is a woman or a man, and the debate hinges on one word in the fifth line of the graffito—whether it modifies the word that follows ("wasted *night*") or references the author ("*I* . . . wasted/lost"). If it references the author, then the author would seem to be female, since the Latin word "wasted" is in feminine form. Leaving that issue aside temporarily, the first four lines read:

> Oh, if only I could hold your sweet
>   arms around my neck
> Entwined in an embrace, and place
>   kisses on your delicate lips.
> Come now, my little darling, entrust
>   your pleasures to the winds,

> Believe me, men have a fickle
>   nature . . .

If the author was a man, the fifth line that follows reads: "Often I have been awake in the middle of the wasted night." If the author was a woman (which would seem to make more sense of the fourth line), the fifth line that follows reads: "Often I have been awake, wasted [unloved], in the middle of the night." If the author was a woman, she hoped to embrace her "little darling" and find there a faithfulness that offsets the (sexual) fickleness of men. Is this the context for interpreting the fresco of the women and the cupids from the Villa Arianna?

206

(Contrast this declaration written by a Pompeian man [*CIL* 4.3932]: "Weep, you girls. My penis has given you up. Now it penetrates men's behinds. Goodbye, wondrous femininity!" Perhaps the "girls" of Pompeii were not, in fact, struck with sorrow at this turn of events.)

The fickleness of men is something Christian leaders sought to eradicate within Jesus-groups. In 1 Corinthians 7:2–5, for instance, Paul urged female Jesus-followers to fulfill their "marital duties" to their husbands and instructed that wives should yield authority over their bodies to their husbands. These might look like routine statements undergirded by conventional values of the Roman world, except for the notable fact that Paul gave the same instructions to male Jesus-followers—husbands are to fulfill their "marital duties" to their wives and yield authority over their bodies to their wives. In speaking this way not just to wives but also to husbands, Paul made it clear that male Jesus-devotees were to conform to a form of sexual practice and restraint that ran against the grain of many strong cultural currents of their day. In this, Paul expected Roman men to avoid "sexual immorality . . . so that Satan will not tempt you because of your lack of self-control [i.e., your fickleness]" (1 Cor. 7:2, 5 [NIV]; for more on this issue, see "Questions to Consider," chapter 16, question 2).

Presenting the Ideal Couple

The Vesuvian towns also provide us with frescos of married couples. One, painted in the final years of Pompeii's existence, depicts an optimistic, upwardly mobile, impressive, and confident household partnership (see figure 16.8). In the portrait, the wife holds a stylus (to her lips, in a pose of contemplation) and

Figure 16.8. The fresco of a man (perhaps Terentius Neo) and his wife (from 7.2.6, MANN 9058)

Figure 16.9. A drawing of a Vesuvian fresco that displayed a householder, with a scroll in one hand and a bucket of scrolls next to him, instructing his inquiring son, who also holds a scroll, while his wife (without a scroll) approvingly observes the pedagogical process (see credits)

207

a notebook tablet, into which she would write notes with her stylus. Her notes would involve things pertaining to the efficient running of the household—memos, reminders, lists, and the like. As we saw in chapter 12, women are often depicted holding tablets of this kind, illustrating their effectiveness as the matron of the household. This woman, then, is advertised as someone who serves her household with effective diligence. Although we don't know the woman's name, her husband is often thought to be Terentius Neo—the name on an electoral campaign notice on the external wall of the residence. He is dressed in a white toga and holds a papyrus scroll. He too is literate, but what he deals with are not the matters of the household (represented by her tablet) but higher matters, things of greater consequence, the things that usually reside within scrolls—literature, philosophy, civic pronouncements, and the like. Advertised within this fresco, then, is a partnership that is effective in its household management (embodied in the diligent wife) and ambitious in its public persona (embodied in the learned husband).

Negotiating Family Bonds among Jesus-Followers

Early Jesus-followers were no different from their contemporaries in wanting the best for members of their families. Jesus was remembered for having expressed the sentiment in this way: "Who among you would give your child a snake if he or she asked for a fish? Or if the child asked for an egg, would you give him or her a scorpion?" (Luke 11:11–12, my translation). Or, "If one of you has a child or an ox that has fallen into a well, will you not immediately pull it out [even] on a sabbath day?" (14:5). Just as Lucretius Fronto wanted his son to succeed in business, so too the mother of two prominent disciples of Jesus came to Jesus and "asked a favor of him," requesting that her two sons would "sit, one at your right hand and one at your left, in your kingdom" (Matthew 20:20–21). Most parents can relate to that kind of request in one way or another. Jesus's reply to her, however, characteristically threw a wrench into things: "Whoever wishes to be great among you must be your servant, and whoever wishes to be first among you must be your slave" (20:26–27).

We have seen that Lucretius Fronto wanted his children not to think too highly of themselves and to think about the needs of others (especially their parents when in need). The same two emphases emerged in the teaching of Jesus, who was remembered as emphasizing the need to obey the commands, "Honor your father and mother, and also love your neighbor as yourself" (Matthew 19:19). The same emphasis on familial duty is replicated in various early Christian texts. Ephesians, for instance, contains this exhortation to children:

> Children, obey your parents in the Lord, for this is right. "Honor your father and mother"—this is the first commandment with a promise—the promise being "so that it may be well with you and you may live long on the earth." (6:1–3)

We usually think that the "children" mentioned here are offspring who aren't yet adults. Clearly, it would have included them, but there is no reason to restrict the admonition to the young; in the ancient world, it would have been heard as an exhortation to offspring of any age, including adult offspring.

Similar concerns for the solidarity of the family are evident in other passages as well. The author of 1 Timothy notes that "if a

208

widow has children or grandchildren, they should first learn their religious duty to their own family and make some repayment to their parents; for this is pleasing in God's sight" (5:4). In the Augustan program to rejuvenate the family, demonstrating one's piety required a person to take care of his or her own family. The pattern is precisely the same here. Caring for the elderly within one's own household is said to be the "religious duty" of adult householders who adopt Jesus-devotion. This is good practice within the Roman world. And against the backdrop of the Augustan ideal, another passage from 1 Timothy fits perfectly within that same context: "And whoever does not provide for relatives, and especially for family members, has denied the [Christian] faith and is worse than an unbeliever" (5:8). "Unbelievers" of the Roman age were expected to provide for family members in need, as Lucretius Fronto reinforced in the frescos of his children's bedroom. If Jesus-followers were to do less than that within their households, they would be denigrating the reputation of their deity and "denying the faith."

These passages, probably datable to the last quarter of the first century, derive from the time when Jesus-groups were realizing the need to settle into their cultural context. The urgent expectation that Jesus Christ might be returning soon had begun to subside, and Jesus-followers found the need to meld into their environment and work more integrally within it. In that context, Jesus-devotion was finding ways to accommodate itself within the culture, as the Christian faith was being handed down from generation to generation. "I am reminded of your sincere faith, a faith that lived first in your grandmother Lois and your mother Eunice and now, I am sure, lives in you" (2 Timothy 1:5). It was in the context of the Christian household

Figure 16.10. A fresco of the deity Juno (or Hera in Greek mythology) being brought in wedding robes to Jupiter (or Zeus in Greek mythology); Juno was the deity of marriage, and she bore many children for Jupiter (from the House of the Tragic Poet [6.8.5], MANN 111441).

that fathers were instructed to raise their children "in the discipline and instruction of the Lord" (Ephesians 6:4)—just as Timothy could be characterized as having "known the sacred writings" even "from childhood" (2 Timothy 3:15). Older women were to teach younger women how to be respectable Christian women when judged by the standards of the Roman world, including being "good managers of the household" (Titus 2:3–5, here verse 5). The same emphasis appears in 1 Timothy, where widows who are young enough to remarry are instructed to "marry, bear children, and manage their households" (5:14).

But the flip side of the coin was being remembered as well. Late in the first century, the author of Luke's Gospel recorded some very harsh words of Jesus. "Whoever comes to me and does not hate father and mother, wife and children, brothers and sisters, yes, and even life itself, cannot be my disciple" (Luke 14:26; see a harsher version of the same pronouncement in the Gospel of Thomas 55, and a softer version of the same in Matthew 10:37). If these words were astonishing in the context of the Jewish homeland, they were just as astonishing in the urban heartland of the Roman world. Taken at face value, these words run against the grain of every form of civilized culture.

Perhaps in the mind of the Gospel writer, the shock value of these words was to provoke reflection on a person's ultimate priorities, without allowing the words to be understood with full literal force. After all, the same Jesus who said these offensive words is depicted only a few chapters later as exhorting a man to "honor [his] father and mother" in order to attain eternal life (Luke 18:20). Perhaps the "hatred" that Jesus was encouraging was a hatred of what the bonds of family stood for in the first-century world—prioritizing the needs of the household's status and placing all other considerations in submission to that goal. Perhaps Luke wanted his audiences to hear that all relationships need to be informed by an underlying form of relationality that usurps all others in terms of importance: one's own loyalty to Jesus Christ. Perhaps this is why Luke remembered Jesus as saying that he came to set "father against son and son against father, mother against daughter and daughter against mother, mother-in-law against her daughter-in-law, and daughter-in-law against mother-in-law" (12:52–53; compare Matthew 10:35–36, as noted at the start of this chapter). The ideals of Jesus-devotion were, in some respects, so counter-cultural that even the ideal Augustan household may not survive their implementation.

Fictive Kinship among Jesus-Followers

Family relationships were to be the most resilient of all relationships and the bedrock for all other forms of productivity. Since the ideals of Jesus-devotion often set households on edge or placed Jesus-followers at odds with their peers, it is hardly surprising that Jesus-devotees often employed the language of familial relationships when referring to each other. Paul, for instance, identified Timothy as his "beloved and faithful child in the Lord" (1 Corinthians 4:17; see also 1 Timothy 1:2, 18; 2 Timothy 1:2; 2:1; Hebrews 13:22), and also as his "brother" (2 Corinthians 1:1; 1 Thessalonians 3:2; Philemon 1; see also Colossians 1:1). Similarly, Titus is both his "loyal child in the faith" (Titus 1:4) and his "brother" (2 Corinthians 2:13). Paul identified Onesimus, the slave of Philemon, as "my child . . . whose father I have become" (Philemon 10) and as a "brother" (Colossians 4:9; Philemon 16). And on almost one hundred occasions, the Pauline letters show Paul as identifying other Jesus-followers as his "brothers (and sisters)." In so doing, Paul places Jesus-followers metaphorically within "the household of faith" (Galatians 6:10, my translation). No longer slaves but children who inherit the riches of the household (4:1–7), these Jesus-followers cry out in prayer, referencing the almighty deity as "Abba, Father" (4:6; also Romans 8:15)— the prayer address used by Jesus himself, the obedient son (as in Mark 14:36). This kind of discourse reinforced relational bonds between Jesus-devotees in a fashion that helped them realign their primary reference groups, affirming their Christian relationality as the arena from which they were to draw their primary identity.

The redefinition of family kinship along lines of fictive (i.e., non-biological) kinship has a strong narrative foothold in each of the four canonical Gospels. Mark narrates a scene in which Jesus's family wants to speak with him, away from the crowds, because he has become something of a public embarrassment to the family's reputation (see Mark 3:21). The episode continues:

> And he replied, "Who are my mother and my brothers?" And looking at those who sat around him, he said, "Here are my mother and my brothers! Whoever does the will of God is my brother and sister and mother." (3:33–35)

Both Matthew and Luke share this episode in which fictive kinship takes priority over expectations regarding the status of the familial household (Matthew 12:46–50; Luke 8:19–21). Luke also has an episode in which Jesus, as a twelve-year-old Judean (or Jewish) youth, caused his mother and father "great anxiety" when he stayed in the temple for three days discussing matters with the Judean leaders; when he is found there, he responds to parental concern by saying, "Didn't you know that I must be concerned with the things of my Father?" (Luke 2:49, my translation). Similarly, John's Gospel realigns family most dramatically as Jesus hangs on the cross in Jerusalem:

> When Jesus saw his mother and the disciple whom he loved standing beside her, he said to his mother, "Woman, here is your son [that is, the disciple]." Then he said to the disciple, "Here is your mother." And from that hour the disciple took her into his own home. (19:26–27)

Each Gospel, then, has at least one episode in which Jesus himself legitimates the prioritization of fictive kinship over the bio-logical family. Mark's Gospel sheds light on why these fictive kinship relationships were so urgently necessary:

> Peter began to say to him, "Look, we have left everything and followed you." Jesus said, "Truly I tell you, there is no one who has left house or brothers or sisters or mother or father or children or fields, for my sake and for the sake of the good news, who will not receive a hundredfold now in this age—houses, brothers and sisters, mothers and children, and fields, with persecutions—and in the age to come eternal life. (10:28–30)

Those who follow Jesus in exclusive terms can expect to experience "persecutions"—a word that slips into the list of otherwise good things that Jesus-followers are said to gain in return for abandoning familial relationships. When old ties become corrosive obstructions, Jesus-followers are to find new lines of relational support in their fictive kin: "brothers and sisters, mothers and children."

In these metaphorical relationships between Jesus-followers, notice that no father is mentioned. The absence of a male overseer in this metaphorical list would have captured attention, with the implied head of the household being the deity worshiped by Jesus-followers. They proclaimed themselves to be "children" of a "father in heaven" (Matthew 5:45; 6:8; 7:11; 23:9), who forgives trespasses (Mark 11:25) and gives "good things to those who ask" (Matthew 7:11; see also Luke 11:13). So Jesus is remembered as instructing his followers, "Call no one your father on earth, for you have one Father, the one in heaven" (Matthew 23:9). And just as sons are to emulate their fathers, so too these children are to emulate their heavenly father by being "merciful, just as [their] Father is merciful" (Luke 6:36).

211

17 Piety and Pragmatism

I [Paul] did not shrink from doing anything helpful, proclaiming the message to you and teaching you publicly *and from house to house* as I testified to both Jews and Greeks about repentance toward God and faith toward our Lord Jesus.

Acts 20:20–21

Space in the House

Jesus-groups often met together in houses (although not exclusively in that context). For us to conceptualize how Jesus-followers expressed their devotion in pragmatic ways in relation to that setting, we need to understand the functionality of space within houses of the Roman world.

Ancient houses were not like twenty-first-century houses. Despite variety in their layout, residences were not devised simply to be private spaces for family members to retreat to after a long day in the public arena. Our twenty-first-century division between private space (i.e., home) and public space (e.g., shopping malls, restaurants, office buildings, places of worship) does not coincide with the way first-century people used their space.

For instance, in houses where the householder had a significant public profile, clients would congregate in the morning outside the residence's entrance and move into the house's atrium when invited to do so by a household slave (by instruction from the householder). As the clients waited to meet individually with the householder, they might pay their respects to the householder's deities displayed in an atrium shrine. When it was their turn to meet with their patron, they would be ushered into the *tablinum* (or office), where (after a few moments of submissive dialogue) they would present their request. They would then be told what was required of them (to enhance the householder's reputation) in exchange for his support. In these instances, the residence doubled as a place of business and politics, overseen by the household deities. Moreover, it was hoped that passersby would glance into the house and see how busy it was inside, thereby reinforcing the importance of its householder.

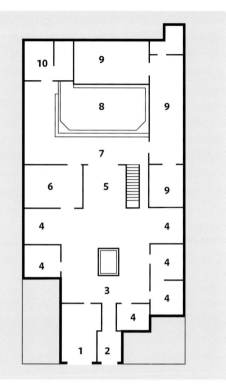

Figure 17.1. The plan of the ground floor of a relatively standard house from the Roman world (in this case, the House of the Bicentenary in Herculaneum, at 5.15). A shop (that opens to the street with access into the house, labeled 1) adjoins the entryway (2); the atrium (3) wraps around the impluvium (or small pool to collect rainwater), with bedrooms and other spaces (4) adjoining it; a staircase is to the right of the *tablinum* (or office, 5), which is to the right of the *triclinium* (or dining room, 6); beyond that lies a truncated two-sided peristyle (7) around a small garden (8), with workspaces (9) and a kitchen (10) adjoining the peristyle.

Meanwhile, other people might come and go within the house, especially if they had rented an apartment above the ground floor that could be accessed only by the internal stairs. Anyone entering or leaving through the front entrance of the house in the afternoon would probably pass the matron in the atrium, spinning cloth at her loom, while slaves prepared the house and food for the evening meal. In the late afternoon, invited guests would arrive to join the householder for the dinner, in which the household deities would again be honored in one way or another. After the meal, the men might enjoy a philosophical symposium while the women listened to the conversations or (in accordance with earlier Greek practice) simply moved themselves to a separate space.

Space within houses was used for a variety of overlapping purposes, especially in the case of houses that were midsized or larger. Smaller houses would have fewer possibilities for configuration, but the same principle often applied. Space in a house was usually multi-purpose. People moved in and out of it for different reasons, and furniture that suited different purposes might be moved around within the home to suit different occasions throughout the day.

Household Devotion

In his letter to Jesus-followers in Rome, Paul spoke of his ministry as having extended "from Jerusalem all the way around to Illyricum" (15:19 NIV, Illyricum being across the Adriatic Sea from the eastern coast of Italy). What might Paul have encountered as he went "from house to house" throughout the Mediterranean basin to proclaim his message?

If the houses of Pompeii and Herculaneum are anything to go by, Paul would inevitably have encountered deeply entrenched forms of household devotion. The deities were not simply worshiped occasionally in the urban temples; devotion to the deities was incorporated within the everyday practices of a Roman household. As we have seen, piety was thought to be the foundation of the household structure—what kept the household together through the proper ordering of relationships within it. Consequently, the focal point of

213

many Vesuvian homes was the devotional shrine (or shrines) to the deities and suprahuman forces. Each month had special days designated to reverence particular deities, and other days were added to the list of celebratory days that required expressions of household piety—such as birthdays of household members or imperial figures, or death dates of deceased ancestors. But there were also practices of devotion that would have happened in ordinary fashion each day—such as offering food on the devotional shrine for the household deities to consume (through spiritual rather than physical ingestion). According to the Roman poet Ovid, "gentle Concord is said to be present" as households "give incense to the deities of the family," or give "an offering of food" to "nourish the *lares* [the guardian spirits of a place]" (*Fasti* 2.631–34). In many ways, then, the hub for efficiency and proper relationality within the household was the shrine of devotional piety. Some shrines from Vesuvian homes have already been highlighted in previous chapters; here it needs to be reinforced that shrines (or *lararia*, from the singular *lararium*, where the *lares* were honored) were the architectural norm for Vesuvian houses and workshops.

One example effectively captures the importance of these shrines. At the beginning

Figure 17.2. A fresco depicting the extended members of a household gathered around an altar while undertaking a sacrifice (from the kitchen of 1.13.2, and directly adjacent to a *lararium*); two large *lares* stand on either side of this scene (beyond the frame), referencing the spirit of the place and its favorable disposition to the household within its premises.

of Plautus's play *Pot of Gold* (from the early second century BCE), a *lar* introduces himself to the audience: "I am the *lar* of the family of this home. . . . I looked after it for the father and grandfather of the present occupant." The *lar* then recounts how the grandfather honored the *lar* properly and entrusted to the *lar* a pot of gold, hidden within the premises of the house. The next householder, however, failed to give due respect to the *lar*, and consequently died. The current householder, the grandson of the man who hid the gold within the house, has a daughter who "is constantly praying to me every day, with gifts of incense or wine or something. She gives me garlands. Because of her devotion, I have caused her father Euclio to discover the treasure here so that he might more easily find her a husband" (the narrative derives from *Pot of Gold* 1–27).

Worshiping the deities and suprahuman forces is on clear display within the House of the Golden Cupids (at 6.16.7/38; we have seen this residence already in chapter 9). A large painted shrine enhanced the walls of the southeast corner of the house's beautiful peristyle, with the shrine dedicated to the worship of Isis, the deity of life (see, for instance, figure 9.3). On the north wall of the peristyle, another ornate shrine resided, crafted as a miniature temple, with two fluted marble columns on each side (see figure 17.3). When archaeologists removed the volcanic debris from this shrine, they found figurines of some traditional deities—Jupiter, Juno, and Minerva. As noted in chapter 4, this "Capitoline Triad" comprised the deities that were worshiped together on Rome's Capitoline Hill, with Jupiter being the high deity of the empire, Juno being the deity of marriage (the wife of Jupiter), and Minerva being the deity

of wisdom (especially in strategy, tactics, and warfare). At least three other figurines also had been placed within the shrine: Mercury, the deity of commerce, and two large figurines of the *lares*, symbolizing the benevolent spirits of the place in which the household resided. Accordingly, when dinner guests walked around the gardened peristyle before or after dinner (perhaps reinforcing the sense of *otium* within the residence), they would inevitably pass each of these two imposing shrines—one honoring the traditional deities of Rome's political heritage and the enrichment of the household, the other honoring the Egyptian deity of personal life in the present and beyond.

Shrines constructed like a miniature monument or temple often appear near the front entrance of Vesuvian residences, being a common feature in house atriums. (This is true, for instance, of the House of Lucius Caecilius Jucundus [5.1.26], the House of Menander [1.10.4], the House of Marcus Epidi Sabini [9.1.22], the House of Marcus Obellius Firmus [9.14.4], and the Villa San Marco.) Sometimes these large shrines were placed at the back of the house, but even then they were usually positioned in the line of vision from the house's front entryway so that a passerby could see the piety of the household on display. It added to the reputation of the household to exhibit its piety prominently, demonstrating that the household was playing its part in the advancement of Roman society.

If one shrine benefited a residence, additional shrines might bring further benefit. Many residences and workshops had two, three, or more shrines. The grand House of Menander (1.10.4), for instance, had at least three impressive shrines (see figure 17.4). The shrine in the atrium would have enabled clients

Figure 17.3. One of the main shrines in the House of the Golden Cupids (6.16.7), with the divine Capitoline Triad (Jupiter and two female deities, Juno and Minerva) on the top platform and the two household *lares* flanking them one platform down (photos of the original figurines have been superimposed onto their original locations, as they were first discovered, although with some artistic license; originally a larger figure of Mercury also sat on the top platform to the left; see credits)

of the wealthy householder to show their respect by extending devotion to his deities as they entered his house. The shrine in the back peristyle (which was found with figurines of the householder's ancestors residing within it) would have done the same for the special guests who were invited past the front of the house and into the back of the residence, where honored guests were made welcome by the head of what was obviously a preeminent household of long-standing reputation. A

third major shrine was in the slave quarters of the residence, ensuring that the piety of the household was shared by its slaves. Other Vesuvian residences share this architectural feature, with the household shrine being placed in the slave quarters (for instance, the House of the Faun at 6.12.2/5, and the Villa of the Mysteries, where household shrines adorned the large kitchen area).

Most Vesuvian shrines were far simpler and/or smaller than the impressive temple shrines

Figure 17.4. Two of the shrines in the House of Menander (1.10.4; left: the peristyle shrine; right: the atrium shrine)

of some of the larger houses. Some shrines were formed simply by painting frescos of shrines onto walls (for example, see figure 7.3). Some shrines were simple niches in walls (see figures 17.5 and 17.6). Within the niches were either frescos or figurines depicting the household *genius*, deceased ancestors, the *lares*, and/or the *penates*—the *penates* symbolizing all the household deities collectively (despite their original significance only as guardians of the storehouse and its provisions).

Besides the obvious variety of shrines on display in Vesuvian residences, the takeaway is simply that the majority of residences had

shrines, often prominently placed, where the deities could be worshiped by the household and its various guests at any point throughout the day. Cicero may give the most poignant commentary on this when he writes (*De domo sua* 41.109):

What is more sacred, what is more inviolably hedged about by every kind of sanctity, than the house of every individual citizen? Within its circle are his altars, his hearths, his household deities, his piety, his observances, his ritual; it is a sanctuary so holy in the eyes of all, that it were sacrilege to tear an owner therefrom.

217

Figure 17.5. Two niche shrines; left: a niche shrine from the House of Marcus Obellius Firmus (9.14.4), depicting the *genius* of the householder; right: a niche shrine from the House of the Triclinium (5.2.4), depicting Jupiter (on his throne) and his eagle

What the Vesuvian remains do not show us, however, is the extent to which household piety played itself out in meals and other situations. This is something we learn about from literary sources of the day. Meals inevitably entailed the worship of deities at some point. This might have involved praying to select deities, requesting the presence of deities at the meal itself, and/or offering sacrifices of some kind to the deities overseeing the meal.

Jesus-Devotion Complicating Household Relationships

If devotion to the deities was a fundamental component of household decorum, and if Jesus-devotion was spread through association with other people attached to households in one fashion or another, how were Jesus-followers to negotiate the worship of deities within households?

The issue was complicated, especially because devotion within the household was structured by the householder, with others in the household needing to fall in line with the devotion dictated by him. What was a slave to do, then, when he or she adopted Jesus-devotion but was embedded within a non-Christian household? That issue (considered already in chapter 15) was not given much space in the texts of the New Testament.

What, then, about wives who adopted Jesus-devotion but whose husbands did not? Paul had a thing or two to say about the issue of marriage between believer and unbeliever:

> If any believer has a wife who is an unbeliever, and she consents to live with him, he should not divorce her. And if any woman has a husband who is an unbeliever, and he consents to live with her, she should not divorce him. (1 Corinthians 7:12–13)

218

Paul gives a rather startling reason why a Jesus-follower should stay married to a non-believer: "For the unbelieving husband is made holy through his wife, and the unbelieving wife is made holy through her husband. Otherwise, your children would be unclean, but as it is, they are holy" (7:14). Does holiness seep through the boundary between belief and unbelief? Two verses later, Paul adds this: "Wife, for all you know, you might save your husband. Husband, for all you know, you might save your wife" (7:16; see also 1 Peter 3:1–2).

Paul may not have considered this to be the ideal situation, of course. Elsewhere he articulated things in sharply contrastive terms:

> Do not be mismatched with unbelievers. For what partnership is there between righteousness and lawlessness? Or what fellowship is there between light and darkness? What agreement does Christ have with Beliar? Or what does a believer share with an unbeliever? What agreement has the temple of God with idols? (2 Corinthians 6:14–16)

This passage articulates a principle that Paul occasionally adopted in which Jesus-followers and non-believers are like oil and water, never mixing (although this is not his only mode of discourse; see 1 Corinthians 5:9–10 for the complexities of the matter). Although Paul was not speaking specifically about the relationship between husbands and wives in this

Figure 17.6. Shrines with elaborate frescos surrounding them, with snakes benefiting from the sacrificial offerings of the shrines; left: a shrine from the House of the Ephebus (1.7.11/12/19); right: a shrine from the House of Pinarius (6.16.15)

219

passage, one can easily be forgiven for interpreting it along those lines (although only by neglecting 1 Corinthians 7:14, quoted above). Notably, however, the way Paul made his point suggests that he had already given thought to Jesus-devotion in relation to pagan worship (as in 1 Corinthians 8–10), since in this passage he articulated his discourse in terms of the contrast between "the temple of God" and "idols," identifying Jesus-followers themselves as "the temple of the living God" (as noted in chapter 4).

That form of contrastive reasoning is not in play, as we have seen, when Paul discussed an unbelieving husband's marriage to a believing wife in 1 Corinthians 7. There, a permeable boundary of holiness is postulated, perhaps in alignment with Paul's concern that Jesus-followers should generally stay where they are placed in order to be used in that position. Paul may not have been wholly satisfied with that view, at least if his words at the end of the chapter are anything to go by, for there he shows that his solution is not the ultimate solution: "The appointed time has grown short . . . for the present form of this world is passing away" (7:29, 31; cf. 7:26). If Paul was thinking through a difficult gray area, his theological deliberations here seem to derive from a context in which the return of Jesus Christ was much closer than the far distant future.

Jesus-Followers and Household Meals

What, then, about meals shared with non-Christians? Should Jesus-followers sever all links with their peers? As we have seen, the author of Revelation seems to have wanted Jesus-devotees to adopt a solution that runs along those lines. Paul was more nuanced. We have already examined his view regarding whether Jesus-followers could eat meat that had been offered as a sacrifice to idols (see chapter 5); here we examine the other dimension of ancient meals that he explores—the devotional aspect that characterized so many dining contexts of the Roman world.

Paul's instructions are sometimes hard to pin down in 1 Corinthians 8–10 since he articulated his view along different lines at different points in his discussion. In 1 Corinthians 8, for instance, Paul seems relatively relaxed about Christians eating in non-Christian contexts, working through an envisaged scenario of a Jesus-follower "eating in the temple of an idol" (8:10). In one sense, Paul was rather unconcerned about the prospect. He agreed with certain Corinthian Jesus-followers that idols do not really exist and that the only true deity is the deity proclaimed by Jesus-devotees (8:4–6), and in light of this, he seems to think that eating in the temple of an idol is just eating, nothing more. Participating in such a meal might even be an opportunity for mission, we might imagine Paul saying. The only problem Paul entertains in this context is what that act of eating in a "pagan" temple might mean for some other Jesus-followers, the "weak" as he calls them (or as other Corinthian Jesus-followers called them). This term has been devised because these Jesus-followers did not feel as free in their convictions as other Jesus-followers did. These Jesus-followers might, therefore, adopt confused actions or beliefs as a consequence of the freer actions of others (8:9–13).

Two chapters later, however, Paul worked the issue from another angle. Although idols might be nothing at all, he nonetheless thought that there were strong spiritual forces at work in "pagan" dining situations. Aware that he almost seems to contradict what he said two chapters earlier, Paul asked, "Do I imply that food sacrificed to idols is anything, or that an idol is anything? No!" (1 Corinthians 10:19–20). Instead, he wanted his readers now to consider another dimension of the situation:

> What pagans sacrifice, they sacrifice to demons and not to God. I do not want you to be partners with demons. You cannot drink the cup of the Lord and the cup of demons. You cannot partake of the table of the Lord and the table of demons. (10:20–21)

If Jesus-followers were invited to meals where pagan deities were worshiped as part of the meal, they should simply avoid those situations altogether (10:14–22). This makes good sense, but it is hard to imagine an instance when "eating in the temple of an idol" (as in 8:10) would not involve worship of a pagan deity (and Paul's advice in 1 Corinthians 8 operates on the basis of this likely scenario being irrelevant to his reflections). In 1 Corinthians 10, Paul also imagined situations where issues may not be clear-cut with regard to the devotional dynamics in play at certain meals. In those instances, he calls for discernment, with the well-being of others being the foremost concern (10:23–30).

The Inspiration of Jesus-Devotees in Household Contexts

Discernment needed to be exercised in other regards as well. Since Jesus-followers often met in houses used for various purposes, they would inevitably have been seen by others who shared the house's space but were not Jesus-followers. Perhaps Jesus-followers were allowed to assemble in the home of a non-Christian householder who permitted his household manager

Figure 17.7. A damaged fresco depicting a meal in progress (from the House of the Chaste Lovers, 9.12.6)

(let's say) to gather with other like-minded individuals in one part of his residence—perhaps in the corner of a house's atrium or a corner of the peristyle. This scenario might be what Paul had in mind when he envisaged other people "entering" into a meeting of Jesus-devotees (1 Corinthians 14:23–24). These other people, whom Paul identifies as "inquirers or unbelievers" (NIV), were not entering an enclosed and self-contained church building. They were entering the space where the Jesus-devotees had assembled within a house or workshop. The passersby would be entering the space used for Christian worship, and they could easily observe what transpired within those worship contexts. We might call the worship of early Jesus-followers "semi-public." And this meant that it had to be regulated to a certain extent by the opinion of those who would inevitably pass by.

Paul raised this scenario of "inquirers or unbelievers" entering their worship service because of the practice of speaking in tongues—

the utterances of linguistic gibberish that transpired within corporate worship (as discussed in chapter 8; see 1 Corinthians 12–14). For those who were passing by, this kind of gibberish could act as an obstacle to the reputation of Jesus-followers through a perceived lack of decorum. For this reason, Paul wanted the Spirit-inspired practice of speaking in tongues to be linked to the Spirit-inspired practice of interpretation. Moreover, Paul was convinced that if "inquirers or unbelievers" would become caught up in the prophecies given within the community, they themselves would be "reproved" and "called to account," with the "secrets of [their] heart" being disclosed in the process (14:24–25). As a consequence, the inquirer would experience transformation and come to worship Jesus Christ, recognizing that "God is really among you" (14:25). If this took place within households, the irony of the situation is not hard to spot, with deity figurines sitting in their shrines nearby (unless the householder himself had adopted an exclusive form of Jesus-devotion and removed those figurines from his household).

Women and Worship in Jesus-Groups

Discernment was also required regarding the place and role of women within Jesus-groups. Here again it was the Corinthian Jesus-followers who gave Paul the occasion to comment. We have already seen that some Corinthian women may have seen their devotion to Jesus as a way of transcending their female gender (discussed briefly in chapter 8). In that instance, Jesus-devotion (perhaps like some forms of Bacchic devotion) was being interpreted as negating the low status of female identity, with women interpreting the phrase "not male and female" (literally translated, from Galatians 3:28) to mean that their lord had raised them to transcend the low status that was generally conferred on the female gender. In the context of worshiping Jesus, they found the freedom of Jesus-devotion to be freedom from the restraints of their gender. In arguing against this view, Paul approached the issue from several different angles, all of which were intended to affirm femaleness as a legitimate identity to be "saved within" rather than something to be "saved from."

This may help to explain why the phrase "not male and female" fails to appear in similar articulations of Christian identity beyond Galatians. After writing Galatians (probably in 50 or 51), Paul may have come to see how that phrase was being used to promote expectations that he himself was concerned about. So, when writing to the Corinthians (probably in 54 or 55), Paul preferred to omit the phrase altogether: "In the one Spirit we were all baptized into one body—Jews or Greeks, slaves or free" (1 Corinthians 12:13). Absent is any mention of male and female. The same is evident in the later letter to the Colossians: "There is no longer Greek and Jew, circumcised and uncircumcised, barbarian, Scythian, slave and free; but Christ is all and in all" (Colossians 3:11). Once again, the phrase "not male and female" fails to appear—the best guess for that omission being that the clause was seen as too problematic because of the way it was sometimes understood to erase gendered identities.

If women did not transcend their femaleness in Christ, what did that mean with regard to women and the practicalities of worship in groups of Jesus-devotion? New Testament voices seem to have differed on that score. Paul himself clearly expected women to be praying aloud (speaking the community's words to their deity) and prophesying aloud (speaking their deity's words to the community) within celebrations of Jesus-devotion (1 Corinthians 11:5, 13), albeit in a manner consonant with their identity as women. This is a feature that Luke depicted as being central to the apostolic articulation of Christian innovation, as Peter announced in Jerusalem:

> In the last days it will be, God declares, that I will pour out my Spirit upon all flesh, and your sons and your daughters shall prophesy, and your young men shall see visions, and your old men shall dream dreams. Even upon my slaves, both men and women, in those days I will pour out my Spirit; and they shall prophesy. (Acts 2:17–18, quoting Joel 2:28–29)

Paul lauded prophesying of this kind as being among the highest spiritual gifts within Jesus-groups, bringing "upbuilding and encouragement and consolation" to the group and thereby "build[ing] up the church" (1 Corinthians 14:1–5). Paul's assumption that women were participating in this gift for the benefit of Corinthian Jesus-groups is highly suggestive, indicating the significance of women in pioneering the devotional practices within the early Jesus-groups that Paul founded.

It is not surprising, then, to hear about particular women who played important roles in Paul's communities. In both Corinth and Ephesus, Paul planted Jesus-groups with the assistance of a wife-and-husband team, Prisca and Aquila, who also sponsored a house church in Rome on their return to that city. Because Prisca is mentioned by name before her husband in certain texts, it seems that she took prominence in some fashion in this ministry (see Romans 16:3; 2 Timothy

Figure 17.8. A fresco of a composed and reflective woman (from the Villa Arianna, MANN 9097)

4:19; and Acts 18:18, 26). Elsewhere Paul mentioned Euodia and Syntyche, two women who had "struggled beside [him] in the work of the gospel" (Philippians 4:3), although we cannot tell the precise role that they played. A woman named Phoebe had served Jesus-groups (as deacon?; Greek: *diakonos*) in Corinth's port city Cenchreae and also supported others as a benefactor of Jesus-groups (Romans 16:1–2, much like Eumachia was a benefactor of the fullers of Pompeii, as noted in chapter 14). The Christian woman Junia was at one time an associate of Paul, together with Andronicus, who was probably Junia's husband. Notably, Paul characterized this team as "prominent among the apostles" (16:7). (And then there is Apphia, mentioned in Philemon 2, about whom Paul says only that she is "our sister," but who was probably a benefactor to the Jesus-group associated with Philemon.)

These were heady days in the early Jesus-movement, and women seem to have been involved in the movement in ways that did not leave them simply as passive observers or inert hangers-on. The best suspicion, in fact, is that when Phoebe delivered Paul's letter to Jesus-groups in Rome, it was she who read the letter aloud and, moreover, offered explanations when its initial audiences in Rome discussed what they heard (as noted in chapter 12).

But Jesus-followers increasingly realized that "the appointed time" had *not*, in fact, "grown short"; they increasingly recognized that "the present form of this world" was *not*, in fact, "passing away"—despite Paul's expectations. And it was in this environment, it seems, that a different line of thought emerged regarding the profile of women within Jesus-groups. We see this in a nutshell in the late first-century text of 1 Peter. The author of that text depicted women as "the weaker sex" and claimed that Christian women are to be adorned with "a gentle and quiet spirit" as they "accept the authority of their husbands" (3:4–7).

Much the same picture emerges from another late first-century Christian text—1 Timothy, a text in which the author sought to speak Paul's voice in a context beyond Paul's own day (and in contrast with other extensions of the Pauline voice in different directions, not least among groups with "gnosticizing" tendencies). The author held the view that, when Jesus-followers meet together, women should "learn in silence with full submission" to the men in the group (2:11). He added: "I permit no woman to teach or to have authority over a man; she is to keep silent" (2:12).

Figure 17.9. A mosaic of a respectable woman (from 6.15.14, MANN 124666)

This ruling might have surprised the women from an earlier generation, such as Prisca, Phoebe, and Junia. Prisca, together with her husband, had "explained more accurately the Way of God" to Apollos, a male leader in the movement's early mission (Acts 18:26). Phoebe had probably explained Paul's letter to audiences that included men in Rome in 57. Junia was said to have been "prominent among the apostles" in the earliest generation of Jesus-devotion (Romans 16:7). For the author of 1 Timothy, however, it was necessary for the Christian mission to situate itself in a way that was culturally familiar and prudently inoffensive within the late first-century context. In that setting, the author considered that Jesus-groups should not be places of relational innovation with regard to the profile and roles of males and females. Instead, a woman was to recognize that her salvation placed her firmly in the role expected of females within respectable households: "She will be saved through childbearing" (2:15). And whereas Paul thought it best for widows not to marry (1 Corinthians 7:8, 39–40; see also his advice to single women in 7:25–26), the author of 1 Timothy thought just the opposite, encouraging them to "marry, bear children, and manage their households" (5:14, as we saw briefly in chapter 16). Since the present form of this world was not seen to be passing away any time soon, the author of this text thought it best to work within the structures of the world in which he was embedded. Doing so would ensure that "the enemy" had "no opportunity for slander" against the Christian movement of his day (5:14 NIV). Managing respectable households was an all-important task for Christian matrons in the late first century of the Roman world.

Managing Respectable Christian Households

The kind of advice given by the author of 1 Timothy about the proper decorum for Christian women coincides with other aspects of his program regarding how Jesus-followers should fit respectably into Roman society: "I urge that supplications, prayers, intercessions, and thanksgivings be made for everyone, for kings and all who are in high positions, so that we may lead a peaceful and quiet life in all godliness and dignity" (2:1–2). Seeking to shore up stable forms of life within the society of the late first century, the author of 1 Timothy adopted the view that

Figure 17.10. A fresco of a meal in progress (from 9.12.6)

respectable life was to be evidenced first and foremost by the male leaders of the church. Here is his brief outline of what the respectable male Jesus-follower should look like in the context of his culture:

> He must manage his own household well, keeping his children submissive and respectful in every way—for if someone does not know how to manage his own household, how can he take care of God's church? . . . Moreover, he must be well thought of by outsiders. (3:4–5, 7)

As the author makes clear (3:15), these instructions were written to ensure that leaders of Jesus-groups would know how to "conduct [themselves] in the household of God"—the household of God that was slowly seeping into a variety of first-century contexts. In that enterprise, the chance that the Christian message would seep into respectable households and permeate out from there was increased by ensuring that those who were already

Jesus-followers managed their households in ways that were respectable to others of their day.

A generation earlier, Paul had preferred to support himself whenever possible, rather than relying on others for financial assistance (for instance, 1 Thessalonians 2:9; 2 Thessalonians 3:7–8). Charlatans seeking economic gain roamed the Roman world, and Paul wanted to avoid appearing like one of them (e.g., 2 Corinthians 12:14–18). At times, however, Paul was able to put those concerns aside. For example, Paul was not averse to hinting that Jesus-followers in Rome may want to assist him financially in spreading his good news to the regions to the west of Rome (so Romans 15:24, 28–29). And Paul wrote appreciatively of the benefaction of Phoebe, a woman who supported him in Corinth from her home in the nearby port of Cenchreae (Romans 16:1–2, evidently referring to the time of Paul's Corinthian residency in 57). This differs from the way Paul depicts his earlier time among the Corinthians (in 50–51), when he strove to support himself (1 Corinthians 9:15–18).

Various concerns may have motivated Paul's hesitancy about accepting financial support. Among them was probably the desire to curtail the influence of those who could set themselves up as Paul's patrons and thereby influence how he presented the good news. Something of this hesitation seems to lie behind Paul's comments in Philippians 4:10–20. When Jesus-followers in Philippi sent financial support to offset a time of hardship, Paul responded not with effusive gratitude (as social mores would have dictated) but by clarifying that he is not indebted to them. Instead of binding them to him, their generous gift binds them to God, who will repay them for their goodness. In fact, Paul notes that he could manage quite well even without their financial support, since he has learned to be content in all things and since God can strengthen him to do all things, regardless of his physical situation. This passage in Philippians, then, is characterized by "thankless thanks" because of Paul's guarded and cautious attitude toward financial support and the strings of relational conformity.

As apostolic figures like Paul increasingly died off, some Jesus-followers (like the author of 1 Timothy) came to see benefits in an alternative mission strategy. In that context, Christian householders were to be held in preeminent esteem within Roman society, in order to be reliable patrons in the expansion of the Christian message in the Roman world. Paul had given a foothold for this approach in his comments about the beneficial initiatives of the householders Stephanas and Philemon (1 Corinthians 16:15–16, 18; Philemon 4–6, as noted in chapter 11). Toward the end of the first century, that model came to dominate the pastoral vision of the author who spoke in Paul's name, with adjustments being made as a consequence, to enable the household to be the place where mission could be effectively carried out within the Roman world.

Powers and Protection

> A leper came to him [Jesus] begging him, and kneeling he said to him, "If you choose, you can make me clean." . . . Jesus stretched out his hand and touched him, and said to him, "I do choose. Be made clean!" *Immediately the leprosy left him*, and he was made clean.
>
> Mark 1:40–42

The Invasion of Spiritual Forces

As one who suffered from a fiercely deforming skin disease, the leprous man depicted in this story would have shared his condition with many others in the first-century world. According to one Roman author, skin diseases began to rise significantly within urban environments of the first century, with such afflictions becoming "so disfiguring that any kind of death would be preferable" (Pliny the Elder, *Natural History* 26.1—and ironically, Pliny the Elder was killed in the eruption of Mount Vesuvius in 79). To the ancient mind, in fact, skin diseases of this kind already testified to the grip of death on a person, with leprosy sufferers essentially being among the living dead. This was even advertised by a sufferer's skin—which probably had a whitish tinge as it hung limp and disfigured from its

frame, replicating characteristics of skin on a dead body.

But the original audiences probably heard this story as more than a miracle story in which physical death was temporarily pushed back; they may well have heard it as an exorcism story in which a malevolent spiritual power was eradicated. To many an ancient mind, physical illnesses and diseases were easily attributable to the influence of suprahuman forces that impacted one's health and tilted it toward death. It is probably not coincidental, then, that the words immediately preceding this episode speak of Jesus's success in "casting out demons" (Mark 1:39). In some ancient mindsets, physical maladies were connected closely to the suprahuman realm of the spirit world, regardless of whether those spiritual entities hijacked the bodies of their victims (as in many of the stories in the Gospels) or simply influenced them from afar. If we ask, for instance, whether the one-sentence miracle story of Matthew 12:22 depicts Jesus working a physical cure or a spiritual exorcism, it is obvious that framing the issue in relation to that "either-or" offers a defective appreciation of the full dynamics within the short episode: "Then they brought to him [Jesus] a demoniac who was blind and mute; and he cured him, so that the one who had been mute could speak and see."

For many in the Roman world, the spiritual forces that frequently bedeviled human beings were rarely in it simply for their own interests. They were often beckoned to work on behalf of someone still living. The spirits of deceased family members were sometimes

Figure 18.1. A mosaic usually interpreted as two women (left and middle) who seek the services of a witch, who is attended to by a girl (from the so-called Villa of Cicero in Pompeii, MANN 9987)

thought to be "on call" (in a sense) to advance the interests of surviving family members. This usually involved seeking vengeance on others or simply disadvantaging others beyond the family in order to keep them from getting ahead. So when a person in the Roman world experienced a setback of some kind (whether physical or otherwise), the suspicion could easily arise that he or she might have been the victim of an attack involving the initiative of suprahuman forces—sometimes "magical" forces. Some philosophers and a few beyond their ranks did not see things this way, but popular opinion often ran deeply along these lines.

The Roman world offers numerous examples of this form of popular opinion regarding the effectiveness of the spirit world in relation to the physical world. Many ancient curse tablets involve people going to a graveyard at sunset and asking Helios, the overlord of spirits, to find the spirit of a deceased corpse and bring it up from the underworld to carry out a magical curse against a person's competitor in love or business (e.g., *PGM* 4.296–466). Forces beyond human existence did not need to inhabit a person's body to effect the curse (unlike the many stories of Jesus casting out demons). More often, those forces could detrimentally affect a person's well-being simply through external influence. Detrimental effects were brought against a person by a competitor, through "magical" means (such as casting curse spells or manipulating physical representations like dolls).

A rather humorous example of this way of seeing the world emerges from the work of the Roman poet Ovid, who was active primarily during the reign of emperor Augustus. On one occasion Ovid spoke bluntly about a recent incident in which he found himself unable to perform sexually with a lover. Instead of considering this to be a sign of the slowly debilitating effects of age on his body, Ovid followed his instinct (trained as it was in ancient perceptions of things) to seek an explanation for that embarrassment in relation to malignant forces within the suprahuman realm. So he wrote (*Amores* 3.7.27–30): "Is it some spell or drug that has brought this misery upon me? Has some sorceress written my name on crimson wax, stuck a pin in my liver?" Ovid could not imagine that his body was simply less efficient than it had been in the days of his youth. Instead, with malignant spirits everywhere in the ancient imagination, he found a convenient explanation in that realm.

Curses and Defense in the Vesuvian Evidence

Ovid was not the only poet who feared the power of incantations harnessing suprahuman forces. As one Pompeian resident pointed out in a graffito, the popular Latin poet Virgil perpetuated the same view. Referring to line 70 of Virgil's eighth eclogue, the Pompeian graffito notes that "With magic charms Circe transformed the companions of Ulysses" (*CIL* 4.1982). If it was good enough for Virgil and the great heroes of the past to believe in the power of sorcery, it was good enough for this Pompeian resident. One of his contemporaries expressed it more simply when she/he wrote on a Vesuvian wall, "I believe in incantations" (*CIL* 4.1635).

Figure 18.2. The tombs along a street in the necropolis beyond Pompeii's Nucerian Gate

So too, evidently, did members of the Epidii family, a leading family in Pompeii in the decades immediately before the eruption. In their family tomb, two curse tablets were found that call on the spirit of a deceased member of the household to act against the face, hair, brain, lungs, and kidneys of a victim whose name is no longer decipherable (*CIL* 4.9251). These curse tablets were buried under a layer of dirt because they were meant to be read not by the living but by deceased household members whose cremated remains had been placed in that location. The powerful spirits of the deceased were expected to facilitate the desires of the living.

Because of this connection between the living and the dead, incantations were often used to promote fear in someone, with the intention of causing them to act in a particular way to avoid a fearful prospect. A simple example is on display with the work of a man named Celer who painted several public notices on the walls of Pompeii (one of them having been painted "on his own by the light of the moon," *CIL* 4.3884, as noted in chapter 12). On one notice (painted to express support for Lucius Statius Receptus for *duovir*), he added a subtle curse at the end: "O you hateful person who erases [this], become ill" (*CIL* 4.3775)—an illness presumably manufactured through a suprahuman entity of some kind.

This connection is more explicit on other graffiti. Three curse graffiti appear on the external wall of the House of Pascius Hermes (3.5.1), each of which plays a role in deterring people from defecating in the alleyway. Two of them read *cacator cave malum*—"defecator, beware evil," or perhaps "defecator, beware the evil eye" (*CIL* 4.7714 and 7115; the "evil eye" was thought to be the means whereby someone could cause harm to others by means

of eye contact motivated by envy). The purpose of these graffiti is clear: spiritual forces were called on to police the area and punish anyone who defecated in the alleyway. A third made the point much more forcefully, by writing in huge letters that extended the graffito to over twenty feet in length: "Defecator, beware evil [or the evil eye], or else, if you disregard this warning, may you incur the wrath of Jupiter" (*CIL* 4.7716). Here again, the wrath of a leading deity was being called on to enact vengeance on the defecating transgressor.

Something similar may be evident in an interesting fresco painted on the wall of a corridor leading to a toilet within the Inn of Tertius at Pompeii (9.7.21/22). Several aspects of the fresco are clear. The deity Isis Fortuna (combining the Egyptian deity Isis with the Roman deity Fortuna) holds a rudder (symbolizing control over the forces of life) and a cornucopia, or horn of plenty (symbolizing abundance). This deity of power and plenty looks over at a naked man who is squatting in the position one would take when defecating. Surrounding him are two snakes that represent the protective spirit of the place (the *genius loci*). Scholars usually adopt one of two ways of interpreting the fresco's meaning. In one interpretation, the snakes are protecting the man from evil as he defecates (especially if evil could be thought to lurk below him in the dark underground sewers). This interpretation makes sense if the fresco relates to the toilet down the hall—that is, the dangers of evil are warded off by the beneficent spirit of the place and by Isis Fortuna, who ensures the good fortune of the toilet user. In another interpretation, however, the snakes are attacking the man, an attack watched over approvingly by Isis Fortuna. This interpretation makes sense if the fresco depicts what may have transpired in the corridor itself—that is, to defecate in the corridor instead of the toilet would cause the guarding spirit of the place and the deity Isis Fortuna to punish the offender. Unfortunately, it is impossible to know which interpretation was intended. This situation is not aided by the fact that someone wrote the phrase "defecator, beware evil" on the fresco (*CIL* 4.3832), since that phrase could assist either interpretation.

Most residents of the Vesuvian towns probably thought they could easily become victims of curses—curses conjured by their peers and executed by powerful spirits of the deceased. Pliny the Elder made the point this way: "There is indeed nobody who does not fear to be spellbound [or cursed] by imprecations" devised by others (*Natural History* 28.19). When the architecture of the world is imagined to be full of various levels of suprahuman powers, spiritual defenses are necessary. It is not surprising, then, that one man had words painted at the entryway of his Pompeian workshop (at 8.4.7), which read: "The son of Zeus, Herakles, dazzling in victory, lives here. Let no evil enter!" (*CIL* 4.733). Here malignant forces are deflected through the power of a deity who is said to reside within the workshop, as if it were a temple itself.

Shrines were essential features in erecting the defenses of households (as we have already seen in chapter 17). But another feature of protective defense was also commonly adopted. It might seem strange to us, but Vesuvian residents found they could lessen their anxieties by depicting an erect phallus somewhere within their premises. This is because the phallus tapped into what Pliny the Elder called "the divine protection of *fascinus*"—the spirit of the life-giving phallus that, according to Pliny, served as the "guardian" for everyone

Figure 18.3. A fresco of a man defecating, while seen by Isis Fortuna and the protective spirits of the location (from 9.7.21/22, MANN 112285)

from the least to the greatest (*Natural History* 28.7.39).

For this reason, the phallic symbol is found throughout the archaeological remains of the Vesuvian towns. It was sculpted in stone and displayed for all to see (including spirits)—often being placed emblematically at the front of houses (see figure 18.4). It was worn on jewelry for women and girls. It was scratched into walls (evidenced at the service entrance to the latrine at Oplontis Villa A). It was cast in bronze as a wind-chime (since the sound of the wind-chime was thought to keep evil spirits at bay, assisted by the phallus). It was placed above bakery ovens (at Herculaneum's Insula Orientalis 2.8; in Pompeii at the House of the Chaste Lovers at 9.12.6), with the phallic symbol above one bakery oven including the words *hic habitat felicitas*, or "Here lives good fortune" (*CIL* 4.1454 at 6.6.17). A phallus was sculpted into a visible stone block of a large three-arched neighborhood shrine at 9.2.1, while another phallus oversaw the spiritual ethos of a neighborhood by standing at the

Figure 18.4. Phallic symbols adorning the front of Pompeian residences at 6.14.28 (left: several phallic symbols appear together with a dice-throwing goblet in the middle) and 7.1.36 (right)

intersection between four insulae (at 3.4.3). Meanwhile, a shrine for the neighborhood at the front of a workshop (9.7.2) featured three phallic adornments that helped to frame a main phallus in the shrine's centerpiece (see figure 18.5).

These are just a few examples of the numerous phallic symbols that appear throughout the Vesuvian towns. We should not get distracted by the apparent strangeness of this and lose sight of what this ubiquitous phenomenon testifies to—that is, the perceived need for protection against dangerous spiritual forces that were thought to course through the urban streets. Even the deities could never be wholly trusted for protection. (Note, for instance, *CIL* 4.1839, "Agato, the slave of Herennius, prays to Venus," while below that, written in another hand, is someone else's comment about Agato himself: "I pray that he [Agato] will die.") Without protection, the residents of the Vesuvian towns thought they were exposed to the predatory impulses of others, who could access spiritual powers as extended vehicles of their reach into the very households and lives of others. When that view of the world

is in play, who can blame people for resorting to whatever means possible to increase their chances of protection?

Spirits of Evil in New Testament Texts

We see something of this view of the world in literature of early Christianity. It is evident, for instance, in the exorcism stories that are common in the first three New Testament Gospels (i.e., the "Synoptic Gospels" of Matthew, Mark, and Luke; exorcisms are absent from John's Gospel). These are stories in which evil spirits have taken up residence in the bodies of their victims—going even further than simply orchestrating their downfall at a distance. This is seen, for instance, in the story of the demon-possessed man who lived "night and day among the tombs" and whose possession caused him to be "always howling and bruising himself with stones" (Mark 5:5, from 5:1–13). In fact, it was not a single spirit that manipulated this man but a collective of them. When Jesus asked "the unclean spirit" what its name was, the spirit

Figure 18.5. A neighborhood shrine featuring a winged phallus in the center, with three other phallic symbols surrounding the shrine (at 9.7.2)

upon the victim (in this case, a boy); it is also a social dishonor, since the victim was not protected properly within the household—which probably explains why the victim's father asks Jesus, "Have pity on *us* and help *us*" (9:22).

In each of these accounts, it is no surprise that Jesus casts these destructive spirits out of their victims. But the three New Testament Gospels that include exorcism stories also add an interpretive layer to these stories that takes these stories to another level of meaning altogether. When depicting Jesus exorcising harmful spirits from the lives of their unfortunate victims, each of the three Synoptic Gospels includes an important explanation about what Jesus was really doing in those incidents. So, for instance, in Matthew's Gospel, after Jesus performs an exorcism, the Pharisees are said to charge him with acting through the power of Beelzebul, or Satan. The story continues with Jesus's reply:

> If Satan casts out Satan, he is divided against himself; how then will his kingdom stand? . . . If it is by the Spirit of God that I cast out demons, then the kingdom of God has come to you. Or how can one enter a strong man's house and plunder his property, without first tying up the strong man? Then indeed the house can be plundered. (Matthew 12:26, 28–29, from the episode in 12:22–29; see also Mark 3:23–27 and Luke 11:14–23)

answered, "My name is Legion; for we are many" (5:9).

We see something similar elsewhere, in the story of a man whose only son is controlled by a spirit that "will scarcely leave him"—a spirit that seizes the boy, causing him to shriek, convulse, and foam at the mouth (Luke 9:38–43). In the Gospel of Mark, this incident is told elaborately, with the evil spirit making his victim "unable to speak, and whenever it seizes him, it dashes him down, and he foams and grinds his teeth and becomes rigid" (Mark 9:17–18). In fact, so alarming was the power of this particular spirit that it had often cast its victim "into the fire and into the water in order to destroy him" (9:22). This is not simply a physical calamity that has come

This puts Jesus's mighty deeds into a much larger narrative context than the exorcism of malignant spirits. The full panoply of his exorcisms is not restricted to the micro-narratives of individual lives; it is now seen to be operating also in relation to the macro-narrative of the cosmos—the cosmos as the battleground between Israel's creator deity and the primary

233

force seeking to undermine the sovereignty of that deity.

The readers of these Gospels, then, are not to think of Jesus's power as simply an ambulatory equivalent to a protective phallic symbol. Instead, Jesus's power is part of a cosmic defense against the influx of chaotic forces that have invaded the created order—and not just a "defense against" but a "demise of" those forces, a "plundering" of the house and property of "the strong man." Relatedly, the story of Jesus existing alone in the wilderness for forty days, being surrounded by wild beasts, surviving the trials of Satan, and being attended to (protected?) by angels (Mark 1:12–13) might well have captured the attention of first-century audiences concerned to enhance their defenses against the ultimate force of concentrated evil, narratively embodied in the figure of Satan.

John's Gospel is devoid of exorcism stories, but this does not mean that protection motifs are missing from that Gospel. In fact, the theme of protection plays a central role in Jesus's final words spoken in the company of his disciples, in a prayer that he says to his heavenly Father just moments before he is arrested prior to his crucifixion. In those final moments, Jesus prays for the protection of his disciples:

> Now I am no longer in the world, but they are in the world. . . . Holy Father, protect them in your name that you have given me. . . . While I was with them, I protected them in your name that you have given me. I guarded them. . . . I am not asking you to take them out of the world, but I ask you to protect them from the evil one. (John 17:11–12, 15)

Much the same derives from the first epistle of John. Toward the close of that letter, the Johannine author writes the following:

> We know that those who are born of God do not sin, but the one who was born of God protects them, and the evil one does not touch them. We know that we are God's children, and that the whole world lies under the power of the evil one. (1 John 5:18–19)

These are stark denunciations of the world in which early Jesus-followers found themselves, with "the evil one" being the one who orchestrates power directed against Jesus-followers. What is notable in these texts is not the need for protection against supernatural forces but the assurance that even the most concentrated form of evil power cannot encroach on the guardianship of the loving deity who protects his followers.

Spiritual Forces and Protection in Galatians

Paul's letter to Jesus-followers in Galatia frequently engages with issues of power, protection, curses, and magical forces. We cannot know for sure what was going on in the Galatian communities, but it is possible that the Galatian Jesus-followers were toying with the idea that obeying the Torah (often translated "law") would be a helpful way to protect themselves from curses and malignant forces of evil. In that scenario, Paul's comments have special force, as he turned their concerns along different lines. Claiming that a curse falls on all people who try but inevitably fail to do the Torah, Paul argued that this curse was placed on Jesus Christ, who became a curse in order to effect redemption for all people ensnared in that curse (3:10–13). For Paul, the divine Spirit (or "the Spirit of [God's] Son," 4:6) flows to everyone in Christ, without the need for supplementation of any kind. Paul wrote:

"I died to the Torah, so that I might live to God. I have been crucified with Christ and it is no longer I who live, but it is Christ who lives in me" (2:19–20). With the Lord of the universe animating his life, Paul understood that no additional supplements were necessary to enhance a person's protection. If the Galatians were seeking additional levels of power, they had misunderstood the full import of the good news that Paul had brought to them. In Paul's view, the divine Spirit had already been given to them (as testified to by the works of power that they had already experienced, 3:5). If the Galatians were wanting more, they were flirting with less. By seeking to supplement what they already had, they were jeopardizing the whole blessing that protected them. It is because of this that Paul framed his letter in the language of a curse, pronouncing a curse on anyone who preached a gospel other than the one he had preached to them (1:8–9, a passage where the simple Greek word "curse" is sometimes translated "God's curse").

Throughout much of Galatians 3–5, Paul continued to borrow terminology from the sphere of "magic" when articulating his theological discourse. If the Galatians were seeking extra protection from curses and malignant spiritual forces, Paul held out the prospect that they had already been attacked by such undesirable influences, which explained why their best interests might already have been compromised: "Who has cast an evil-eye spell on you?" (a literal translation of 3:1). Later, Paul recounted how he arrived in Galatia with an illness, calling his illness "a trial" for the Galatians (4:13–14). This "trial" put them to the test, in a sense, precisely because illnesses could be thought of as having been induced by an evil spirit. And people with illnesses might themselves cast the evil eye against others, in

Figure 18.6. A mosaic of Medusa (from 6.1.7; without an inventory number); the head of Medusa was often depicted to keep evil away, especially (as in this mosaic) in connection with geometric shapes that were probably intended to distract and confuse evil spirits.

an attempt to capture health from them by means of spiritual powers. In those situations, one form of protection against the evil eye was thought to be spitting—which is precisely why Paul wrote that when he arrived as an ill man among the Galatians, they "did not scorn or spit" at him (4:14, usually translated "scorn or despise"). These terms derive their meaning from cultural customs regarding the world of evil spirits and forms of protection against those spirits.

One other word that Paul used later in Galatians is also important in this regard. It appears in his list of things that Jesus-followers are set free from: "witchcraft," or sorcery (5:20). This word appears nowhere else in Paul's extant letters, so it might have found its way into the letter because of the situation that his Galatian audience was concerned

235

Figure 18.7. A mosaic depicting life in the frail balance, which could easily tilt toward poverty or riches at any moment (even through something as insignificant as the flapping of a butterfly's wings), with death as the one thing that all people have in common (from 1.5.2, MANN 109982)

it with additional forms of protection (3:3): "Having started with the Spirit, are you now ending with the flesh?"

The Protecting Power of the Christian Deity

One of the reasons why Paul was so confident that Jesus-devotees should have nothing to do with sorcery must have been his confidence in the overwhelming power of the Spirit. When Paul called this "the Spirit of [God's] Son" (Galatians 4:6), his audience might have conceived this initially as the *genius* of Jesus Christ. Paul, however, seems to have thought more in terms of what might be called a proto-trinitarianism, in which the creator deity is evidenced in the Father, the Son, and the Spirit (see, for instance, 1 Corinthians 12:4–6). Paul repeatedly claimed that "the Holy Spirit has been given to us" (Romans 5:5) and "dwells in you" (8:9). The Spirit was sent "into our hearts" (Galatians 4:6), and there it cries out to the Father using the same prayer language that characterized the prayer language of Jesus, "Abba! Father!" (4:6; see also Romans 8:15 and Mark 14:36). Replicating Jesus's address to his divine Father is part of a larger complex in which the same "Holy Spirit" that empowered Jesus's ministry empowers the lives of Jesus's followers.

This Spirit emerges from the heart of divine power—the life-giving power of resurrection (Romans 8:11). Consequently, Paul frequently spoke of "the power of the Holy Spirit, . . . the power of the Spirit of God" (15:13, 19). This power generates "the new life of the Spirit" (7:6). In a world of threatening spirits, fearful curses, and malignant entities of all kinds, this message of power might well have attracted the attention of

about. Perhaps they (like almost everyone else in the Roman world) felt they needed as much protection as possible from the threat of malicious spirits that were orchestrated by the practice of sorcery. This is why it is easy to imagine the Galatians thinking that observing the Torah would offer an additional form of protection over and above simply having faith in Jesus Christ. If they already imagined their Jesus-devotion to be a form of protection from spiritual forces, it would have been natural for them to imagine that the more defenses they could add to their faith, the more effective their faith would be. Paul saw things differently. In a simple sentence, he inverted their order of starting with faith and completing

236

many people. The Vesuvian remains (like the material remains from Greco-Roman sites in general) testify to the tremendous measures that people of that ancient world undertook in their search for enhanced protection. People of their world must have been curious to hear about "the immeasurable greatness of God's power for us," not least since this deity was proclaimed to be "far above all rule and authority and power and dominion" (Ephesians 1:19 and 21 respectively). Jesus-devotees were said to have "power through the Spirit of God" (3:16).

Because of his confidence that Jesus-followers had access to unlimited and superior forms of suprahuman power, Paul offered Jesus-groups instruction that was counterintuitive to the curse-laden culture of his day: "Bless those who persecute you; bless and do not curse them" (Romans 12:14). This instruction removed one form of self-protection from the survival strategies of Jesus-followers. Its

challenging vision no doubt emerged from a conviction established earlier in the letter, with this simple rhetorical question: "If God is for us, who can be against us?" (8:31 NIV). We see a similar conviction when Acts recounts how some Jesus-devotees were so convinced of the power of their deity that "a number of those who practiced magic collected their books [of magic spells] and burned them publicly; when the value of these books was calculated, it was found to come to fifty thousand silver coins" (19:19). By the late first century, Jesus-followers had written narratives that depicted their lord encountering the spirits of the underworld and trouncing them "with authority," having "command[ed] even the unclean spirits" so that "they obey[ed] him" (Mark 1:27). Evidently, when Jesus-followers recited the prayer that Jesus had taught his followers to pray, they urgently believed that their "Father in heaven" had the power to act on their bidding: "Deliver us from evil" (Matthew 6:9, 13 RSV).

19

Banqueting and the Dead

The Lord Jesus on the night when he was betrayed took a loaf of bread, and when he had given thanks, he broke it and said, "This is my body that is for you. Do this *in remembrance of me*." In the same way he took the cup also, after supper, saying, "This cup is the new covenant in my blood. Do this, as often as you drink it, *in remembrance of me*." For as often as you eat this bread and drink the cup, you proclaim the Lord's death until he comes.

1 Corinthians 11:23–26

Shaping the Social Memory

"While I am alive, you, hateful death, are coming." This graffito (*CIL* 4.5112, beside the entrance to 9.5.18) captures what we all know to be true: death comes for everyone. In the Roman age, a significant aspect of death was remembrance—remembering a person's significance. Remembrance was so important to social honor that people in the Roman world often strove to dictate, even prior to their death, how they should be remembered after their death.

For the vast majority of people, of course, preserving the social memory of who they had been was not an option. The socially "inferior" regularly passed from this life relatively unnoticed, being remembered by only a few people who themselves played virtually no role in the corporate imagination or the social memory. Only those who enjoyed a certain level of social prominence could meaningfully invest time and energy to shape how they would be remembered after death.

Perhaps the most well-known example of this was the emperor Augustus (emperor from 27 BCE to 14 CE). Prior to his death, the emperor had an oration drafted that heralded all the honors of his impressive reign—the many public offices he had held, the public awards he had received, and the many benefactions he had undertaken to benefit his empire. Titled "The Deeds of the Divine Augustus" (or *Res Gestae Divi Augusti*), this extensive list was inscribed on sizeable stone monuments and set up in strategic urban centers throughout his empire. In the years before his death, Augustus

238

Figure 19.1. The inscription on the tomb of Marcus Arrius Diomedes (HGE42), with the word "memoriae" clearly advertised on the second line

had been fine-tuning how the list would read, to ensure that it was ready to be published to his liking when his inevitable passing was imminent.

Augustus was not the only one who sought to control his own postmortem reputation by means of a memorial monument. In the Roman age, people with some degree of public profile were interested in creating memorials for themselves in the public sphere, thereby ensuring that they had some control over how they would be remembered. Of course, some people were publicly memorialized only after their death. But there are also a good number of tomb monuments that honored people even before their death, often set up by the individuals honored by the memorial.

Shaping Social Memory in Pompeii

We have already seen an instance in which a resident of Pompeii used his tomb as a way of attempting to control his social identity in life and the social memory of himself after death—the case of Publius Vesonius Phileros (who was discussed in chapter 13). Much

the same was the case for a freedman named Marcus Arrius Diomedes. He rose to civic prominence in Pompeii and established a tomb there in memory of himself and his family, even while he was alive: "Marcus Arrius Diomedes (freedman of a woman) [set this up] in memory of himself and his household; [he was] president of the Fortunate Augustan Suburban Country District" (*CIL* 10.1042; see figure 19.1). In this case, Diomedes (who seems to have owned a villa virtually across the street from this monument, outside the walls of Pompeii) erected a monument to people (members of his household) while they were still living and took the occasion to control the social memory of his own life by highlighting his single most significant identity marker— his role as president of a prestigious group.

Constructing social remembrance by means of memorialization is evident also in the interesting case of the tomb of Gaius Munatius Faustus—or better, the tombs of Gaius Munatius Faustus, since there are two tombs honoring him in Pompeii outside two of the town gates (both tombs seeming to date between 50 and 60). The first is a tomb set up by Faustus himself just beyond Pompeii's Nucerian

Gate, in the southeast of the town (see figure 19.2). It is the tomb he was buried in, as indicated by a *columella* that bore his name (a *columella* being a headstone marking where the cremated remains of a person had been placed under the ground). Some of his household were also buried there (as noted in chapter 15). The inscription above the entrance of this tomb reads: "Gaius Munatius Faustus, a member of the *Augustales* and a suburban supervisor by decree of the councilors, to himself and to Naevoleia Tyche, his wife" (DADC, at tomb 9ES). As we have seen in chapter 11, the *Augustales* were expected to use their wealth for purposes of public benefaction, much like those rich freeborn men who were elected to public office. Not all *Augustales* were former slaves, so perhaps Faustus was born free. But neither tomb inscription references his father (which is expected in cases of freeborn citizens), and from his second tomb we see that his wife was herself a former slave. These indicators tip the balance toward Faustus also having been a former slave. Most likely, then, Faustus's story went from birth in slavery to freedom, to acquiring significant wealth, to public status (as an *Augustalis*) and public benefaction. This tomb inscription, however, only remembers the parts of his life story that feature his relatively high civic status.

Figure 19.2. The tomb of Gaius Munatius Faustus (in a state of disrepair) in the necropolis beyond Pompeii's Nucerian Gate

The second of his tombs, outside the Herculaneum Gate in the northwest of the town, is the much more elaborate of the two (see figure 19.3). It was erected by Faustus's wife, Tyche, after Faustus's death and adds further significant features in the public remembrance of Faustus's impressive civic career.

Naevoleia Tyche, a freedwoman of Lucius, [built this] for herself and for Gaius Munatius Faustus, an *Augustalis* and suburban supervisor, to whom the town councilors (with the people's agreement) decreed an honorific chair for his merits. Naevoleia Tyche had this monument made in her lifetime for her own freedmen and freedwomen and for those of Gaius Munatius Faustus. (*CIL* 10.1030)

A *columella* honoring Tyche was not found in either tomb, so we cannot know which tomb was used to hold her cremated remains. The tomb Tyche constructed had only two *columellae*—one for Gaius Munatius Atimetus, a former slave of the household who lived fifty-seven

Figure 19.3. The memorial tomb to Munatius Faustus (HGW22) erected by his wife, Naevoleia Tyche, with an entrance to the left that allowed household members to access it

241

years, and one for Salvus, a boy who lived six years, probably one of Tyche's household slaves. The remains of other household members may well have been interred in this tomb as well.

There are probably two reasons why Tyche built this second tomb, while she was alive, in honor of herself and her husband (presumably after his death), along a busy road out of Pompeii. Faustus's first tomb, erected by him while he was alive, went some way in advertising his civic importance, but it failed to mention a few particulars of his noteworthy public career. The original memorial did not point out, for instance, that the town councilors had awarded Faustus an honorific chair for his merits (*merita*). This would have been quite a notable honor. It meant that, whenever Faustus attended theatrical performances in one of Pompeii's two theaters, he could sit in his chair of honor in a prominent position among the civic elite who held public office. (Compare Holconius's seat in the Large Theater, mentioned in chapter 11.)

If Faustus's honors were more explicitly referenced in the inscription on the second memorial, they were also visually displayed on that tomb. One side of the memorial erected by Tyche graphically depicts the honorific chair awarded to Faustus (see figure 19.4), and the front of this second monument re-creates a scene of a celebratory parade that must have been a high point in Faustus's civic career (see figure 19.5). For Tyche, these were the moments that defined who Faustus was and how he was to be remembered, in return for his generous gifts to the community. In her view, it seems, the first memorial tomb was deficient in constructing the social remembrance of Faustus's identity sufficiently. There was more to his career that needed to be announced publicly, more beneficence and status to be en-

tered into the public registry (for the benefit of survivors within Faustus's household). So Tyche undertook the responsibility of enhancing the social memory of her husband's identity by constructing a second memorial in his honor. (Unlike Vesonius Phileros, Tyche did not simply upgrade an inscription or add a new inscription to Faustus's original tomb monument; instead, she undertook the building of a completely new memorial—itself an impressive and expensive undertaking.)

There was a second motivation for Tyche's initiative. She used her husband's second memorial tomb to insert herself more securely

Figure 19.4. The marble representation of the chair awarded to Faustus in recognition of his outstanding civic service, highlighted on a side of the monument erected by Tyche

Figure 19.5. The marble representation of a public moment in Faustus's civic career, perhaps a procession honoring him or his distribution of bread to the people

into Faustus's impressive narrative—so much so, in fact, that his narrative almost gets overshadowed by hers. Getting first mention in the inscription, Tyche later highlights that she has made this monument "for her own freedmen and freedwomen and for those of Gaius Munatius Faustus." That is to say, she, formerly a slave within someone else's household, had become an impressive *materfamilias* herself, with her own household slaves—some of whom she had released to become her freedmen and freedwomen, who have then gone on to play their own roles within the town. Tyche has become a patroness to an enclave of Pompeii's constituency. Her personal narrative, then, was one of long-standing upward mobility, and she wanted to advertise that fact, using a second tomb to Faustus as her means of doing that. In a sense, she felt that she deserved to get in the picture with more than the simple credential of being Faustus's wife, which was her only credit in the inscription left by Faustus in his original tomb.

Putting herself in the picture is literally what she did in this impressive tomb. On the very front of the inscription, a figure is popping out of a window at the top. An early archaeological drawing of this artifact clearly shows that this figure is a woman rather than a man. That woman must be Tyche herself. She has been overseeing the whole process of her husband's success, this detail seems to suggest. Tyche wanted it to be known that she epitomized the (modern) saying "Behind every great man there stands a great woman." Evidently Tyche did all that she could to bolster prospects for herself and her family after Faustus's death. This may be the tomb in memory of Faustus, but it is very much in honor of his wife, Tyche, who helped to engineer the social remembrance of herself while she was living.

Memorializing the Social Memory of the Beneficent Deity

When first-century urbanites heard the narrative recounted in 1 Corinthians 11 about what Jesus did "on the night when he was betrayed," their primary context for understanding it

243

might well have been the memorials honoring prominent figures in the socio-political arena. This is not to suggest that tomb memorials provide the *specific* backdrop for understanding Paul's instructions. Nor is it to suggest that tomb memorials informed Jesus's own awareness of what he did on that night (since the theme of "remembrance" in that context would probably have been drawn from the Passover ceremony of the Judean people, in which they remember their exodus from slavery in Egypt). But the tomb memorials are easy examples of the ubiquitous phenomena that Paul's audiences would have experienced, providing them with a filter through which to receive the story of Jesus's final night. Tomb memorials are phenomena that served to craft social remembrance. Members of Paul's communities would have been keenly aware of the precedents in which people crafted their identities on memorials prior to their deaths for purposes of posthumous remembrance; the evidence was all around them in their towns and cities—whether in remembrance of the "acts of the divine Augustus" or the monuments heralding generals victorious in battle or the initiatives undertaken by prominent civic leaders on behalf of local urban centers. In a certain sense, "the Jesus memorial" could sit alongside the rest of them as a variation on the common theme uniting them all: "for others" and "in remembrance of me."

Unlike "the divine Augustus," however, the divine Jesus Christ is memorialized in only two simple actions he commanded his followers to perform—"eat this bread and drink the cup" (1 Corinthians 11:26). Those symbolic acts memorialize what he stood for. Together, those two acts encapsulate one thing in particular: his death. This was emphasized with the words, "As often as you eat this bread

and drink the cup, you proclaim the Lord's death until he comes" (11:26). The sense is captured also in Luke's Gospel, where Jesus highlights that single act of self-giving as the act by which he is to be remembered: "This is my body, which is given for you. Do this in remembrance of me" (Luke 22:19). The one thing that unites all humanity is death (despite vast differences in status while living), but it is precisely death that characterizes the unique identity of Jesus Christ. His memorial of benefaction for others is centered on his death.

There is an oddity in this regard, however, and that is the vast disparity between the memorials of the great civic benefactors on the one hand and the memorial of Jesus Christ on the other. Why would Jesus's rather insignificant form of benefaction be of any attraction to first-century urbanites? Jesus's actions might have been admirable, even heroic perhaps, but in terms of benefaction they would have appeared paltry and uninteresting compared to, say, the gifts given by the civic elite. Those benefactors were abundantly rich, and their public gifts were evident in impressive stones for all to see. How could a relatively insignificant death be a form of beneficence? It wasn't even close to being on the same scale of generosity as the multiple gifts of benefaction advertised on memorials everywhere throughout ancient urban centers.

But to frame the issue in those terms misses the point, since the same Jesus Christ who gave himself in death was proclaimed to have been resurrected as a mighty deity—in fact, a deity that stood above all other claimants to divinity. In this light, the disparity in forms of benefaction might well have been understood by Jesus-followers to tilt in favor of Jesus Christ. The beneficence of even the most generous benefactors came to an end with their deaths; their memorials tell the stories of generosity past and generosity localized. Even in cases where their beneficence continued to have an effect beyond their lives, the effectiveness of that beneficence diminished as the future stretched out ahead. By contrast, Paul imagined the death of a relatively poor Galilean to become the fount of an ongoing divine beneficence. The memorial of Jesus Christ features his "death until he comes" (1 Corinthians 11:26). His memorial tells the story of a beneficence that drives increasingly into the future, and in doing so, it is beneficence that drives beyond boundaries. This is because the suffering benefactor of Paul's proclamation was not simply a man "born of a woman, born under the law" (Galatians 4:4) who would otherwise have played no significant role in the cultural imagination of the Roman age; instead, this man was raised to life to be recognized as the powerful creator deity. Alongside "the Father, from whom are all things and for whom we exist," Paul's proclamation featured the "Lord Jesus Christ, through whom all things come into being and through whom we exist" (1 Corinthians 8:6). This shifts the memorial of Jesus's beneficence from being the end of the line in his own life story; instead, it is the beginning of the line in the dynamic life story of devotional communities gathering in his name and generously embodying his powerful grace—thereby proclaiming "the Lord's death until he comes." What Paul preached was not simply an instance of altruistic benefaction by means of a curious death; he preached an altruistic death of the only deity that mattered, whose communities participated in manifold beneficence. This was a story of beneficence on steroids—or, in Paul's theological terms, beneficence enlivened by the Spirit of the

Son, "who loved me and gave himself for me" (Galatians 2:20). When the memorial of the beneficent deity is seen in this light, we can start to glimpse a bit of why the so-called good news of the early Jesus-followers might have caught the imagination of some urbanites of the Roman world—perhaps with an appeal that could at times outstretch the magnificent appeals of other deities, such as Isis or Bacchus.

In this light, there are further points to consider regarding the disparity in the memorials commemorating the urban elite on the one hand and Jesus Christ on the other. The elite were memorialized in grand public tombs; by contrast, Jesus was memorialized in a short ritual within a simple meal. Moreover, the tombs of the urban elite were expected to stand as testimonials in perpetuity, but everyone knew that those memorials could not last; there would come a time when the memories of the elite would fall into disrepair or (more likely) be replaced by the memorials of later elite urbanites. By contrast, the memorialization of Jesus Christ was not to fade away and be replaced by another. The simple memorial to Jesus Christ and his main act of benefaction (his death) would continue as a proclamation "until he comes." Only then would his memorial, repeatable throughout the world by his followers, no longer be necessary. So whereas the deceased benefactors would not be returning to their former civic positions, Jesus Christ was expected to return and be revealed as the sovereign of the world.

Dining with the Departed

In the meantime, Jesus-followers met to celebrate their participation in the benefaction of their deity. This often happened in meal settings, as Paul's discussion of "the Lord's Supper" indicates. It was there that they enjoyed the innovative spirit/Spirit of their deity's benefaction.

This, too, would not have been out of the ordinary in the Roman age. As we have seen, many people of that world imagined there to be only a thin partition between the living and the dead. For this reason, tombs of the elite sometimes became miniature banquet halls. When a prominent person died, the members of his or her household would gather at the memorial tomb on the anniversaries of that person's birth and death to participate in a celebratory meal commemorating the life of the deceased. But more than commemoration was taking place in these meals. The Roman poet Ovid speaks of offerings given at the tombs as a means of "appeasing the paternal spirits" (*Fasti* 2.537; also 2.545). The spirits of the deceased could be harnessed for the benefit of the household and its members, but only if those spirits were properly honored. This is referred to in a Jewish text from the second century BCE, which denounces gentile

nations as "unclean" for a variety of reasons, including the fact that they "offer their sacrifices to the dead and they worship evil spirits, and they eat over the graves" of their departed (Jubilees 22:16–17).

The practice of celebratory meals commemorating a family's deceased members is reflected in the archaeological finds of Pompeii. Tombs there were frequently constructed to facilitate a gathering of household members, with ample space for a celebratory banquet to be conducted within the confines of the tomb itself. For instance, the first of Faustus's tombs had space behind the entrance so the household could gather for a meal that joined them to Faustus's spirit. Sometimes the tombs had inner spaces that permitted living members of the household to visit the cremated remains of deceased predecessors—as in the case of the memorial that Tyche constructed for Faustus (see figure 19.6). Tombs sometimes included openings that allowed sustenance to be passed from the outside to the spirits of the dead inside, and many *columellae* were fitted with tubes allowing food and drink to be passed down to the spirits (as noted in chapter 7). One tomb from Pompeii even had a *triclinium*, or dining space, built into its very fabric, needing only to be populated by celebrants at any given time (see figure 19.7).

Some of the frescos in the tomb of Gaius Vestorius Priscus highlight many of these aspects of social remembrance. The tomb for this twenty-two-year-old civic official was erected by Priscus's mother after his early death, probably in the year 76 (just three years before the eruption). When his household visited his tomb after his death, they were surrounded by a feast of beautiful frescos that served various purposes. Some depict aspects of Priscus's public profile. We have already

Figure 19.6. The interior of the memorial tomb for Munatius Faustus erected by Naevoleia Tyche, with space to allow the living to visit the cremated remains of the dead, which would have been held in cremation urns placed in the various niches

Figure 19.7. A drawing of a *triclinium*, or dining space, erected within a Pompeii tomb (HGW23) to facilitate the household's celebratory meals honoring the deceased; the drawing shows the *triclinium* in its condition from two hundred years ago in the early nineteenth century, since this location is now in a state of notable disrepair (see credits).

seen the fresco of a gladiatorial contest from his tomb (see figure 13.2), suggesting that Priscus had sponsored at least one such event for the people of Pompeii. Another fresco within his tomb depicts him making a speech among local politicians, who seem to gaze up at him approvingly (see figure 19.8, left). Another displays Priscus's fine selection of silver banquet utensils, showcasing his opulence and the expensive meals he hosted for his peers (see

figure 19.9). This young man was certainly impressive in his lifetime.

One part of Priscus's memorial tomb seems to pertain to his afterlife. It is a fresco of an open door (see figure 19.10). Placed next to the literal door of the tomb, this interior fresco seems to be the door for Priscus's spirit to move in and out of the tomb as necessary (or at least a symbol of that movement), representing Priscus's ability to enter the tomb from the

Figure 19.8. Two poorly preserved frescos in the tomb of Gaius Vestorius Priscus; left: a scene recalling Priscus's civic involvement as outstanding among his peers; right: a banquet scene (with a slave serving from a table at the right), depicting either the kind of thing Priscus normally did in life or an assembly of his family at his tomb after his death

Figure 19.9. A fresco from the tomb of Gaius Vestorius Priscus depicting ornate silver dining utensils, bowls, and pitchers, all useable at celebratory meals

and some have died," Paul said when discussing an aberrant version the Lord's Supper (1 Corinthians 11:30). Paul thought that the power of the almighty deity coursed through the community's memorialization of their lord. If that memorialization ran contrary to what their lord continues to stand for "until he comes," then the community's access to life-affirming power would be changed into a dire situation.

What would it take for the memorialization of the Lord to run against the grain of that Lord's identity? In this instance, it was the community's compliance with the value system of their world. Paul identified the problem in general terms when he said, "There are divisions among you" (1 Corinthians 11:18). What these divisions looked like in practice is indicated in one short sentence: "For when you

spirit world. Whereas the living members of his household would celebrate with him by entering through the physical doorway, the frescoed doorway reminded them of his presence with them, as his spirit accessed their assembly through a "doorway" of a different kind.

Dining with the Deity of Jesus-Devotees

In one sense, the first urban Jesus-followers had a very similar understanding of their corporate meal celebrations, which were animated by spiritual dynamics. We have seen this already with Paul's discussion about whether Jesus-followers should participate in non-Christian meals. Paul thought meals inevitably involved associating with suprahuman forces of one kind or another. For Paul, if the spiritual dynamics of a meal celebration went wrong, detrimental consequences followed. "That is why many of you are weak and ill,

Figure 19.10. A fresco in the tomb of Gaius Vestorius Priscus depicting an open door, seemingly representing the ability of his spirit to move between this world and the afterlife

are eating, some of you go ahead with your own private suppers; as a result, one person remains hungry and another gets drunk" (11:21 NIV alt.). Whatever divisions were evidenced in Corinthian Jesus-groups seem to have been configured along lines of social status. Those with higher status enjoyed the benefits of a good meal and drink, while those with low social status did without those benefits. It was the custom for hosts to provide substantial meals for their peers—that is, for others who were endowed with similar levels of status. This seems to be what Paul envisaged with regard to some Corinthian Jesus-followers; some went ahead with their own private suppers while others went hungry. Perhaps the hungry ones were relatively impoverished artisans who, after a full day in their workshops, joined the celebratory meal relatively late in the day, after most of the community's food was consumed by those who had the luxury of arriving earlier in the late afternoon.

It is, of course, possible that Paul's reconstruction of the Corinthian situation is more stark than the reality among the Corinthians. Nonetheless, the "divisions" that Paul highlighted pertained to a socio-economic distinction between those who enjoyed a healthy amount of social status and "those who [had] nothing" (1 Corinthians 11:22). The offense may well have been unintentional, a simple case of following the patterns of behavior that everyone was accustomed to. But this was what Paul found so discouraging. The Corinthians had failed to think through their inherited practices in light of the story of Christ's self-giving for others—a story that does the heavy lifting in Paul's instructional discourse (11:23–26). Had they properly re-

flected on those practices, the Corinthians would have leaned into new patterns of corporate behavior. Instead, Paul identifies their inherited practices as "humiliating" some of Jesus's devotees (11:22). As a consequence, their meetings did "more harm than good" (11:17 NIV).

Dining with their deity would have been wondrously exciting. But if that deity's patience was tested by his devotees, disadvantages came to them. Even in that situation, however, Paul did not imagine that his Lord allowed his devotees to fall away from him. Instead, even when illness and death came among them, this itself was thought to be a form of discipline rather than rejection. So, said Paul, "When we are judged in this way by the Lord, we are being disciplined so that we will not be finally condemned with the world" (1 Corinthians 11:32 NIV).

Paul's perception of the Lord's Supper as a spiritual meal involving spiritual power was completely at home in the first-century world. Even at that distance from our world, however, Paul's vision still poses a challenge. Nowhere is this clearer than in the way he saw the Lord's Supper as radicalizing the valuing of status. For Paul, those with higher levels of social prestige were not more significant than those whose social identity was deemed less significant. To bring a highly differentiated system of social stratification to the Lord's Supper was, for Paul, wholly at odds with the transforming power of the deity proclaimed by the early Jesus-followers. The supper of their lord was to testify "until he comes" that inherited patterns of social status are at odds with the value system of their almighty deity.

Looking Further

A Conclusion

There is more that could be said. Each of the probes of the previous chapters could be developed beyond its introductory character, correlating the relevant material from the Vesuvian towns with (1) other material remains of the ancient world, (2) the ancient discussions of relevant topics from Greco-Roman literary texts, and (3) the full spread of texts from early Christian writers. And no doubt further probes could be added to explore additional topics and to consider additional complexities. But while expanding the coverage would add greater depth and nuance, it would also impede the nature of the introductory overviews offered in the previous chapters. So while more can be said, enough has been said, at least for the purposes of this book.

In the preceding chapters, we have at times heard apostolic voices of the early Jesus-movement articulating perspectives that highlight the innovative creativity of their theological worldview. Embedded in their discourse were certain ideological commitments that ran against the grain of perspectives and practices commonly entrenched within the Greco-Roman world. At much the same time, however, we have also seen how some forms of early Christian discourse and practice were aligned in general conformity with the first-century contexts. And we have seen apostolic voices sometimes differing in their assessment of how the novelty of their worldview was to take shape in concrete form in their first-century world.

If more can be said, some of it lies beyond the interface of the Vesuvian towns and the early Jesus-movement. For instance, although some Judeans resided in Pompeii, we know very little about them in that context, so there has been little about them in this book. Of course, the first Jesus-followers often drew on Judean traditions and devotional practices when interpreting their devotion to their risen Lord, but those dimensions are not at our interface and so have not been assembled here to the extent that they are reflected in early Christian texts. Or again, there are points of comparison between the early Christian message and the outlook of Stoic philosophers (as well as clear differences, not least in the narrative configurations that undergird their discourse), but since Stoicism has left almost no distinct impression on the material remains of the Vesuvian towns, Stoicism and early Christianity haven't been compared in this book.

Further, the poor were everywhere in the Roman world, and the New Testament provides plenty of resources for significant engagement with the poor and the societal structures that perpetuated forms of poverty in the Roman world. Unfortunately, the Vesuvian remains give us very little hard data regarding the ubiquitous poor. We probably need to imagine the destitute populating Pompeii's forum and congregating outside the public buildings and temples, with the hope that someone would offer them assistance in their plight. By night, they must have slept rough in the streets or in crevices around the town or beyond the town walls or farther afield in the countryside. They were neighbors of those who have served as guides in this book, and they must have been numerous, but we know almost nothing of them. Here the Vesuvian towns, destroyed by tremendously hot flows of pyroclastic ash, offer almost no specific points of entry into the fragile world of the ubiquitous destitute, now lost to us.

We might want to devise an impressionistic calculation of how many destitute people populated Pompeii. If we imagine that the destitute of Pompeii composed only 5 percent of the population (and usually estimates of the urban poor put the figure much higher than that), and if we imagine the population of Pompeii to have been approximately twelve thousand, then there would have been roughly six hundred utterly destitute people living (or more likely dying) in Pompeii at any given time. Even doubling that number would easily fall within the bounds of reasonable expectation. In any responsible estimate of the population's demographics, the destitute would have been far more numerous than the socially prominent people whom we have met along the way—people like Eumachia, Mamia, Marcus Nonius Balbus, Marcus Holconius Rufus, Gnaeus Alleius Nigidius Maius, Gaius Munatius Faustus, Marcus Arrius Diomedes, Naevoleia Tyche, and Publius Vesonius Phileros. In contrast to those prominent residents who had resources enough to build a life of significance within the public realm, there were hundreds of others whose desperate lack of basic resources placed their life in precarious straits. While well-placed people were building tombs and statues and monuments to themselves, these people were hoping for a way to survive, usually only through the generous initiatives of others.

We know from one graffito that at least one person in Pompeii (I'll assume it was a male) prided himself on not being generous to the destitute. Here is a short extract from a graffito he wrote: "I detest the destitute [*pauperos*]" (*CIL* 4.9839b; see also the destitute of *CIL* 4.9932a, as noted in chapter 10). As the full graffito illustrates, the person who wrote it thought a destitute person was a "fool" who simply wanted a free handout. If John the author of Revelation saw connections between all spheres of life, the author of this graffito was at the other end of the spectrum, failing to see that many people had been forced into situations of poverty as by-products of the social systems and economic structures of their world. Of course, giving free handouts to

Figure Concl.1. A fresco variously interpreted, but probably depicting a person giving a drink to a hungry traveler, accompanied by his dog (from 6.9.6, MANN 9106)

lazy fools is not something we find advocated within the New Testament. For instance, Paul noted that some Jesus-followers were taking advantage of the goodwill and resources of other Jesus-followers, and he gave instructions that this form of behavior should stop (see 2 Thessalonians 3:6–13; compare 1 Timothy 5:3–16; Titus 1:12; Matthew 25:26). But Paul was also able to differentiate between callous laziness on the one hand and unavoidable destitution on the other (see below)—a distinction that the author of this Pompeian graffito seems oblivious to, since he indiscriminately characterized all the destitute as lazy fools. The graffito's author shows no cognizance of the deeply entrenched economic systems that structured so much of ancient society. Those systems often predetermined where people

fell on the economic spectrum, with relative stability for the few at one end and dangerous instability for the many at the other end. The graffito, then, illustrates the author's failure to connect the dots between lived experience and social structures (as evidenced in the charge that the destitute "should pay for it [their food]"), resulting in a graffito that can appear trite in its ignorance and oblivious in its smugness.

The attitude expressed in the graffito is very different from the one attributed to Jesus in the New Testament. Jesus is remembered as saying, "Blessed are you who are poor, for yours is the reign of God" (Luke 6:20). Conversely, he commanded a rich man, "Sell your possessions and give to the poor" (12:33); on another occasion, he exhorted an elite ruler, "Sell all

252

that you own and distribute the money to the poor, and you will have treasure in heaven" (18:22). In the Wisdom of Sirach (a text widely known among Judeans of the first century), "the poor" are said to be "an abomination to the rich" (13:20), but in Jesus-traditions the rich are often "strangely moved" so that they come to recognize their responsibility toward those in need. For instance, when a wealthy man promised to give half of his goods to the poor and to ensure that the rest of his resources could be claimed by those whom he had defrauded, Jesus pronounced, "Today salvation has come to this house" (Luke 19:8–9). Jesus is remembered to have told a story about a Samaritan who cared for a struggling stranger out of his own resources, despite significant inconvenience and danger to himself (10:29–37). He told another story of a rich fool (unlike our Pompeian graffito writer, who thought the poor were fools); in this story, the rich man is judged as foolish for hoarding his possessions (rather than sharing them with those in need, as implied in 12:13–21). In another story, Jesus contrasted a rich man and a poor man, with the rich man eventually finding himself tormented in Hades as a consequence (it seems) of his failure to recognize the needy people around him (16:19–31). And in this same story, Jesus suggested that the scriptural texts written by "Moses and the prophets" are properly interpreted in contexts where the needs of the poor are not overlooked (16:29). This is the same Jesus who is remembered for summing up his ministry with the words, "The Spirit of the Lord is upon me, because he has anointed me to bring good news to the poor" (4:18; compare Matthew 11:2–6 and Luke 7:18–23).

New Testament texts and other texts beyond them demonstrate repeatedly that Jesus-followers of the first few centuries often sought to maintain this openness to the stories of the vulnerable (as chapters 10, 11, and 14 have gone some way to demonstrate, but there is still more that cannot be entertained here). In this way, the early followers of Jesus were aligning themselves with the one who "became poor" for their sake (2 Corinthians 8:9). Moreover, they were embracing the decision of the first ecumenical council of the fledgling Jesus-movement (probably held in the year 48), where it was agreed that the exhortation to "remember the poor" should characterize the practice of Jesus-devotees in all indigenous forms of Christian identity (see Galatians 2:10).

Evidently, then, Jesus-followers were to see past the lazy prejudices exhibited by our Pompeian graffito writer. Others within Pompeii held a view much more in tune with Jesus's sentiments. Frescos in the country club of Julia Felix, for instance, portray scenes of ordinary life that would have been seen on any given day in Pompeii's forum (as noted above; see figure 12.3). One of those frescos shows a woman offering financial assistance to a destitute beggar in the forum (see figure Concl.2). Since the gesture is seen only by the woman's daughter or slave, it seems virtually devoid of the quest for status (almost contrary to what we might have expected); instead, what is on display seems to be a rarely depicted form of simple humanitarian concern for a person in need. (Perhaps the woman is training her daughter in the art of generous living.) The attitude is completely different from the blanket expression of loathing for the destitute in a nearby Pompeian graffito.

The fresco's depiction of the poor beggar offers a rare glimpse into ancient destitution. Although we seldom see the first-century destitute in the material remains of the Vesuvian

253

similar initiatives (for example, Acts 4:34–35; 20:35; Ephesians 4:28; 1 Timothy 6:18; Titus 3:14; 1 John 3:17). Some of the destitute were evidently finding new resources for living in spirited communities of Jesus-devotion, where relational innovation was being enacted—often in experimental form, as they sought to find their way in the aftermath of a new day in obedience to the one whom they called their lord.

If we could ask those Jesus-devotees to summarize their contribution to the search for human meaning in no more than a dozen words, perhaps they might have said something like this: "Rethink your deities; recalculate your status; reinvigorate your relationality with the distressed." These three interconnected convictions helped to inject fresh resources into the ideologies of the Roman world, sometimes enabling Jesus-followers to lean into bold configurations of adventurous novelty within their corporate relationships. Perhaps these same convictions have a role to play even in the twenty-first-century tournament of narratives about healthy forms of human life, meaning, and flourishing.

Figure Concl.2. A drawing of a Pompeian fresco (MANN 9059, from the country club of Julia Felix at 2.4) depicting a destitute man receiving aid from a "middle-class" woman and her daughter or slave (see credits); the fresco is in poor condition today.

towns, the New Testament brings their world alive time after time, with their stories having some prominence within its covers. At much the same time that a fresco painter depicted a woman extending generosity to the needy in the forum of Pompeii, some of the earliest followers of Jesus were acting corporately to undertake

Questions to Consider

To help you dig deeper into the issues presented in the main chapters of this book (chapters 4 through 19), forty-eight "things to consider" are offered here (three per chapter). These are intended to draw your attention to other early Christian texts that were not considered in those chapters and are suitable for either individual consideration or group discussion.

Chapter 4: Deities and Temples

1. Read and consider selected passages in 1 Peter: 2:12, 20; 3:9–11, 15–17; and 4:19. What advice does that text give regarding how first-century Jesus-followers should position themselves within a non-Christian society?

2. We have seen that Paul identifies the Christian community as "the temple of God" in both 1 Corinthians (3:16–17; see also 6:19) and 2 Corinthians (6:16). Read 1 Corinthians 3:16–17 again, noting that the word "you" is always plural but the word "temple" is always singular. Is there significance in that?

3. When Paul spoke to philosophers of Athens (recounted in Acts 17), he noticed an altar with the inscription "To an unknown deity" (17:23). Why would the people of an ancient city have such an altar? How would it have operated in relation to all the other altars in the temples of the same city? Even if Paul "was deeply distressed to see that the city was full of idols" (17:16), would his contemporaries in Athens have agreed that their statues of deities (i.e., idols) illustrated a belief that "the divine being is like gold or silver or stone—an image made by human design and skill" (17:29 NIV), or is that rhetorical exaggeration on Paul's part? What aspect of Paul's worldview enabled him to announce that "in the past God overlooked such ignorance, but now he commands all people everywhere to repent" (17:30 NIV)?

Chapter 5: Sacrifice and Sin

1. Paul filters his discourse through the prism of sacrificial language in various ways in his letters.

- Sometimes he depicts himself as a sacrifice, as in Philippians 2:17 (NIV): "But even if I am being poured out like a drink offering on the sacrifice and service coming from your faith, I am glad and rejoice with all of you."
- Sometimes the financial support of his own ministry by communities he founded is depicted as a sacrifice, as in Philippians 4:18 (NIV): "They are a fragrant offering, an acceptable sacrifice, pleasing to God."
- Sometimes gentile Jesus-followers whom Paul has converted to the gospel are themselves depicted as a sacrificial offering, as in Romans 15:16 (noted in chapter 5).

Why might Paul refract the imagery of sacrificial offerings in such diverse ways in his letters to urban Jesus-followers?

2. According to John's Gospel, when John the Baptist saw Jesus, he declared: "Behold the Lamb of God who takes away the sin of the world" (1:29 RSV). Why would this symbolism of Jesus as "the Lamb of God" pertain more to the Judean sacrificial system based in Jerusalem than to sacrificial practices in urban centers beyond that setting? What would an Epicurean think of John the Baptist's declaration?

3. Prayer was an important part of presenting sacrifices to the Greco-Roman deities,

making the offerings acceptable and more effective. Some passages in the New Testament might strike familiar chords with people in the Roman world. Consider, for instance, this passage from James:

> The prayer offered in faith will make them [the sick] well; the Lord will raise them up. If they have sinned, they will be forgiven. Therefore confess your sins to each other and pray for each other so that you may be healed. The prayer of a righteous person is powerful and effective. (5:15–16 NIV)

Consider other passages in this regard: Romans 15:30; Ephesians 6:18; Philippians 4:6; 1 Peter 3:12.

Chapter 6: Peace and Security

1. As noted in chapter 6, the Gospel of Luke remembers Jesus as saying, "Do you think that I have come to bring peace to the earth? No, I tell you, but rather division" (12:51). Matthew records this saying in this way: "Do not think that I have come to bring peace to the earth; I have not come to bring peace, but a sword" (10:34). Give further consideration to how these statements might have been heard in first-century urban centers in relation to the vision of imperial rule propagated by Rome—both appreciatively and apprehensively. When linked to a narrative of resurrection power, what reactions might such statements have stirred up?

2. The Gospel of John records Jesus as saying the following:

> Peace I leave with you; my peace I give you. I do not give to you as the world gives. . . . I have told you these things, so that in me you

may have peace. In this world, you will have trouble. But take heart! I have overcome the world. (14:27; 16:33)

What is the relationship between the peace that Jesus leaves with his followers and the trouble that awaits his followers "in this world"? In this regard, consider also 1 Peter 4:12–19.

3. According to Ephesians 2:14–18,

What is the barrier to peace?

What is being united in peace?

What is the true goal of peace?

Chapter 7: *Genius* and Emperor

1. In Philippians 1:27, Paul writes, "I will know that you are standing firm in one spirit, striving side by side with one mind for the faith of the gospel." Explain the concept of "in one spirit" in relation to the ideas outlined in chapter 7. Some translations of the Bible employ a capital *S* when translating the word, "in one Spirit." In that interpretation, how is the notion of the corporate spirit (or the "one mind" of the community) related to "the Holy Spirit"? In this regard, also give consideration to 1 Corinthians 12:13 and Ephesians 4:4.

2. Read 1 Corinthians 5:3–5, where Paul gives instructions to the Corinthians about how they are to discipline a man whose transgression is causing confusion among the community. Can the ideas outlined in chapter 7 shed light on Paul's depiction of his own spirit and the spirit of the man in question? See also the depiction of Paul's own spirit in Colossians 2:5.

3. In John 19:15 we read an exchange between the Judean chief priests and the Roman prefect in Jerusalem regarding the fate of Jesus. "They cried out, 'Away with him! Away with him! Crucify him!' Pilate asked them, 'Shall I crucify your King?' The chief priests answered, 'We have no king but the emperor.'" How does the story continue in 19:16? Does Pilate's action there suggest that he may have manipulated the situation to extract a declaration of political allegiance from the chief priests?

Chapter 8: Mysteries and Knowledge

1. What does Paul imagine "the mystery of God" to be, and in what fashion is it revealed? Consult his argument in 1 Corinthians 2:1–16, where he ends with the claim "We have the mind of Christ." Consider further how all this might relate to what Paul says in 13:2: "If I understand all mysteries and all knowledge . . . but do not have love, I am nothing."

2. Imagine you are a resident of a first-century urban center. How might you hear the story of Jesus turning water into wine in John 2:1–11 if you were also familiar with the nature of Bacchus celebrations? Read the story in full and comment on points of potential contrast and commonality. Then do the same for Ephesians 5:18–20.

3. Read 1 Peter 4:3–5. How many of the entries that the author lists when describing "what the gentiles like to do" overlap with Bacchic celebrations? How does a form of "end-time theology" assist the author in his instruction concerning the form of lifestyle expected of Jesus-followers? Apply the same questions to Romans 13:11–14.

Chapter 9: Death and Life

1. Imagine you are a first-century urban dweller. How would you hear the following verse if you were a devotee of a mystery deity? "This is how God showed his love among us: He sent his one and only Son into the world that we might live through him" (1 John 4:9 NIV). How would an Epicurean (discussed in chapter 5) respond to such a claim?

2. Because Isis suffered loss and grief when Osiris was murdered, her devotees considered her able to understand their own sorrows and suffering. Against this backdrop, read Hebrews 4:14–16 and consider the possibility that those verses might have a polemical edge in relation to these Egyptian deities.

3. Interpret the Lazarus account in John 11:1–53 as if you were a first-century devotee of Jesus explaining the passage to a devotee of Isis. In what ways does it correspond with your understanding of Isis, and in what ways might it differ?

Chapter 10: Prominence and Character

1. In 1 Corinthians 1:10–17, Paul raises the issue of quarreling and divisions among Corinthian Jesus-followers. In 1:18–2:16 he looks at those social problems through a theological lens focused on divine wisdom in Christ. Compare Paul's elaborate theological analysis in 1:18–2:16 with the simpler advice about "bitter envy and selfish ambition" in James 3:14–18. What commonalities do these two passages have in their discourse about social prominence? What aspects of character do they seek to promote within communities of Jesus-followers?

2. Read 1 Corinthians 1:19–21 and 2:6–8. In these passages, it is unlikely that Paul was simply challenging the use of the mind (since elsewhere he wants Jesus-followers to make good use of their minds). Instead, his comments seem to be directed against using the mind in accordance with a particular way of thinking, a specific kind of "wisdom." It is a way of thinking that props up the rulers of this age and the machinery that supports them. It is a way of thinking that entices other people into its deceptive power. What kind of "wisdom" do the rulers of this age perpetuate in order to maintain their positions of power? How is the wisdom of God different from the wisdom of the socially powerful?

3. The author of 1 Timothy thought that the "elders who rule" should be "considered worthy" of their position (5:17). According to 5:19–22, what procedures should be followed in cases where a leader is thought to have engaged in activities demeaning of their position?

Chapter 11: Money and Influence

1. If civic benefactors were seen as bestowing "gifts" on local communities, how might the "good news" regarding the ultimate divine "gift" be heard in urban centers of the Greco-Roman world?

2. Read the story of the poor widow in Mark 12:41–44. What does Jesus do with the "micro-narrative" of the woman over against the powerful characters in the story, and how might that correlate with the Pompeian graffito that lauds "fullers and the owl" rather than "arms and a man"?

3. In 1 Corinthians 16:1–4, Paul encourages Jesus-followers to take steps to support his collection for "the poor among the saints in Jerusalem" (as he calls it in Romans 15:26). Notice who the intended audience is in 1 Corinthians 16:2. Was Paul giving ownership of this initiative to those like Stephanus who were relatively well off—Jesus-followers who were probably among the "middling groups" of the Roman world? Or is Paul giving ownership of this economic initiative to people with a different socio-economic profile? Whose money counts the most in this enterprise and why?

Chapter 12: Literacies and Status

1. Read John 7:14–15 and consider the significance of these verses in terms of the competition for perceived status. How does "learning" play into that competition?

2. Read John 8:7–8 (a passage added to the Gospel of John probably in the early third century). Readers of this passage frequently ponder what Jesus might have written. What are we to imagine Jesus did with his finger?

3. Read Luke's depiction of the early years of Paul's life in Acts 22:3–5. In that passage, what nuances in Paul's self-presentation pertain to the issue of literacy?

Chapter 13: Combat and Courts

1. Read Galatians 5:26 and James 4:1–2. Paul and James agree that certain kinds of "conflicts" or "competition" derive from a particular kind of moral character. What is that moral character, and why do you think a character of that kind can produce such antagonistic

results? (See also the larger context in Galatians 5:13–15 and 5:22–26.)

2. "You have heard that it was said, 'You shall love your neighbor and hate your enemy.' But I say to you, Love your enemies and pray for those who persecute you, so that you may be children of your Father in heaven" (Matthew 5:43–45). This instruction is part of the larger Sermon on the Mount, where Jesus says other things along similar lines (see 5:38–42). Theologians have interpreted these radical sayings in a variety of ways. What is your view regarding the instructive force of Jesus's radical pronouncements? What steps can be taken to evaluate the strengths of other interpretations?

3. In Luke 21:12–19, Jesus portrays the prosecution system gone wrong, under the auspices of "kings and governors." Read that passage and consider how it depicts popular social opinion and the prosecution of civic offenders. How might this help to shed light also on Hebrews 13:3?

Chapter 14: Business and Success

1. The author of Hebrews contrasts

   a. those who exhibit "the love of money" and
   b. those who are "content with what [they] have" and who say, "I will not be afraid" because "the Lord is my helper" and the Lord "will never leave [me] nor forsake [me]" (13:5–6).

In the eyes of the author of Hebrews, which of these two forms of life is more secure? What does he mean when he has the "content" person say, "What can anyone do to me?" How does this compare with the voice of Jesus in Luke 12:32–34? Or the voice of Paul in Philippians 4:10–13?

2. In light of early Christian exhortations to "keep your lives free from the love of money" (Hebrews 13:5; see also 1 Timothy 6:6–10), how would early Jesus-devotees have heard the story about Ananias and Sapphira in the broader narrative of Acts 4:32–5:11? What does contentment have to do with all this?

3. Consider how the story of Acts 16:16–24 compares to the issues presented in chapter 14 (for instance, the identity of the person through whom money is made in 16:16–24, the reaction of the entrepreneurs, and the reaction to the apostles).

Chapter 15: Household and Slaves

1. Compare (1) the situation between the servile household manager described in Matthew 18:23–27 and (2) the situation described in 18:28–31. What does the second of these scenarios suggest about what happens when someone gets a bit of power in their grip? What do you make of the end of the story, described in 18:32–35?

2. Contrast (1) the relatively healthy situation between the servile household manager and the rest of the household slaves described in Matthew 24:45–47 (also Luke 12:42–44) with (2) the unhealthy situation described in Matthew 24:48–51 (also Luke 12:45–48). What does the second of these scenarios suggest about what happens when someone gets a bit of power in their grip? What does it suggest

about early Christian attitudes toward what is "just and fair"?

3. The message "neither slave nor free" must have had special attraction for slaves of the Roman world. What might their expectations have been upon hearing about that message, and how would 1 Timothy 6:1–2 have addressed those expectations?

Chapter 16: Family and Solidarity

1. Most urban residents in the Roman world would never have met a Pharisee from Judea or Galilee. What might they have thought of the Pharisees after reading how they are depicted in relation to their familial duties in Mark 7:9–13 or Matthew 15:1–6?

2. A clash of values was frequently evident when the idealized values of Christian apostolic discourse met the realities of the Roman world. How does Hebrews 13:4 play into that scenario, both in relation to what it says about marriage and about the deity of the Christian gospel in relation to other deities of the Greco-Roman world? Consider the same in relation to 1 Thessalonians 4:1–8.

3. Titus 2:3–5 instructs "older women" to be "reverent" in their behavior "so that the word of God may not be discredited." Reverent behavior for a woman is thought to include the following characteristics: love your husband and children, be self-controlled, be chaste, be good managers of the household, be kind, be submissive to your husband. How different might the list have been if Lucretius Fronto had written it? Titus 2:6–8 instructs "younger men" to be "self-controlled" in everything. This includes the following characteristics:

modeling good works, having integrity, displaying gravitas, and modeling reliable speech. How different might this list have been if Lucretius Fronto had written it?

Chapter 17: Piety and Pragmatism

1. The author of 1 John ends his five-chapter tractate on eternal life and sin with one simple instruction: "Keep yourselves from idols" (5:21). In what ways might an enslaved Jesus-follower in a pagan household have wanted to know more about the practicalities of that instruction? Or a woman who became a Jesus-follower after marrying a pagan householder?

2. In several early Christian texts, conversion seems to happen within whole households. Read, for instance, 1 Corinthians 1:16 (Stephanas and his household); Acts 16:11–15 (Lydia and her household); Acts 16:25–34 (a jailer and his household); and Acts 18:8 (Crispus and his household). What advantages might this model of conversion have had in the first century? What disadvantages might it have had? And consider the implications of Philemon 10, where Paul identified the slave Onesimus as "my child" because Paul had recently "fathered" him spiritually. Does this suggest that Onesimus had not adopted Jesus-devotion while he resided within the residence of his master Philemon, who was himself a Jesus-follower?

3. In 1 Corinthians 14:34–36, women are instructed to "be silent in the churches" since "it is shameful for a woman to speak in church." Many scholars consider this to be a later scribal insertion into Paul's letter to the Corinthians, and there are good reasons for that view. Those reasons cannot be considered here, except to note that the verses appear at 14:34–36 in some ancient manuscripts and after 14:40 in other ancient manuscripts; displacement of this kind is usually a sign that the words may have started life in the margin of a manuscript as a scribal comment and were subsequently inserted directly into the text at one position by one later scribe and into another position by another later scribe.

Give some thought to this thorny issue by comparing 1 Corinthians 14:34–36 with two other passages:

   a. Paul's discussion in 1 Corinthians 11:1–16, where he simply assumes that women regularly prophesy aloud within Christian communities, and
   b. the Pauline author's discussion in 1 Timothy 2:11–15 (perhaps a generation or two after Paul) about how women are to be silent and express their salvation in childbearing.

If 1 Corinthians and 1 Timothy were written by different authors separated by several decades, whose voice does 1 Corinthians 14:34–36 align with more successfully?

Chapter 18: Powers and Protection

1. Imagine you are a first-century reader of the Gospel of Mark. Interpret the significance of Mark 3:13–19 (the calling of the disciples, who are given power to cast out demons) followed immediately by 3:20–27 (the debate about Jesus's suprahuman power). What frame of reference does this narrative sequence construct as the lens for interpreting the miraculous powers of the apostolic figures of the early Christian movement?

261

2. Acts 19:19 notes that when people in Ephesus heard the powerful message of the early Christian movement, "a number of those who practiced magic collected their books and burned them publicly; when the value of these books was calculated, it was found to come to fifty thousand silver coins." What does this text suggest about the prominence of magical practices in the Roman world? When the text goes on to claim that "the word of the Lord grew mightily and prevailed" (19:20), what might this tell us about (1) the anxiety that people felt concerning the spirit world and (2) the power they expected to have available to them when adopting Jesus-devotion?

3. Read the account of Paul's encounter with the magician in Acts 13:4–12. Read also a similar encounter featuring Philip and Simon in 8:9–13. Consider the effect of these stories on people whose mental universe was populated by spirits that could be conjured by magicians and others for malignant purposes. What might ancient audiences have made of such stories about the power of early Christian leaders?

Chapter 19: Banqueting and the Dead

1. Acts 10 introduces its audience to Cornelius, a gentile who was devout and "God-fearing": "He gave generously to those in need and was constantly in prayer to God" (10:2 NIV alt.). When Cornelius sees a vision, he is told by an angel, "Your prayers and your alms have ascended as a memorial before God" (10:4). Compare and contrast this instance of the word "memorial" (in Greek, *mnēmosynon*) with its only other instance in the New Testament—referencing the woman who anointed Jesus's head with expensive perfume "to prepare [him] for burial," so that "wherever this good news is proclaimed throughout the world, what she has done will also be told, in memory [*mnēmosynon*] of her" (Mark 14:3–9; Matthew 26:6–13).

2. Some Corinthian Jesus-followers evidently began to practice "baptism on behalf of the dead" (1 Corinthians 15:29). While it is difficult to know what this practice entailed, the most likely option is that they were undergoing baptism for the benefit of those who had already died without being united with Christ in baptism—perhaps children, parents, and other members of the family. (This may coincide with Paul's view that holiness "spreads out" within families, as he noted in 1 Corinthians 7:12–14.) How does the ancient view of the interpenetration of the living and the dead assist us in understanding the Corinthian view of "baptism on behalf of the dead"?

3. Consider these three meals:

a. Jesus's last supper before his death (Luke 22:14–38, here at 22:15–16): "He [Jesus] said to them [his disciples], 'I have eagerly desired to eat this Passover with you before I suffer; for I tell you, I will not eat it again until it is fulfilled in the kingdom of God.'"

b. The post-resurrection meal that Jesus eats with two disciples on the road to Emmaus (Luke 24:13–35, here 24:30–31, 35—keeping in mind that ghosts do not ingest physical forms of food, only the "spiritual" nutrients from them): "When he was at the table with them, he took bread, blessed and broke it, and gave it to them. Then their eyes were opened, and they recognized him; and he vanished from their sight. . . . Then they told what had happened on the road, and how he had been made known to them in the breaking of the bread."

c. The meal promised to his followers by the ascended heavenly Lord (Revelation 3:20 NIV alt.): "Here I am! I stand at the door and knock. If anyone hears my voice and opens the door, I will come in and eat with them, and they with me."

Consider how aspects of these three meals might converge with or diverge from the expectations of many in the Roman world regarding postmortem celebratory gatherings.

Abbreviations

AE	*Année épigraphique*, various volumes
alt.	altered
CErc	Cronache Ercolanesi
CIL	*Corpus Inscriptionum Latinarum*, various volumes
DADC	D'Ambrosio, A., and S. De Caro. *Un impegno per Pompei: Fotopiano e documentazione della Necropoli di Porta Nocera.* Milan: Touring Club Italiano, 1983.
EE	*Ephemeris Epigraphica*, various volumes
HG	Herculaneum Gate
ILLRP	*Inscriptiones Latinae Liberae Rei Publicae*, various volumes
LCL	Loeb Classical Library, various volumes
MANN	Museo Archeologico Nazionale di Napoli (National Archaeology Museum of Naples) inventory number
OGIS	*Orientis graeci inscriptiones selectae.* 2 volumes, ed. W. Dittenberger. Leipzig: Apud S. Hirzel, 1903–5.
OS	West Side
NG	Nucerian Gate
PGM	*Papyri Graecae Magicae: Die griechischen Zauberpapyri.* 2 volumes, ed. K. Preisendanz et al. Stuttgart: Teubner, 1973–74.
RICIS	Bricault, Laurent. *Recueil des inscriptions concernant les cultes isiaques.* 2 volumes. Paris: Diffusion de Boccard, 2005.
Tab.	plate
VAR	Arangio-Ruiz, V. "Tavolette ercolanesi (il processo di Giusta)." *Bullettino dell'istituto di diritto romano*, 3rd series 1 (1959): 223–45.

Glossary

aedile: an elected civic official, prominent among the populace but a lower-level magistrate nonetheless, charged with overseeing urban infrastructures such as the maintenance of public buildings and roads.

Aesculapius (originally Asclepius in Greek mythology): the deity of healing; in Greek mythology, his father was the deity Apollo and his mother was a human woman named Koronis.

amphitheater: the large oval outdoor building whose arena was the location for "spectacles," such as gladiatorial combat and wild beast fights.

Apollo: a Greek Olympian deity, son of Zeus/Jupiter.

associations: groups that gathered together for congenial and supportive purposes.

atrium: an open central court with multi-functional purposes, found in many of the more well-off Roman houses.

Augustales (singular, *Augustalis*): the name given to the group of men honored as priests of the emperor; they were usually former slaves who, upon gaining their freedom, went on to acquire significant amounts of money.

Bacchus (originally Dionysus in Greek mythology): a deity of wine, conviviality, and "mystery" initiation.

basilica: the court building where legal disputes were heard; business was often conducted in its adjoining aisles.

Capitoline Triad, the: the three deities that were worshiped on Rome's Capitoline Hill. Jupiter was the high Olympian deity; as his wife, Juno was the deity of marriage; and Minerva was the deity of wisdom—or more specifically, warfare tactics and strategy.

Ceres (originally Demeter in Greek mythology): the Olympian deity of agriculture and life-producing productivity (a mystery cult arose around Demeter and her daughter Persephone); her wrath was deemed to bring drought and famine.

Cicero: an influential Roman orator and politician from the first century BCE.

columella (plural, *columellae*): a simple basic tombstone, carved to approximate a human head and upper torso.

cult: a form of devotion to a particular person or deity (or persons and deities), often enhanced by and enhancing a particular group identity in relation to distinctive worship practices and interests

Cybele: a female deity from Anatolia, who was known as Magna Mater (or "the Great Mother") and whose priests (the *galli*) were usually castrated.

265

denarius (plural, denarii): a Roman coin worth approximately a full day's wage for the average worker (Matthew 20:1–16); it was worth four sesterces. See also sesterce.

Diana (originally Artemis in Greek mythology): the Olympian deity of the hunt, and the sister of Apollo.

dipinti: public announcements and advertisements supporting political candidates, painted on the external walls of a building.

duoviri (singular, *duovir*; plural sometimes written *duumviri*): the senior magistracies (or "the two men") of the town, elected for a three-year term; they chaired the urban council meetings and were responsible to ensure that the decrees of the council were fulfilled.

Erotes: small cupids and permutations of the deity Eros, a deity of love and sexual desire who was the offspring of Venus and Mars.

eschatological: pertaining to the culmination of time, the ultimate end or goal (or "telos") of history (i.e., the eschaton)

fascinus: the life-giving spirit of protection, symbolized most often by a phallus.

Fortuna: a Roman female deity of good fortune.

forum: a central hub of a Roman urban center, with open public space adjoining a number of buildings used for any number of functions (civic, commercial, legal, devotional).

freedman/freedwoman: a former slave who, having been freed, had one of two forms of citizenship—an initial form of pseudo-citizenship for those who were "Junian Latins" (released prior to thirty years of age) and full citizenship for others. Even after gaining their freedom, former slaves still had obligations to their former masters, and men born as slaves could never hold public office as an urban magistrate. Freedwomen could be citizens but, like all women, could not vote.

fresco: a painting that has been embedded in the plaster of a wall by painting the wall before the plaster dries.

fullery: a business in which workers (fullers) cleaned and treated wool clothing.

genius: a male's life force, thought to transcend his physical identity; also used in relation to the life force of certain spaces (for instance, the neighborhood and the colony). See also *juno*.

gnosticizing: the tendency to interpret life through lenses that denigrated the created order and its deity, with salvation coming in the form of secret knowledge ("gnosis") within the soul, enabling the soul to transcend to its true origins in the "heavenly" or spiritual sphere.

grand palaestra: a palaestra is a public courtyard dedicated to exercise and/or military training and/or gladiatorial training; Pompeii had what archaeologists have called a "grand palaestra" near its amphitheater that served these and a number of other functions that often resembled those of a modern park.

imperial cult: the cult (which grew from the grassroots of the Roman empire) dedicated to veneration of the emperor (or his *genius*) and his imperial family.

in situ: in its original place.

insula (literally, "island"; plural, *insulae*): an urban block composed of residences, commercial premises, workshops, and public buildings, in various concentrations (the word is also used at times to refer to a multi-story building made up of apartments, but that meaning is not used in this book).

ira deorum: "the wrath of the deities" was thought to be a pressing threat and avoidable through sacrifices to the deities in temple precincts.

Isis: a popular Egyptian deity who offered those initiated into her mysteries an enhanced life in the present and better prospects in the afterlife.

juno: a female's life force, thought to transcend her physical identity. See also *genius*.

Juno (originally Hera in Greek mythology): a female Olympian deity, the deity of marriage, married to Jupiter, one of the Capitoline Triad (the trio of deities worshiped on the Capitoline Hill of Rome—Jupiter, Juno, and Minerva).

Jupiter (originally Zeus in Greek mythology): the high Olympian deity, one of the Capitoline Triad (the trio of deities worshiped on the Capitoline Hill of Rome—Jupiter, Juno, and Minerva).

lar (plural, *lares*): the guardian spirit of a place (e.g., the guardian spirit of the home in which a household resided, the guardian spirit of a neighborhood).

lararium: the shrine or shrines (plural, *lararia*) where offerings were made to specific guardian spirits. See also *lar*.

macellum: the market in which fish and meat were sold.

Mars (originally Ares in Greek mythology): the deity of war.

Mercury (originally Hermes in Greek mythology): the deity of commerce and financial gain.

Minerva (originally Athena in Greek mythology): an Olympian deity, the deity of wisdom (especially in strategy, tactics, and warfare), one of the Capitoline Triad (the trio of deities worshiped on the Capitoline Hill of Rome—Jupiter, Juno, and Minerva).

otium: the Latin word that denoted fruitful leisure and balanced personal growth.

paterfamilias: the male head of the household, who (in theory) held authoritative power over all others within his household.

pax deorum: "peace with the deities" benefited people by means of sacrifices to the deities in temple precincts.

Pax Romana: the "peace" that Rome was rumored to have effected throughout its empire.

penates: the deities protecting a household (and therefore mobile, unlike the *lares*).

peristyle: the columned porch that (in its full form) encircled the inner garden of many Roman houses.

realia: archaeological artifacts that, having been discovered, reveal aspects of ancient life.

sesterce (plural, sesterces): a Roman coin worth one quarter of a denarius.

sistrum: a musical shaker used by Isis-devotees to assist them in worship of the Egyptian deity.

Social War, the: a brutal conflict in 91–89 BCE between the Roman forces and the Italian Federation of urban centers, resulting in (among other things) the Roman colonization of Pompeii in 80 BCE.

spectacula: the Latin word usually used to describe gladiatorial events.

tablinum: in its original function, this room served as the householder's office, ideally situated between the front atrium and the back peristyle of the house and showing the householder's significance to passersby looking into the house; increasingly, this original function for the room gave way to other functions, and the *tablinum* may have receded in its significance within the structure of the house.

toga: a wool robe that distinguished an adult male as a Roman citizen.

triclinium: the dining room with three couches assembled in the shape of a U to allow the diners to recline on their left side (usually three to a couch), with the center area between the couches being the area for wine and food, which diners consumed using their right hands.

Venus (originally Aphrodite in Greek mythology): the deity of love and sexual attraction (among a vast number of other functions as well), who served as Pompeii's patron deity.

villa: a private residence of unusually large proportion, often beyond the walls of an urban center; some were working villas dedicated to harvesting agricultural produce, others were dedicated primarily to the pursuit of *otium*, and others were a combination of the two; the suburban villa was situated much closer to the walls of an urban center and was similar to any of the larger Roman residences within the urban walls.

Further Reading

Readers who want to delve deeper into aspects of Pompeian life discussed in this book will do well to consult one of the introductory books found in the first paragraph of the "Studies of Pompeii" listed below. Being books of an introductory nature, they almost inevitably articulate the larger contexts in which those aspects can be considered.

More specific studies pertaining to issues mentioned in the chapters of this book are found in the chapter-by-chapter listings below. I have not tried to list every possible resource on any given topic mentioned in the main chapters of this book; these entries (usually listed in chronological order) are simply helpful starting points for exploring relevant publications beyond this book. Beyond these lie many other helpful studies, including many written in languages other than English. (Moreover, the fact that a resource is listed here does not necessarily mean that I agree with its contents.)

Studies of Pompeii

The best overall introduction to Pompeii is Joanne Berry, *The Complete Pompeii* (London: Thames & Hudson, 2007). For other recent works, see Mary Beard, *Pompeii: The Life of a Roman Town* (London: Profile Books, 2008; also published as *The Fires of Vesuvius: Pompeii Lost and Found* [Cambridge, MA: Harvard University Press, 2010]); Roger Ling, *Pompeii: History, Life and Afterlife* (Stroud, UK: History Press, 2009); Paul Roberts, *Life and Death in Pompeii and Herculaneum* (London: British Museum Press, 2013). See also the excellent DVD lecture series by Steven L. Tuck, *Pompeii: Daily Life in an Ancient Roman City*, The Great Courses, 2010.

An engrossing reconstruction of the town's final twenty-five years can be found in Alex Butterworth and Ray Laurence, *Pompeii: The Living City* (London: Weidenfeld & Nicolson, 2005).

The best introduction to Herculaneum is Andrew Wallace-Hadrill, *Herculaneum Past and Future* (London: Francis Lincoln, 2011).

For studies of Pompeii that are more academic, see L. Richardson Jr., *Pompeii: An Architectural History* (London: Johns Hopkins University Press, 1988); Andrew Wallace-Hadrill, *Houses and Society in Pompeii and Hercula-*

neum (Princeton: Princeton University Press, 1994); John J. Dobbins and Pedar W. Foss, eds., *The World of Pompeii* (London: Routledge, 2007).

On economic aspects of Pompeian life, see Miko Flohr and Andrew Wilson, eds., *The Economy of Pompeii* (Oxford: Oxford University Press, 2017), which offers some important qualifications to the issues recorded by Willem M. Jongman, *The Economy and Society of Pompeii* (Amsterdam: Gieben, 1988). See also Eric Poehler, Miko Flohr, and Kevin Cole, eds., *Pompeii: Art, Industry, and Infrastructure* (Oxford: Oxbow Books, 2011).

For interesting studies on Pompeii's street system (on which so much of the town's social life was built), see Jeremy Hartnett, *The Roman Street: Urban Life and Society in Pompeii, Herculaneum, and Rome* (Oxford: Oxford University Press, 2017); Eric E. Poehler, *The Traffic Systems of Pompeii* (Oxford: Oxford University Press, 2017)—the latter improving on an earlier work by Ray Laurence, *Roman Pompeii: Space and Society* (London: Routledge, 1994). See also the photographic reconstruction of Pompeii's main east-west street in Jennifer F. Stephens and Arthur E. Stephens, *Pompeii, A Different Perspective: Via dell'Abbondanza* (Atlanta: Lockwood, 2017). For the "religious register" of the streets, see especially Harriet I. Flower, *The Dancing Lares and the Serpent in the Garden: Religion at the Roman Street Corner* (Princeton: Princeton University Press, 2017).

General Studies of Pompeii's Relevance for Understanding Early Christianity

On the presence of Jesus-devotion within Pompeii, a fresh case that sets out new evidence can be found in Bruce W. Longenecker, *The Crosses of Pompeii: Jesus-Devotion in a Vesuvian Town* (Minneapolis: Fortress, 2016).

On Pompeii as offering resources for helping to understand early Christianity, see Bruce W. Longenecker, ed., *Early Christianity in Pompeian Light: Texts, People, Situations* (Minneapolis: Fortress, 2016)—a collection of academic essays by a variety of scholars.

For a reading of Romans with the help of Pompeian material realia, see Peter Oakes, *Reading Romans in Pompeii: Paul's Letter at Ground Level* (Minneapolis: Fortress, 2009).

General Studies of Early Christianity in the Roman World

An introduction to some of the issues discussed in this book can be found in Paul Duff, *Jesus Followers in the Roman World* (Grand Rapids: Eerdmans, 2017).

For other studies of early Christianity in urban contexts of the Greco-Roman world, see especially Wayne A. Meeks, *The First Urban Christians: The Social World of the Apostle Paul* (1983; repr., New Haven: Yale University Press, 2003); Todd D. Still and David G. Horrell, eds., *After the First Urban Christians: The Social-Scientific Study of Pauline Christianity* (New York: T&T Clark International, 2009); Luke Timothy Johnson, *Among the Gentiles: Greco-Roman Religion and Christianity* (New Haven: Yale University Press, 2009); Moyer Hubbard, *Christianity in the Greco-Roman World: A Narrative Introduction* (Grand Rapids: Baker Academic, 2010); N. T. Wright, *Paul and the Faithfulness of God* (Minneapolis: Fortress, 2013), 197–347, 1271–407; M. David Litwa, *Iesus Deus: The Early Christian Depiction of Jesus as a Mediterranean God* (Minneapolis: Fortress, 2014); James R. Harrison and L. L. Welborn, eds., *The First Urban Churches 1:*

Methodological Foundations (Atlanta: SBL Press, 2015); James R. Harrison and L. L. Welborn, eds., *The First Urban Churches 2: Roman Corinth* (Atlanta: SBL Press, 2016); James R. Harrison and L. L. Welborn, eds., *The First Urban Churches 3: Ephesus* (Atlanta: SBL Press, 2018); C. Kavin Rowe, *One True Life: The Stoics and Early Christians as Rival Traditions* (New Haven: Yale University Press, 2016); J. Paul Sampley, ed., *Paul in the Greco-Roman World: A Handbook*, volumes 1 and 2, rev. ed. (New York: Bloomsbury T&T Clark, 2016); Steve Walton, Paul R. Trebilco, and David W. J. Gill, eds., *The Urban World and the First Christians* (Grand Rapids: Eerdmans, 2017); Robert Knapp, *The Dawn of Christianity: People and Gods in a Time of Magic and Miracles* (Cambridge, MA: Harvard University Press, 2017); Jan N. Bremmer, *Maidens, Magic and Martyrs in Early Christianity* (Tübingen: Mohr Siebeck, 2017); Harry O. Maier, *New Testament Christianity in the Roman World* (Oxford: Oxford University Press, 2018).

For discussion of Christians in rural contexts prior to the Constantinian revolution (although primarily in the second and third centuries), see Thomas A. Robinson, *Who Were the First Christians? Dismantling the Urban Thesis* (Oxford: Oxford University Press, 2017).

Chapter 1: Human Meaning in Stone and Story

On story as a central aspect of human identity, see Jonathan Gotschall, *The Storytelling Animal: How Stories Make Us Human* (Boston: Houghton Mifflin Harcourt, 2012).

The standard compilation of Vesuvian graffiti and inscriptions is Alison E. Cooley and M. G. L. Cooley, *Pompeii and Herculaneum: A Sourcebook* (New York: Routledge, 2013).

Recent studies of the graffiti of Pompeii include Kristina Milnor, *Graffiti and the Literary Landscape in Roman Pompeii* (Oxford: Oxford University Press, 2014); Peter Keegan, *Graffiti in Antiquity* (New York: Routledge, 2014); Rebecca Benefiel and Peter Keegan, eds., *Inscriptions in the Private Sphere in the Greco-Roman World* (Boston: Brill, 2016). For an earlier study, see Helen H. Tanzer, *The Common People of Pompeii: A Study of the Graffiti* (Baltimore: Johns Hopkins Press, 1939). On the "love inscriptions" of Pompeii, see Antonio Varone, *Erotica Pompeiana: Love Inscriptions on the Walls of Pompeii*, translated by Ria P. Berg (Rome: L'Erma di Bretschneider, 2001).

Chapter 2: Fire in the Bones

On status as the primary commodity of the Roman world, see especially Carlin Barton, *Roman Honor: Fire in the Bones* (Berkeley: University of California Press, 2001).

On the complex phenomenon of manumitted slaves and the role of freedmen in the Roman world, see Lauren Hackworth Petersen, *The Freedman in Roman Art and History* (Cambridge: Cambridge University Press, 2011); Henrik Mouritsen, *The Freedman in the Roman World* (Cambridge: Cambridge University Press, 2011).

On the complexities of identity pertaining to manumitted women, see Matthew J. Perry, *Gender, Manumission, and the Roman Freedwoman* (Cambridge: Cambridge University Press, 2014).

Chapter 3: Accessing the First-Century World

On Greco-Roman urbanism in general, see the valiant attempt to construct an "urban geography" by J. W. Hanson, *An Urban Geography of the Roman World, 100 BC to AD 300* (Oxford: Archaeopress, 2016).

For discussion of the growth in the number of Christians, see Keith Hopkins, "Christian Number and Its Implications," *Journal of Early Christian Studies* 6 (1998): 185–226. Hopkins's work meshes well with the proposals of Rodney Stark in *The Rise of Christianity: How the Obscure, Marginal Jesus Movement Became the Dominant Religious Force in the Western World in a Few Centuries* (San Francisco: HarperSanFrancisco, 1997). See also Roderic L. Mullen, *The Expansion of Christianity: A Gazetteer of Its First Three Centuries* (Leiden: Brill, 2004). Note, however, the important qualifications to the numerical figures suggested in these studies in Thomas A. Robinson, *Who Were the First Christians? Dismantling the Urban Thesis* (Oxford: Oxford University Press, 2017).

On the term "Judean," see especially Steve Mason, "Jews, Judaeans, Judaizing, Judaism: Problems of Categorization in Ancient History," *Journal for the Study of Judaism* 38 (2007): 457–512.

For discussions of Pompeian art and architecture, see especially Amedeo Maiuri, *Roman Painting* (New York: Skira, 1953); Paul Zanker, *Pompeii: Public and Private Life*, translated by Deborah Lucas Schneider (Cambridge, MA: Harvard University Press, 1998); Antonella Magagnini and Araldo de Luca, *The Art of Pompeii* (Vercelli, Italy: White Star, 2010). For an extensive (although optimistic) analysis of the relevance of Vesuvian art for our understanding of early Christianity, see David L. Balch, *Contested Ethnicities and Images: Studies in Acts and Art* (Tübingen: Mohr Siebeck, 2015); also David L. Balch and Annette Weissenrieder, eds., *Contested Spaces: Houses and Temples in Roman Antiquity and the New Testament* (Tübingen: Mohr Siebeck, 2012).

Chapter 4: Deities and Temples

On "religion" in the Roman world, see Mary Beard, John North, and Simon Price, *Religions of Rome*, volume 1, *A History* (Cambridge: Cambridge University Press, 1998), and its accompanying volume, Mary Beard, John North, and Simon Price, *Religions of Rome*, volume 2, *A Sourcebook* (Cambridge: Cambridge University Press, 1998). See also Denis Feeney, *Literature and Religion at Rome: Cultures, Contexts, and Beliefs* (Cambridge: Cambridge University Press, 1998); Valerie M. Warrior, *Roman Religion: A Sourcebook* (Newburyport, MA: Focus, 2002), and its accompanying volume, Valerie M. Warrior, *Roman Religion* (Cambridge: Cambridge University Press, 2006); John Scheid, *An Introduction to Roman Religion* (Bloomington: Indiana University Press, 2003); James B. Rives, *Religion in the Roman Empire* (Hoboken, NJ: Wiley-Blackwell, 2006); Jörge Rüpke, *Religions of Rome* (Cambridge: Polity Press, 2007); Rüpke, *From Jupiter to Christ: On the History of Religion in the Roman Imperial Period* (Oxford: Oxford University Press, 2014); Rüpke, *On Roman Religion: Lived Religion and the Individual in Ancient Rome* (Ithaca, NY: Cornell University Press, 2016); Rüpke, *Pantheon: A New History of Roman Religion* (Princeton: Princeton University Press, 2018).

On monotheistic strands even within Greco-Roman polytheism, see Polymnia Athanassiadi and Michael Frede, eds., *Pagan Monotheism in Late Antiquity* (Oxford: Clarendon, 1999); Stephen Mitchell and Peter van Nuffelen, eds., *One God: Pagan Monotheism in the Roman*

Empire (Cambridge: Cambridge University Press, 2010).

On the role of women serving in public cultic contexts, see Meghan diLuzio, *A Place at the Altar: Priestesses in Republican Rome* (Princeton: Princeton University Press, 2016).

On the religious context as it pertains to early Christianity, see Hans-Josef Klauck, *The Religious Context of Early Christianity: A Guide to Graeco-Roman Religions* (Edinburgh: T&T Clark, 2000); James B. Rives, "Graeco-Roman Religion in the Roman Empire," *Currents in Biblical Research* 8 (2010): 240–99.

On Jesus-devotion in polytheistic contexts, see Luke Timothy Johnson, *Religious Experience in Earliest Christianity* (Minneapolis: Fortress, 1998).

On temple imagery in John's Gospel, see Mary L. Coloe, *God Dwells with Us: Temple Symbolism in the Fourth Gospel* (Collegeville, MN: Liturgical Press, 2001); Alan R. Kerr, *The Temple of Jesus' Body: The Temple Theme in the Gospel of John* (New York: Bloomsbury T&T Clark, 2002).

Chapter 5: Sacrifice and Sin

On the notion of sin in the ancient Hellenistic world, see Andrej Petrovic and Ivana Petrovic, *Inner Purity and Pollution in Greek Religion*, volume 1, *Early Greek Religion* (Oxford: Oxford University Press, 2016).

On the overlap between philosophical ethics and "popular morality" in the first century, see Teresa Morgan, *Popular Morality in the Early Roman Empire* (Cambridge: Cambridge University Press, 2007).

On sacrifice in the Greco-Roman world, see F. S. Naiden, *Smoke Signals for the Gods: Ancient Greek Sacrifice from the Archaic through*

Roman Periods (Oxford: Oxford University Press, 2015).

On the use of sacrificial metaphors in two early Christian texts, see Jane Lancaster Patterson, *Keeping the Feast: Metaphors of Sacrifice in 1 Corinthians and Philippians* (Atlanta: SBL Press, 2015).

On the possibility that the man of 1 Corinthians 5 is having sexual relations with his father's second wife while his father is still alive, see Joshua M. Reno, "γυνὴ τοῦ πατρός: Analytic Kin Circumlocution and the Case for Corinthian Adultery," *Journal of Biblical Literature* 135 (2016): 827–47.

On sacrifice in Judaism and early Christianity, see Henrietta L. Wiley and Christian A. Eberhart, eds., *Sacrifice, Cult, and Atonement in Early Judaism and Christianity: Constituents and Critique* (Atlanta: SBL Press, 2017).

Chapter 6: Peace and Security

On the Roman view that war is a necessary instrument to establish peace, see Hannah Cornwell, *Pax and the Politics of Peace: Republic to Principate* (Oxford: Oxford University Press, 2017).

On Roman imperial propaganda, see Clifford Ando, *Imperial Ideology and Provincial Loyalty in the Roman Empire* (Berkeley: University of California Press, 2013); Bruce W. Longenecker, "Peace, Prosperity, and Propaganda: Advertisement and Reality in the Early Roman Empire," in *An Introduction to Empire in the New Testament*, ed. Adam Winn, 15–45 (Atlanta: SBL Press, 2016)—a book that offers readings of early Christian texts in relation to Roman imperial ideologies.

On the interpretation of the political graffito "I sing of launderers and the owl . . . ," see Peter Keegan, *Graffiti in Antiquity* (New

York: Routledge, 2014), 153; on the interpretation of the explicit political graffito "screwed, I say . . . ," see Kristina Milnor, *Graffiti and the Literary Landscape in Roman Pompeii* (Oxford: Oxford University Press, 2014), 122–23.

On early Christianity and Roman imperial ideology, see books listed as further reading for chapter 7.

Chapter 7: *Genius* and Emperor

On the *lares* and frescoed snakes as "the spirits of the place" (and other important issues), see especially Harriet I. Flower, *The Dancing Lares and the Serpent in the Garden: Religion at the Roman Street Corner* (Princeton: Princeton University Press, 2017).

On the Roman imperial cult, see Ittai Gradel, *Emperor Worship and Roman Religion* (Oxford: Oxford University Press, 2002); Duncan Fishwick, *The Imperial Cult in the Latin West* (Boston: Brill, 2004); Gwynaeth McIntyre, *A Family of Gods: The Worship of the Imperial Family in the Latin West* (Ann Arbor: University of Michigan Press, 2016).

On Mamia's temple to "the *genius* of the colony," see Duncan Fishwick, "The Inscription of Mamia Again: The Cult of the *Genius Augusti* and the Temple of the Imperial Cult on the Forum of Pompeii," *Epigraphica* 57 (1995): 17–38.

On the Roman imperial cult and early Christianity, see Bruce W. Winter, *Divine Honours for the Caesars: The First Christians' Responses* (Grand Rapids: Eerdmans, 2015). More generally, see Jeffrey Brodd and Jonathan L. Reed, eds., *Rome and Religion: A Cross-Disciplinary Dialogue on the Imperial Cult* (Atlanta: SBL Press, 2011).

For the political critique of Rome in Revelation, see Adela Yarbro Collins, *Crisis and Catharsis: The Power of the Apocalypse* (Philadelphia: Westminster, 1984); Richard Bauckham, *Climax of Prophecy: Studies on the Book of Revelation* (Edinburgh: T&T Clark, 1993); Steven J. Friesen, *Imperial Cults and the Apocalypse of John: Reading Revelation in the Ruins* (Oxford: Oxford University Press, 2001).

For political dimensions of the Gospel of John, see Warren Carter, *John and Empire: Initial Explorations* (London: T&T Clark, 2008); Tom Thatcher, *Greater Than Caesar: Christology and Empire in the Fourth Gospel* (Minneapolis: Fortress, 2009).

For political dimensions of the Acts of the Apostles, see C. Kavin Rowe, *World Upside Down: Reading Acts in the Graeco-Roman Age* (Oxford: Oxford University Press, 2009); Drew W. Billings, *Acts of the Apostles and the Rhetoric of Roman Imperialism* (Cambridge: Cambridge University Press, 2017).

For discussion of the potential of political critique in Paul, see John M. G. Barclay, *Pauline Churches and Diaspora Jews* (Grand Rapids: Eerdmans, 2011), 341–86; N. T. Wright, *Paul and the Faithfulness of God* (Minneapolis: Fortress, 2013), 1271–319; Bruce W. Longenecker and Todd D. Still, *Thinking through Paul: A Survey of His Life, Letters, and Theology* (Grand Rapids: Zondervan, 2014), 334–46; Christoph Heilig, *Hidden Criticism? The Methodology and Plausibility of the Search for a Counter-Imperial Subtext in Paul* (Minneapolis: Fortress, 2017).

On Hebrews as resistance literature, see Jason A. Whitlark, *Resisting Empire: Rethinking the Purpose of the Letter to "the Hebrews"* (New York: Bloomsbury T&T Clark, 2014).

On the interpretation of the "angels of the churches" in Revelation, see Jeremiah N. Bailey, "Spheres and Trajectories: The Angels of the Churches (Revelation 1–3) in Context," in *Early Christianity in Pompeian Light: Texts, People, Situations*, ed. Bruce W. Longenecker, 167–92 (Minneapolis: Fortress, 2016).

On spiritual aspects of the material world in theological perspective, see especially the stimulating works of Walter Wink: *Naming the Powers: The Language of Power in the New Testament* (Minneapolis: Fortress, 1984); *Unmasking the Powers: The Invisible Forces That Determine Human Existence* (Minneapolis: Fortress, 1986); *Engaging the Powers: Discernment and Resistance in a World of Domination* (Minneapolis: Fortress, 1992).

Chapter 8: Mysteries and Knowledge

On the Villa of the Mysteries in Pompeii, see Elaine K. Gazda, ed., *The Villa of the Mysteries in Pompeii: Ancient Ritual, Modern Muse* (Ann Arbor: Kelsey Museum of Archaeology and the University of Michigan Museum of Art, 2000).

The long-standing standard work on ancient mystery cults is Walter Burkert, *Ancient Mystery Cults* (Cambridge, MA: Harvard University Press, 1987), although he slightly underplays the extent to which mystery cults at times were seen to promise life after death. For more recent discussions, see Hugh Bowden, *Mystery Cults of the Ancient World* (Princeton: Princeton University Press, 2010); Jan N. Bremmer, *Initiation into the Mysteries of the Ancient World* (Boston: de Gruyter, 2014).

On Dionysus/Bacchus, see Renate Schlesier, ed., *A Different God? Dionysos and Ancient Polytheism* (Boston: de Gruyter, 2011); Alberto Bernabe, Miguel Herrero de Jauregui, Ana Isabel Jimenez San Cristobal, and Raquel Martin Hernandez, eds., *Redefining Dionysos* (Boston: de Gruyter, 2013).

On the revelation of divine mystery in Judaism and Paul, see Markus Bockmuehl, *Revelation and Mystery in Ancient Judaism and Pauline Christianity* (Eugene, OR: Wipf & Stock, 2009). On Judean groups that gathered in secret to share divine mysteries, see Michael Stone, *Secret Groups in Ancient Judaism* (Oxford: Oxford University Press, 2018). On the question of the extent to which mystery devotion influenced the apostle Paul, see Alexander J. Wedderburn, *Baptism and Resurrection: Studies in Pauline Theology against Its Graeco-Roman Background* (Tübingen: Mohr Siebeck, 1987).

On the potential influence of Bacchic devotion on Christians (and others), see Courtney Friesen, *Reading Dionysus: Euripides' Bacchae and the Cultural Contestations of Greeks, Jews, Romans, and Christians* (Tübingen: Mohr Siebeck, 2015).

On the "once hidden but now revealed" motif in first- and second-century Christian apologetics about divine mystery, see T. J. Lang, *Mystery and the Making of a Christian Historical Consciousness: From Paul to the Second Century* (Boston: de Gruyter, 2015).

On speech and prophecy especially as it pertains to (women in) Corinthian Jesus-groups, see Antoinette Clark Wire, *The Corinthian Women Prophets: A Reconstruction through Paul's Rhetoric* (Minneapolis: Fortress, 1990); Anna C. Miller, *Corinthian Democracy: Democratic Discourse in 1 Corinthians* (Eugene, OR: Pickwick, 2015); Jill E. Marshall, *Women Praying and Prophesying in Corinth: Gender and Inspired Speech in First Corinthians* (Tübingen: Mohr Siebeck, 2017).

Chapter 9: Death and Life

Beyond the books on mystery cults listed as further reading for chapter 8, on ancient

Isis-devotion see Jaime Alvar, *Romanising Oriental Gods: Myth, Salvation, and Ethics in the Cults of Cybele, Isis, and Mithras*, translated by Richard Gordon (Boston: Brill, 2008). On Isis-devotion in Pompeii (and other aspects of the town's "spiritual ethos" in the aftermath of the earthquake of 62), see Bruce W. Longenecker, "The Empress, the Goddess, and the Earthquake: Atmospheric Conditions Pertaining to Jesus-Devotion in Pompeii," in *Early Christianity in Pompeian Light: Texts, People, Situations*, ed. Bruce W. Longenecker (Minneapolis: Fortress, 2016), 59–91.

On the diverse views toward resurrection in early Judaism, see C. D. Elledge, *Resurrection of the Dead in Early Judaism: 200 BCE–CE 200* (Oxford: Oxford University Press, 2017). On Paul's apocalyptic understanding of resurrection, see especially J. C. Beker, *Paul the Apostle: The Triumph of God in Life and Thought* (Minneapolis: Fortress, 1980), 135–81.

On the emotions of Jesus in the Gospel of John, see Stephen Voorwinde, *Jesus' Emotions in the Fourth Gospel: Human or Divine?* (New York: T&T Clark International, 2005).

On the Gospel of John as a series of "philosophical" discourses on how Jesus Christ brings eternal life to his devotees, see Troels Engberg-Pedersen, *John and Philosophy: A New Reading of the Fourth Gospel* (Oxford: Oxford University Press, 2017).

Chapter 10: Prominence and Character

On Pompeian elections, see James L. Franklin, *Pompeii: The Electoral Programmata: Campaigns and Politics, AD 71–79* (Rome: American Academy in Rome, 1980); Henrik Mouritsen, *Elections, Magistrates and Municipal Elite: Studies in Pompeian Epigraphy* (Rome: L'Erma Di Bretschneider, 1988).

On social prominence and personal character, see Catalina Balmaceda, Virtus Romana*: Politics and Morality in the Roman Historians* (Chapel Hill: University of North Carolina Press, 2017).

On women in the public arena, see Emily Hemelrijk, *Women and the Roman City in the Latin West* (Leiden: Brill, 2013); Hemelrijk, *Hidden Lives, Public Personae: Women and Civic Life in the Roman West* (Oxford: Oxford University Press, 2015).

On Jesus-followers in Corinth in relation to structures of social prominence, see John K. Chow, *Patronage and Power: A Study of Social Networks in Corinth* (Sheffield: Sheffield Academic Press, 1992); Peter Oakes, "Urban Structure and Patronage: Christ Followers in Corinth," in *Understanding the Social World of the New Testament*, ed. Dietmar Neufeld and Richard E. DeMaris, 178–93 (New York: Routledge, 2010); Mark Finney, *Honour and Conflict in the Ancient World: 1 Corinthians in Its Greco-Roman Social Setting* (London: T&T Clark International, 2013).

On Paul's theology of "the body of Christ" as protection against prioritizing financial gifting over other forms of gifting, see Bruce W. Longenecker, "Paul, Poverty, and the Powers: The Eschatological Body of Christ in the Present Evil Age," in *One God, One People, One Future: Essays in Honor of N. T. Wright*, ed. John Anthony Dunne and Eric Lewellen, 363–87 (Minneapolis: Fortress, 2018).

Chapter 11: Money and Influence

On money in the Roman age, see David Jones, *The Bankers of Puteoli: Finance, Trade and Industry in the Roman World* (Stroud, UK: Tempus, 2006)—a book that explores the relevance of over one hundred business contracts from first-century Puteoli, just down the road from the Vesuvian towns. See also David B. Hollander, *Money in the Late Roman Republic* (Leiden: Brill, 2007); Andrew Wilson and Alan K. Bowman, eds., *Trade, Commerce, and the State in the Roman World* (Oxford: Oxford University Press, 2018); Daniel Hoyer, *Money, Culture, and Well-Being in Rome's Economic Development, 0–275 CE* (Leiden: Brill, 2018).

On coins and their importance for understanding the Greco-Roman context of emergent Christianity, see David H. Wenkel, *Coins as Cultural Texts in the World of the New Testament* (New York: Bloomsbury T&T Clark, 2016).

On the currency of honor in early Christianity, see Stephen C. Barton, "Money Matters: Economic Relations and the Transformation of Value in Early Christianity," in *Engaging Economics: New Testament Scenarios and Early Christian Reception*, ed. Bruce W. Longenecker and Kelly D. Liebengood, 37–59 (Grand Rapids: Eerdmans, 2009); Bruce W. Longenecker, "'Do Good to All' (Gal. 6.10): Assets, Capital and Benefaction in Early Christianity," in *Poverty in the Early Church and Today: A Conversation*, ed. Steve Walton and Hannah Swithinbank, 43–53 (London: Bloomsbury T&T Clark, 2019).

On James and money, see Miriam Kamell, "The Economics of Humility: The Rich and the Humble in James," in Longenecker and Liebengood, *Engaging Economics*, 157–76.

Chapter 12: Literacies and Status

On the Villa of the Papyri, see David Sider, *The Library of the Villa dei Papiri at Herculaneum* (Los Angeles: J. Paul Getty Museum, 2005).

On education in the Greco-Roman world, see Judith Evans Grubbs and Tim Parkin, eds., *The Oxford Handbook on Children and Education in the Classical World* (Oxford: Oxford University Press, 2013); and (with reference to Egypt) Raffaella Criboire, *Gymnastics of the Mind: Greek Education in Hellenistic and Roman Egypt* (Princeton: Princeton University Press, 2001). On forms of education in Pompeii, see Laurentino García y García, *Pupils, Teachers and Schools in Pompeii: Childhood, Youth and Culture in the Roman Era* (Rome: Bardi Editore, 2005). On ancient training for education, discussion, and dispute, see Eleanor Dickey, *Stories of Daily Life from the Roman World* (Cambridge: Cambridge University Press, 2017).

On writing in the Roman age, see Hella Eckhardt, *Writing and Power in the Roman World: Literacies and Material Culture* (Cambridge: Cambridge University Press, 2018).

On the literacy (or otherwise) of Jesus, see Chris Keith, *Jesus against the Scribal Elite* (Grand Rapids: Baker Academic, 2014).

On literacy in Greco-Roman Judea, see Michael Owen Wise, *Language and Literacy in Roman Judaea: A Study of the Bar Kokhba Documents* (New Haven: Yale University Press, 2015); see also the helpful corrective to Wise's view in Pieter W. van der Horst, review of Michael Owen Wise, *Language and Literacy in Roman Judaea: A Study of the Bar Kokhba Documents*, in *Review of Biblical Literature*, August 25, 2016, http://www.bookreviews.org.

On corporate reading in early Christianity, see Dan Nässelqvist, *Public Reading in Early Christianity: Lectors, Manuscripts, and Sound in the Oral Delivery of John 1–4* (Leiden: Brill, 2016); Brian J. Wright, *Communal Reading in the Time of Jesus: A Window into Early*

Christian Reading Practices (Minneapolis: Fortress, 2017).

Chapter 13: Combat and Courts

On gladiators in Pompeii, see Luciana Jacobelli, *Gladiators at Pompeii* (Los Angeles: Getty, 2003). On the rituals surrounding gladiatorial combat as a form of "performing the deities," see Jacob A. Latham, *Performance, Memory, and Processions in Ancient Rome: The* Pompa Circensis *from the Late Republic to Late Antiquity* (New York: Cambridge University Press, 2016).

On Roman warfare, see Adrian Goldsworthy, *The Complete Roman Army*, 2nd ed. (London: Thames & Hudson, 2011); Joanne Berry and Nigel Pollard, *The Complete Roman Legions* (London: Thames & Hudson, 2012); Simon Elliott, *Empire State: How the Roman Military Built an Empire* (Oxford: Oxbow Books, 2017).

On Roman courts and the Roman legal system, see Peter Garnsey, *Social Status and Legal Privilege in the Roman Empire* (Oxford: Oxford University Press, 1970); Jill Harries, *Law and Empire in Late Antiquity*, rev. ed. (Cambridge: Cambridge University Press, 2001).

The issue of Corinthian Jesus-followers taking each other to court has been studied from a number of angles (some more successful than others). See Bruce W. Winter, "Civil Litigation in Secular Corinth and the Church: The Forensic Background to 1 Corinthians 6:1–8," *New Testament Studies* 37 (1991): 559–72; J. D. M. Derrett, "Judgment and 1 Corinthians 6," *New Testament Studies* 37 (1991): 22–36; A. C. Mitchell, "Rich and Poor in the Courts of Corinth: Litigiousness and Status in 1 Corinthians 6:1–11," *New Testament Studies* 39 (1993): 562–86;

Michael Peppard, "Brother against Brother: *Controversiae* about Inheritance Disputes and 1 Corinthians 6:1–11," *Journal of Biblical Literature* 133 (2014): 179–92.

On Paul and warfare with spiritual forces, see Lisa M. Bowens, *An Apostle in Battle: Paul and Spiritual Warfare in 2 Corinthians 12:1–10* (Tübingen: Mohr Siebeck, 2017).

For the significance of the trial motif in the Johannine Gospel, see Andrew T. Lincoln, *Truth on Trial: The Lawsuit Motif in the Fourth Gospel* (Peabody, MA: Hendrickson, 2000); P. J. Bekken, *The Lawsuit Motif in John's Gospel from New Perspectives: Jesus Christ, Crucified Criminal and Emperor of the World* (Leiden: Brill, 2015). For an earlier study of the topic, see A. E. Harvey, *Jesus on Trial* (London: SPCK, 1976).

Chapter 14: Business and Success

On occupational groups at Pompeii, see Jinyu Liu, "Pompeii and Collegia: A New Appraisal of the Evidence," *Ancient History Bulletin* 22 (2008): 53–70. On associations in the Greco-Roman world, see Richard S. Ascough, Philip A. Harland, and John S. Kloppenborg, eds., *Associations in the Greco-Roman World: A Sourcebook* (Waco: Baylor University Press, 2012).

On associations in relation to Judaism and early Christianity, see Philip A. Harland, *Dynamics of Identity in the World of the Early Christians* (New York: T&T Clark International, 2009); John S. Kloppenborg, *Christ's Associations: Connecting and Belonging in the Ancient City* (New Haven: Yale University Press, 2019).

On associations, the imperial cult, its economic connections, and Revelation, see Philip A. Harland, *Associations, Synagogues, and Congregations: Claiming a Place in Ancient Mediterranean Society* (Minneapolis: Fortress, 2003); Steven J. Friesen, *Imperial Cults and the Apocalypse of John: Reading Revelation in the Ruins* (Oxford: Oxford University Press, 2001).

Chapter 15: Household and Slaves

On slavery in the Greco-Roman world, see Sandra R. Joshel and Lauren Hackworth Petersen, *The Material Life of Roman Slaves* (Cambridge: Cambridge University Press, 2015). See also Sandra R. Joshel, *Slavery in the Roman World* (Cambridge: Cambridge University Press, 2010). On the manumission of men and women, see the entries for Hackworth Petersen, Mouritsen, and Perry cited as further reading for chapter 2. On the progressive views on slavery held by Bryson (the first-century Neopythagorean philosopher), see Simon Swain, *Economy, Family, and Society from Rome to Islam: A Critical Edition, English Translation, and Study of Bryson's Management of the Estate* (Cambridge: Cambridge University Press, 2013).

On prostitution in Pompeii, see Thomas A. J. McGinn, *The Economy of Prostitution in the Roman World: A Study of Social History and the Brothel* (Ann Arbor: University of Michigan Press, 2004); Sarah Levin-Richardson, *The Brothel of Pompeii: Sex, Class, and Gender at the Margins of Roman Society* (Cambridge: Cambridge University Press, 2019). On prostitutes in the Greco-Roman world, see Anise K. Strong, *Prostitutes and Matrons in the Roman World* (New York: Cambridge University Press, 2016).

On sex in the Roman world, see John R. Clarke, *Looking at Lovemaking: Constructions of Sexuality in Roman Art, 100 BC–*

AD 250 (Berkeley: University of California, 2001); John R. Clarke, *Roman Sex: 100 BC to AD 250* (New York: Harry N. Abrams, 2003); Rebecca Langlands, *Sexual Morality in Ancient Rome* (Cambridge: Cambridge University Press, 2009).

On the "zebra patterns" of the Vesuvian towns, see L. Laken, "Zebra Patterns in Campanian Wall-Painting: A Matter of Function," *Bulletin Antieke Beschauing* 78 (2003): 167–89.

On the issue of slavery in early Christianity in its Roman context, see Jennifer A. Glancy, *Slavery in Early Christianity* (Minneapolis: Fortress, 2006); James Albert Harrill, *Slaves in the New Testament: Literary, Social and Moral Dimensions* (Minneapolis: Fortress, 2009); Katherine Ann Shaner, *Enslaved Leadership in Early Christianity* (Oxford: Oxford University Press, 2018). See also the broader study by Ilaria L. E. Ramelli, *Social Justice and the Legitimacy of Slavery: The Role of Philosophical Asceticism from Ancient Judaism to Late Antiquity* (Oxford: Oxford University Press, 2016).

With regard to slavery and house churches in Colossians, see Margaret Y. MacDonald, "Slavery, Sexuality, and House Churches: A Reassessment of Colossians 3:18–4:1 in Light of New Research on the Roman Family," *New Testament Studies* 53 (2007): 94–113.

On the question of slavery in Philemon, see Bruce W. Longenecker, "Philemon," in James W. Thompson and Bruce W. Longenecker, *Philippians and Philemon*, 149–95 (Grand Rapids: Baker Academic, 2016).

On Christian attitudes toward sex in the context of the Roman world, see William Loader, *Making Sense of Sex: Attitudes towards Sexuality in Early Jewish and Christian Literature* (Grand Rapids: Eerdmans,

2013); Kyle Harper, *From Shame to Sin: The Christian Transformation of Sexual Morality in Late Antiquity* (Cambridge, MA: Harvard University Press, 2016); and David Wheeler-Reed, *Regulating Sex in the Roman Empire: Ideology, the Bible, and the Early Christians* (New Haven: Yale University Press, 2017).

On the relevance of the "zebra patterns" in relation to ideologies of slavery in early Christianity, see Bruce W. Longenecker, "Slave and Free: Ideal Ideologies in Vesuvian Villas and in Galatians 3:28," in *A Temple Not Made with Hands: Essays in Honor of Naymond H. Keathley*, ed. Mikeal C. Parsons and Richard Walsh, 85–102 (Eugene, OR: Wipf & Stock, 2018).

Chapter 16: Family and Solidarity

On the political configuration of family in the Roman world, see Susan M. Elliott, *Family Empires, Roman and Christian* (Salem, OR: Polebridge, 2018).

On women in the Roman world, see Suzanne Dixon, *Reading Roman Women: Sources, Genres, and Real Life* (London: Duckworth, 2007). On women and household structures with regard to Roman law, see Judith Evans Grubbs, *Women and the Law in the Roman Empire: A Sourcebook on Marriage, Divorce, and Widowhood* (London: Routledge, 2002). On educated elite women, see Emily A. Hemelrijk, *Matrona Docta: Educated Women in the Roman Elite from Cornelia to Julia Domna* (London: Routledge, 1999).

On the construction of masculinity in the Roman world, see Maud W. Gleason, *Making Men: Sophists and Self-Presentation in Ancient Rome* (Princeton: Princeton University Press, 1995).

On family in the Augustan period, see Beth Severy, *Augustus and the Family at the Birth of the Roman Empire* (London: Routledge, 2010).

On children and early Christianity, see Margaret Y. MacDonald, *The Power of Children: The Construction of Christian Families in the Greco-Roman World* (Waco: Baylor University Press, 2014); Sharon Betsworth, *Children in Early Christian Narratives* (New York: Bloomsbury T&T Clark, 2016).

On women and early Christianity, see Margaret Y. MacDonald, *Early Christian Women and Pagan Opinion: The Power of the Hysterical Woman* (Cambridge: Cambridge University Press, 1996); Bruce W. Winter, *Roman Wives, Roman Widows: The Appearance of New Women and the Pauline Communities* (Grand Rapids: Eerdmans, 2003); Carolyn Osiek and Margaret Y. MacDonald with Janet H. Tulloch, *A Woman's Place: House Churches in Earliest Christianity* (Minneapolis: Fortress, 2006); Lynn Cohick, *Women in the World of the Earliest Christians: Illuminating Ancient Ways of Life* (Grand Rapids: Baker Academic, 2009); Cynthia Long-Westfall, *Paul and Gender: Reclaiming the Apostle's Vision for Men and Women in Christ* (Grand Rapids: Baker Academic, 2016); Carolyn Osiek, "Growing Up Female in the Pauline Churches: What Did She Do All Day?," in *Early Christianity in Pompeian Light: Texts, People, Situations*, ed. Bruce W. Longenecker, 3–22 (Minneapolis: Fortress, 2016); Lynn H. Cohick and Amy Brown Hughes, *Christian Women in the Patristic World: Their Influence, Authority, and Legacy in the Second through Fifth Centuries* (Grand Rapids: Baker Academic, 2017); Kaisa-Maria Pihlava, *Forgotten Women Leaders: The Authority of Women Hosts of Early Christian Gatherings in the*

First and Second Centuries C.E. (Helsinki: Finnish Exegetical Society, 2017); Alicia D. Meyers, *Blessed among Women? Mothers and Motherhood in the New Testament* (Oxford: Oxford University Press, 2017).

On families and early Christianity, see Stephen C. Barton, *Discipleship and Family Ties in Matthew and Mark* (Cambridge: Cambridge University Press, 1994); Carolyn Osiek and David L. Balch, *Families in the New Testament World: Households and House Churches* (Louisville: Westminster John Knox, 1997).

On reconfiguring Roman masculinity in early Christianity, see Colleen M. Conway, *Behold the Man: Jesus and Greco-Roman Masculinity* (Oxford: Oxford University Press, 2008); Brittany E. Wilson, *Unmanly Men: Refigurations of Masculinity in Luke-Acts* (Oxford: Oxford University Press, 2015).

Chapter 17: Piety and Pragmatism

On locations where early Christians gathered (as testified to by sources from the first three centuries), see Edward Adams, *The Earliest Christian Meeting Places: Almost Exclusively Houses?* (New York: Bloomsbury T&T Clark, 2015). See also the imaginative exercise on this topic by Peter Oakes, "Nine Types of Church in Nine Types of Space in the Insula of the Menander," in *Early Christianity in Pompeian Light: Texts, People, Situations*, ed. Bruce W. Longenecker, 22–58 (Minneapolis: Fortress, 2016).

On the after-meal symposium as a context for early Christian teaching and ritual, see Dennis E. Smith, *From Symposium to Eucharist: The Banquet in the Early Christian World* (Minneapolis: Fortress, 2003). On meals as a context for reinforcing the corporate identity of Jesus-followers, see Hal Taussig, *In the Beginning Was the Meal: Social Experimentation and Early Christian Identity* (Minneapolis: Fortress, 2009).

On "faith" (and its cognates) in Roman and Christian contexts, see Teresa Morgan, *Roman Faith and Christian Faith: Pistis and Fides in the Early Roman Empire and Early Churches* (Cambridge: Cambridge University Press, 2015); and see the journal essays that deal with her work in *New Testament Studies* 64 (2018): 243–61.

On Paul's conviction that the holiness of a believing partner spreads out within a non-Christian household, see Caroline Johnson Hodge, "Married to an Unbeliever: Households, Hierarchies, and Holiness in 1 Corinthians 7:12–16," *Harvard Theological Review* 103 (2010): 1–25; Stephen C. Barton, "Sanctification and Oneness in 1 Corinthians with Implications for the Case of 'Mixed Marriages' (1 Corinthians 7.12–16)," *New Testament Studies* 63 (2017): 38–55.

On the Pastoral letters as crafting an identity that unites Christian commitments and Roman values, see T. Christopher Hoklotubbe, *Civilized Piety: The Rhetoric of Pietas in the Pastoral Epistles and the Roman Empire* (Waco: Baylor University Press, 2017).

Chapter 18: Powers and Protection

On the use of "magic" and protection against evil in the ancient world, see Andrew T. Wilburn, *Materia Magica: The Archaeology of Magic in Roman Egypt, Cyprus, and Spain* (Ann Arbor: University of Michigan Press, 2012); Justin Meggitt, "Did Magic Matter? The Saliency of Magic in the Early Roman Empire," *Journal of Ancient History* 1 (2013): 1–60; Eleni Pachoumi, *The Concepts of the Divine in the Greek Magical Papyri* (Tübingen: Mohr Siebeck, 2017; this book might benefit from substituting the term "suprahuman forces," or some equivalent, for the misleading term "divine" in the title).

On Judean use of magic, see Gideon Bohak, *Ancient Jewish Magic: A History* (Cambridge: Cambridge University Press, 2008); Michael D. Swartz, *The Mechanics of Providence: The Workings of Ancient Jewish Magic and Mysticism* (Tübingen: Mohr Siebeck, 2018).

On early Christian texts in a world of suprahuman powers, see Bruce W. Longenecker, "Until Christ Is Formed in You: Suprahuman Forces and Moral Character in Galatians," *Catholic Biblical Quarterly* 61 (1999): 92–108; Hans-Josef Klauck, *Magic and Paganism in Early Christianity: The World of the Acts of the Apostles* (Minneapolis: Fortress, 2003); Clinton E. Arnold, "'I Am Astonished That You Are So Quickly Turning Away!' (Galatians 1.6): Paul and Anatolian Folk Belief," *New Testament Studies* 51 (2005): 429–49; Arnold, *Ephesians, Power, and Magic: The Concept of Power in Ephesians in Light of Its Historical Setting* (Cambridge: Cambridge University Press, 2009); Natalie R. Webb, "Powers of Protection in Pompeii and Paul: The Apotropaic Function of the Cross in the Letter to the Galatians," in *Early Christianity in Pompeian Light: Texts, People, Situations*, ed. Bruce W. Longenecker, 93–122 (Minneapolis: Fortress, 2016); John H. Elliott, *Beware the Evil Eye*, volume 4, *The Evil Eye in the Bible and the Ancient World—Postbiblical Israel and Early Christianity through Late Antiquity* (Eugene, OR: Cascade, 2017).

On stories of miracles in early Christianity and its Roman context, see Wendy Cotter, *Miracles in Greco-Roman Antiquity: A Sourcebook for the Study of New Testament Miracle Stories* (New York: Routledge, 1999);

Cotter, *The Christ of the Miracle Stories: Portrait through Encounter* (Grand Rapids: Baker Academic, 2010); Lee M. Jefferson, *Christ the Miracle Worker in Early Christian Art* (Minneapolis: Fortress, 2014).

On Mark's Gospel as functioning to move people past a simplistic understanding of Jesus as a deity of protective power, see Bruce W. Longenecker, "Mark's Gospel for the Second Church of the Late First Century," in *The Fullness of Time: Essays on Christology, Creation and Eschatology in Honor of Richard Bauckham*, ed. Daniel M. Gurtner, Grant Macaskill, and Jonathan T. Pennington, 197–214 (Grand Rapids: Eerdmans, 2017).

Chapter 19: Banqueting and the Dead

On the many aspects of death in the Roman world, see Valerie M. Hope, *Death in Ancient Rome: A Sourcebook* (New York: Routledge, 2007); Hope, *Roman Death: The Dying and the Dead in Ancient Rome* (New York: Continuum, 2009). Most books on the subject of the afterlife in the Roman world (often in connection with "mystery religions") are fairly hefty. See, for instance, Katharina Waldner, Richard Gordon, and Wolfgang Spickermann, eds., *Burial Rituals, Ideas of Afterlife, and the Individual in the Hellenistic World and the Roman Empire* (Stuttgart: Franz Steiner Verlag, 2016); Fritz Graf and Sarah Iles Johnston, *Ritual Texts for the Afterlife: Orpheus and the Bacchic Gold Tablets* (New York: Routledge, 2007). Somewhat easier to digest (but also ranging widely) is John Davies, *Death, Burial and Rebirth in the Religions of Antiquity* (New York: Routledge, 1999).

On the memorializing of memory in a Pompeian necropolis (especially Vesonius Phileros, discussed in chapter 13), see Henri Duday and William Van Andringa, "Archaeology of Memory: About the Forms and the Time of Memory in a Necropolis of Pompeii," in *Ritual Matters: Material Remains and Ancient Religion*, ed. Claudia Moser and Jennifer Knust, 73–86 (Ann Arbor: University of Michigan Press, 2017).

On death and the afterlife in early Christianity, see Richard N. Longenecker, ed., *Life in the Face of Death: The Resurrection Message of the New Testament* (Grand Rapids: Eerdmans, 1998); Peter G. Bolt, *Jesus' Defeat of Death: Persuading Mark's Early Readers* (Cambridge: Cambridge University Press, 2003); Peter Brown, *The Ransom of the Soul: Afterlife and Wealth in Early Western Christianity* (Cambridge, MA: Harvard University Press, 2015); Stephen E. Potthoff, *The Afterlife in Early Christian Carthage: Near-Death Experiences, Ancestor Cult, and the Archaeology of Paradise* (New York: Routledge, 2016).

Looking Further: *A Conclusion*

On initiatives of Jesus-followers in relation to the poverty of their world, see Bruce W. Longenecker, *Remember the Poor: Paul, Poverty, and the Greco-Roman World* (Grand Rapids: Eerdmans, 2010). For a precursor along different lines, see Justin J. Meggitt, *Paul, Poverty and Survival* (Edinburgh: T&T Clark, 1998). The subject has been explored in numerous ways since then (with varying results). See, for instance, David J. Armitage, *Theories of Poverty in the World of the New Testament* (Tübingen: Mohr Siebeck, 2016); Thomas R. Blanton and Raymond Pickett, eds., *Paul and Economics: A Handbook* (Minneapolis: Fortress, 2017); Thomas R. Blanton, *A Spiritual Economy: Gift Exchange in the Letters of Paul of Tarsus* (New Haven: Yale University Press, 2017).

On poverty and wealth in early Christianity, see Bruce W. Longenecker and Kelly D. Liebengood, eds., *Engaging Economics: New Testament Scenarios and Early Christian Reception* (Grand Rapids: Eerdmans, 2009); Helen Rhee, *Loving the Poor, Saving the Rich: Wealth, Poverty, and Early Christian Formation* (Grand Rapids: Baker Academic, 2012); Peter Brown, *Through the Eye of a Needle: Wealth, the Fall of Rome, and the Making of Christianity in the West* (Princeton: Princeton University Press, 2012); Brown, *Treasure in Heaven: The Holy Poor in Early Christianity* (Charlottesville: University of Virginia Press, 2016).

On the economic relationships embedded within "the parable of the Good Samaritan," see Bruce W. Longenecker, "The Story of the Samaritan and the Inn-Keeper (Luke 10:30–35): A Study in Character Rehabilitation," *Biblical Interpretation: A Journal of Contemporary Approaches* 17 (2009): 422–47.

Credits

My thanks go to colleagues who have helped in one way or another with the processing of this book: Greg Barnhill (who compiled the indexes), Susan Benton, John Genter, David Goh, Rodney Kilgore, Samuel Otwell, and Stephanie Peek (who introduced me to the phrase "in stone and story"). I am appreciative to students at Baylor University and Regent College from whom I have learned much in our courses on early Christianity in the Greco-Roman world. Melisa Blok at Baker Academic has been the best editor I have ever worked with, and I am very grateful to her for making the production process so enjoyable. I also thank Fiona Bond, Callum Longenecker, and Torrin Longenecker for their persistent patience regarding my fascination with the matters contained in this book.

This study was supported in part by funds from the University Research Committee and the Vice Provost for Research at Baylor University, by the Department of Religion at Baylor University, and by the funders of the W. W. Melton Chair of Religion at Baylor University.

Unless otherwise stated, the photos in this book were taken by Bruce Longenecker and are used here with the permission of The Ministry of Cultural Heritage, Activities and Tourism—Special Superintendency for Archaeological Heritage of Pompeii, Herculaneum and Stabiae. The reproduction of images of realia from the Vesuvian towns contained in this book is prohibited by the Superintendency for Archaeological Heritage of Pompeii, Herculaneum and Stabiae. The other graphics in this book were created by Bruce Longenecker, except the ones listed below.

Most quotations of the Bible in this book derive from the New Revised Standard Version, although sometimes I have tweaked the translation to do better justice to the original Greek in relation to the point being discussed. Whenever another translation is used, it is cited.

Quotations of Greco-Roman literature in this book are usually from standard editions in the Loeb Classical Library, although I have sometimes adjusted the translation slightly to better capture the point. Quotations from Lucretius derive from Ronald Melville's *On the Nature of Things* (Oxford: Oxford University Press, 2009). Quotations from Musonius Rufus derive from Cynthia King and William

Irvine, *Musonius Rufus: Lectures and Sayings* (Scotts Valley, CA: CreateSpace, 2011). The quotation from *OGIS* in chapter 6 is from Barbara Levick, *The Government of the Roman Empire: A Sourcebook*, 2nd ed. (New York: Routledge, 2000), 141.

In general, translations of Vesuvian graffiti and inscriptions are indebted to Alison E. Cooley and M. G. L. Cooley, *Pompeii and Herculaneum: A Sourcebook* (New York: Routledge, 2013), although with slight adjustments as deemed necessary. The translation of the graffito describing Pompeians as "bleating sheep" (see chapter 10) for having elected Proculus derives from Erich Lessing and Antonio Varone, *Pompeii* (Paris: Éditions Pierre Terrail, 1995), 184, where the *CIL* number is not listed.

The following graphics have been sourced or adjusted as follows:

Intro.2. This photo was taken by Massimo Finizio, in the public domain, available at Wikimedia Commons, https://upload.wikimedia.org/wikipedia/commons/f/f7/Vesuvius_from_Naples_at_sunset.jpg.

1.10. *Il Vesuvio visto dagli scavi di Pompei* was painted by Giuseppe Laezza (1835–1905); in the public domain, available at Wikimedia Commons, http://img-fotki.yandex.ru/get/6738/96386024.2a0/0_fce8d_bf86e6a0_XXL.jpg.

3.2. *The First Discovery of the Temple of Isis at Pompeii* was painted by William Hamilton (1757–1804); in the public domain, available at Wikimedia Commons, https://upload.wikimedia.org/wikipedia/commons/5/5c/The_first_discovery_of_the_Temple_of_Isis_at_Pompeii_Wellcome_L0050597.jpg.

3.6. This photo was taken by Giorgio Sommer in 1865; in the public domain, available at Wikimedia Commons, https://upload.wikimedia.org/wikipedia/commons/c/cd/1865_Sommer_Pompeij_anagoria.JPG.

9.8. This drawing is from F. Piranesi, *Antiquites de la Grande-Grece: Tome 2* (Paris: Piranesi & Le Blanc, 1804), plate 69 (in the public domain).

12.1. These drawings are from P. Carcani, ed., *Delle antichità di Ercolano*, vol. 7 (Naples: Regia Stamperia, 1765), 245 (in the public domain).

12.3. These drawings are from P. Carcani, ed., *Delle antichità di Ercolano*, vol. 3 (Naples: Regia Stamperia, 1767), 213 and 227, respectively (in the public domain).

12.5. This drawing is from O. A. Baiardi, ed., *Delle antichità di Ercolano*, vol. 2 (Naples: Regia Stamperia, 1760), 7 (in the public domain).

12.6. This drawing is from P. Carcani, ed., *Delle antichità di Ercolano*, vol. 4 (Naples: Regia Stamperia, 1765), 305 (in the public domain).

13.3. This drawing is from Francois Mazois, *Les Ruines de Pompei*, vol. 1 (Paris: Didot Frères, 1824), plate 30 (in the public domain).

14.9. This drawing is from P. Carcani, ed., *Delle antichità di Ercolano*, vol. 5 (Naples: Regia Stamperia, 1757), 41 (in the public domain).

16.9. This drawing is from P. Carcani, ed., *Delle antichità di Ercolano*, vol. 7 (Naples: Regia Stamperia, 1779), 237 (in the public domain).

17.3. Using Photoshop, I superimposed the collage of the Capitoline deities and the household *lares* onto the shrine of the House of the Golden Cupids.

19.7. The figure of the tomb *triclinium* is from Francois Mazois, *Les Ruines de Pompei*, vol. 1 (Paris: Didot Frères, 1824), plate 20.3 (in the public domain).

Concl.2. This drawing is from P. Carcani, ed., *Delle antichità di Ercolano*, vol. 3 (Naples: Regia Stamperia, 1767), 227 (in the public domain).

Scripture and Ancient Writings Index